PSALMS & READINGS
FOR EVERY SEASON

PSALMS & READINGS
FOR EVERY SEASON

A PRAYER BOOK

For Individuals, Families, Communities

Containing a New Translation of
THE PSALMS IN VERSE
and Guides to
THE READINGS FROM THE LECTIONARY

Arranged for Daily Use Throughout
THE CHRISTIAN YEAR

COMPOSED BY
JAMES KRAUS, STD

T R E E H A U S
TREEHAUS COMMUNICATIONS, INC. • P.O. BOX 249 • LOVELAND, OH 45140

PUBLISHER:
Treehaus Communications, Inc.
P.O. Box 249
Loveland, OH 45140-0249
Phone: 1-800-638-4287
E-mail: Treehaus1@earthlink.net
Website: Treehaus1.com

The design of this book is by Treehaus.
The typeface is Americana.
Printed and bound in the United States.
First printing, September 1999.
ISBN 1-886510-33-4

ACKNOWLEDGEMENTS

I wish to express my deep gratitude to the following:

Dr. Albert Kuhn, English scholar and
former Provost of the Ohio State University.
Without his constant encouragement and careful criticism
the translation of the Psalms would never have been made.

Gerard Pottebaum, President of Treehaus Communications and a
leading authority on the spiritual development of children. Without
his experience, many contributions, and extraordinary efforts, the
Prayer Book would never have come into existence.

My family, sons Isaiah and Justin, and most of all, my wife, Judy.
During the final hectic months of putting this book together, they
came together to type and read, support and advise. It became a
family production.

JAMES KRAUS

CONTENTS

INTRODUCTION

The purpose of this prayer book is to make the Psalms and the Scripture readings of the lectionary the basis of our own personal prayer, our daily conversation with God.

From the beginning the Bible has been the prayer book of the church. The Psalms were its first hymnbook, and readings from the other books its first lectionary. In the course of time, the church saw fit to rearrange the order of the Psalms to fit the prayer life of the monastery in the Divine Office, and to select and arrange passages from the Scriptures for the official Lectionary to be read to the people throughout the Liturgical Year.

In our day that Lectionary has been greatly revised and expanded to provide a rich feast for the faithful. Since it was a cooperative effort of a number of churches it is also an extraordinary instrument of ecumenical reconciliation. It remains for us to make it more available to the people.

The present situation with the Psalms is not as favorable. Obviously, reciting the entire 150 Psalms each week as the monks still do in the Divine Office is out of the question for the ordinary Christian. This prayer book attempts to remedy that by distributing them over a thirteen week cycle, so the entire Psalter is read each of the four seasons of the year rather than each week.

Thus this prayer book remains faithful to the basic structure of traditional Christian prayer. But instead of nine monastic hours, it has two: a longer morning prayer and a short evening prayer. The longer prayer has two basic parts: the Psalms and the Scripture readings, followed by prayers that flow from them. And all is arranged to follow the feasts and seasons of the Christian Calendar, the liturgical year.

Happily, that calendar divides itself naturally into four seasonal quarters, or two quarters and a half. The first or Winter quarter, the Advent-Christmas season, begins with December. The second or Spring quarter, the Lenten-Easter season, usually begins about March, depending on the date of Easter. The rest of the year of about 26 weeks, the Summer and Fall quarters, begins about June with the feast of Pentecost. A calendar in the Appendix serves as a guide for the years ahead.

The Arrangement in Detail

The prayer for each weekday is laid out on facing pages. Sundays require an additional page because of the length and variety of the Sunday readings. The longer morning prayer can be used at any time of the day that is convenient. A brief explanation of each section follows.

I. THE PSALMS

• I chose seven of the shorter Psalms (Psalm 95, the traditional "invitatory" Psalm used every day in the Office, and six similar Psalms) to be recited each day of the week as "Morning Psalms".

• I chose seven more short Psalms (Psalm 23, Psalm 4, and five of the shorter "penitential" Psalms) to be recited each day as "Evening Psalms".

• I added to the Evening Prayer seven psalm-like hymns from the New Testament: the Canticles of Mary, Zachary, and Simeon from the Gospel of Luke; three early Christian hymns from the Epistles of Paul, and one song from the Book of Revelation.

• The Psalms traditionally associated with the great feasts and Sundays, for example, Psalm 104 on Pentecost and Psalm 96 on Christmas, were then placed on those days.

• The rest of the Psalms were distributed over the 13 week cycle in roughly sequential order, from 1 to 150, but with these provisos in mind: we tried to place the Psalms of joy and gratitude on Mondays and Thursdays; the laments, community and individual, on Tuesdays and Fridays; and the wisdom and historical Psalms on Wednesdays and Saturdays. Of course, the Psalms are not so easily classified, nor do they come in the right numbers for that, but it worked often enough to give each day a special character. One gets about 50 verses of the Psalms a day.

II. THE READINGS & PRAYERS

• You will need your Bible to use this prayer book because you will find here only the references to the readings for each day. That solved the problems of having an enormous unwieldy book and of choosing among the many translations. It also enables you to use your own familiar and preferred translation. Moreover, it reminds us that the readings are only selections from the Bible, made by the church and scholars, but still a selection, and that they have a context. With the readings, I have included new translations of the ancient hymns that the church includes in the liturgy of the great feasts.

• I tried to assist the reader by providing for each day's readings:

1) a suggested focus taken from the readings as a whole;

2) a short statement highlighting the content of each reading; and,

3) the brief beginning of a prayer.

These are not intended to take the place of the readings or the readers' prayers, but only to invite them to go further.

• The prayers, based on the readings, and done in the style of the Psalms, are intended only to initiate the readers own thoughts and prayers. Nor should the personal prayers of a lifetime be abandoned, when they can be integrated with the Psalms and readings of the Christian Year. After the Psalms and the Scriptures, my morning meditation and evening prayer still end with prayers our family said for many years, even before I was born.

• The material provided for one day should never be thought of as an "Office", an obligation that has to be performed in its entirety to be effective, even at breakneck speed, as some used to do with the Office. Rather, it is a menu from which you may select according to your time and taste, what appeals, what serves. One Psalm, one reading, and the Lord's Prayer would work; or the Psalms alone; or, if you have the appetite and time, the whole menu is a possibility. It provides a full and balanced meal.

The Translation of the Psalms

This arrangement of Psalms and readings could have used existing translations. But the character of the available translations of the Psalms made the creation of a new translation desirable. In fact, this prayer book began as a study and translation of the Psalms.

It is not useful here in a prayer book to go into a critique of existing translations, or a discussion of the issues involved, scholarly and literary, ecclesiastical and liturgical. But it may be helpful to the reader for me to state my basic principles and purposes.

First, every effort was made to produce a faithful, accurate translation, acceptable to scholars. It is not a paraphrase of the Psalms, not hymns or poems based on the Psalms, or inspired by them, but a translation of them.

Second, I used the traditional formats of poetry: regular lines and stanzas, meter, rhyme, and structure, so that the result is a poem or hymn that can be read aloud or sung to contemporary music composed for it.

Third, I tried to achieve simplicity and clarity, a transparent style, because these are meant to be the popular songs of the People of God.

Fourth, I chose a language, generally inclusive rather than gendered, to speak to and reflect an emerging consciousness among the people of God. After initially doing the translations in traditional gendered language, that is, using "man" and other such words in their generic sense to refer to all persons of both sexes, and using only male pronouns to refer to God, I decided to try a generally inclusive version, and found that it was not only possible, but often more effective. It reduces the exclusively masculine imagery, and, by switching more often to the second person, as the Psalms frequently do themselves, I was still able to preserve much of their intimacy and warmth.

In these principles my only agenda, my only purpose is this: I want the reader to be prayerful rather than puzzled, to be in a conversation with God, not an argument with the text.

JAMES KRAUS

Psalms for Each Day of the Week

PSALMS FOR EVERY SUNDAY

MORNING PSALM / Ps. 95

O my people, now listen to me.

1 Let us come, let us sing to the Lord;
Sing with joy, raise a shout to our God,
To the rock of salvation, the Lord.
2 Let us come with our praise to our God.
Raise your voices in song to the Lord;
Sing your praise
in the presence of God.

You are Lord,
a great God, a great king.
3 All the lords of the earth you command.
4 You created the earth, everything,
From the depths of the sea and the land
5 To the tops of the mountains, all things
Come from you,
are the work of your hand.

6 Let us worship, bow down,
bend the knee.
Let us kneel to the Lord, let us pray.
7 The Lord made us, God's people are we,
And the flock the Lord guides on its way.
O my people now listen to me,
To the charge that I give you today:

8 Do not harden your hearts as before,
When my people put me to the test.
9 What I did they would see and ignore.
10 Forty years
they were senseless at best;
11 Hearts would stray,
leave my way, till I swore
That they never would enter my rest.

EVENING PSALM / Ps. 23

The Lord will give me rest.

1 My shepherd is the Lord, I nothing lack.
2 To pastures green
the Lord will bring me back.

To rest by waters fresh my shepherd leads
3 And there restores my soul,
fills all my needs.

Lord, to your name be true,
show me your way.
4 And though it be a dark and gloomy day,

I shall not fear, you will be there for me,
Your rod and staff with you
to comfort me.

5 My table you will set before my foe,
Anoint my head with oil,
my cup oe'rflows.

Your goodness and your faithful love
are true.
6 Forever I shall be at home with you.

CANTICLE OF MARY / LUKE 1:46-55

Behold the handmaid of the Lord.

My soul proclaims
the greatness of the Lord;
My spirit sings to God, my Savior,
Who looked with favor on my lowliness.
All ages from now on
will call me blest.

The Mighty One
has done great things for me;
And holy is God's name. Eternally.
Your mercy is for those who fear you, Lord.
The mighty arm of God dispersed the proud.

The Lord brings down the mighty
from their thrones.
The Lord will lift the lowly to their own.
The hungry get the bounty of the land;
The rich have been dismissed
with empty hands.

On lowly Israel the Lord above
Did not forget to shower faithful love.
To Abraham the promises God made,
And to his children, too,
will never fade.

PSALMS FOR EVERY MONDAY

MORNING PSALM / PS. 24

Let the King of glory in.

1 The earth is God's, and all it holds,
The world and all who here abide.
2 God made it all and fixed it firm
Against the surging seas and tides.

3 But who shall climb the hill of God,
And dwell within the holy place?
4 The clean of hands and pure of heart
Who seek the God of Jacob's face.

5 Their hearts not fixed on vanity,
They do not swear and then deceive.

6 These are the ones the Lord will bless,
Who their salvation shall receive.

7 Rejoice, O earth, lift up your gates
And let the King of glory in!
8 Who is this King, this glorious King?
A warrior, one sure to win!

9 Rejoice, O earth, lift up your gates
And let the King of glory in!
10 Who is this King, this glorious King?
The Lord of all, who conquers sin!

EVENING PSALM / PS. 4

I go to sleep in peace.

2 Lord, answer me, and vindicate me, God.
You set me free of grief;
now hear my plea.
3 How long, O people,
will you mock our God,
Put faith in frauds, trust idols foolishly?

4 God hears all those who faithfully implore,
The Lord will answer when we call aright.
5 Be anxious therefore, yes,
but sin no more.
Reflect on this in silence, in the night.

6 Then bring your sacrifice to God,
and trust.
7 Though others clamor:
"Who will bring us rain?"
Or, "God has turned away,
abandoned us."
8 You lift your hearts,
your harvest you'll obtain.

9 I go to sleep in peace, for I am sure
That God will keep
my dwelling place secure.

CANTICLE OF ZACHARY / LUKE 1:68-79

Prepare the way of the Lord.

Blest be the God of Israel
Who came to set our people free.
Who raised for us a savior
From faithful David's family.

Of old, through holy prophets' mouths
God spoke to us, God promised us
Salvation from our enemies,
The grasp of those who hated us.

God's faithful love for those of old
Held true, so too the covenant,
The oath once sworn to Abraham,
The promise that the Lord would grant:

That rescued from our enemies
We fearlessly might sing God's praise

In holiness and righteousness
Before the Lord, for all our days.

And you my child, you shall be called
The prophet of the most high God.
For you shall go before the Lord,
Prepare the path that he must plod;

Shall tell the people how God saves,
That God forgives the sins of all;
Shall promise them God's faithful love
Will come at dawn and on us fall;

Shall light the way for those who sit
In darkness and the shade of death;
Shall guide our feet in paths of peace,
And keep us from the paths of death.

PSALMS FOR EVERY TUESDAY

MORNING PSALM / PS. 5

At dawn I pray to you.

2 O hear my words, Lord, hear my sighs.
3 I cry to you, my God and King.
4 At dawn I pray to you, O Lord,
  I plan and hope for everything.

5 The wicked gods delight in evil;
  Wicked people join them too.
6 No wicked one may stand with God.
  I hate them, Lord, I stand with you!

7 All wickedness, idolatry,
  Lord, you despise, and I do, too.
8 But by your love I enter in
  The praise of those who honor you.

9 O lead me, Lord, make straight my path.
  I have a lot of enemies.
10 There is no truth in them. Their hearts
  And tongues are full of treachery.

11 Lord, let them perish, let them fall,
  For all their schemes that challenge you.
12 Let all who seek you, Lord, rejoice,
  Forever singing praise to you.

Lord, shelter those who love your name.
  A smile of joy bring to their face.
13 So that with you, as with a shield,
  They are protected by your grace.

EVENING PSALM / PS. 6

My bed is wet with tears.

2 Correct me not in anger, Lord,
  Nor punish me in wrath.
3 Have mercy, Lord, for I am weak,
  My bones and spirit racked.

4 How long, O Lord? Turn back to me.
5 Deliver me from death.
6 For there, there is no thought of you,
  No praise, no grateful breath.

7 My sobs and cries have worn me out;
  My bed is wet with tears.
8 My eyes grow dim, my heart grows cold
  From sorrow and from fears.

9 Away from me, you wicked ones!
  The Lord has heard my prayer.
10 God heeds my plea, my enemy
  Turns back in deep despair.

THE CHRIST HYMN / PHILIPPIANS 2:6-11

Our mind should be the mind of Christ.

Though he was in the form of God,
He did not think equality
With God a thing that had to be.

Instead, he emptied out himself,
Became a slave, a man like us;
In every way, a man, like us.

Still more would he debase himself,
Obediently take all loss,
To death itself upon a cross.

Because of this God raised him up,
Bestowed on him alone a name
That stands above all other names.

At Jesus' name, all bend the knee.
Let every living thing bow low:
In heaven, earth, and all below.

Let every tongue this truth proclaim:
That Jesus is the Lord of all;
To God the Father, praise and awe.

PSALMS FOR EVERY WEDNESDAY

Morning Psalm / Ps. 101

A royal pledge.

¹ I sing of justice, faithfulness.
　　To you, Lord, make this plea:
² I seek your way, a blameless life.
　　When shall it come to me?

　Within my palace I shall walk
　　In my integrity.
³ No sordid sight before my eyes,
　　No crooked deals for me.

⁴ Perversity be far from me,
　　The wicked I know not.
⁵ The slanderers I shall destroy;
　　Let silence be their lot.

The haughty-eyed, the proud of heart,
　　These I cannot abide.
⁶ I seek the faithful of the land,
　　To have them at my side.

Whoever walks a blameless way
　　I want to serve with me.
⁷ But they shall never stay with me
　　Who deal deceitfully.

⁸ I rise each morning to destroy
　　The wicked of the land,
　To free the city of the Lord
　　From evildoers' hands.

Evening Psalm / Ps. 13

Let me have hope.

¹ How long, O Lord, will you forget,
　　And hide your face from me?
² How long must I in sorrow sigh,
　　In grief eternally?
　How long endure the victory
　　Of every enemy?

³ Look down, and answer me, O God,
　　Send light that I may see.
⁴ Let not my enemies rejoice
　　That they have conquered me.
⁵ But let me hope, rejoice and sing:
　　"How good is God to me!"

The Love of God in Christ / Romans 8:35-39

If God is for us, who can be against us?

If God forgives, who will condemn?
Our intercessor is the Lord.
Can anything keep us from Christ?
Will anguish, famine, or the sword?
Indeed we suffer all day long;
Are killed like sheep as our reward.

But I am sure, not death nor life,
Not angels high, nor earthly kings,
No power present, none to come,
Not height, nor depth, nor anything
Can keep from us the love of God
That comes to us in Christ our King.

PSALMS FOR EVERY THURSDAY

MORNING PSALM / PS. 100

Praise God from whom all blessings flow.

1 Let all the earth acclaim the Lord,
2 Come in with joy, let all adore,
   And sing to God with voices deep!

3 We know that you are God and King;
   You made us, Lord, and so we sing;
   We are your people and your sheep!

4 Come in the gate, go in the court,
   With songs of praise of every sort,
   With hymns of thanks from every page.

5 Lord, you are good. Throughout the land
   Your faithful love will ever stand,
   Will never fail, from age to age!

EVENING PSALM / PS. 131

A child in your mother's arms.

1 O Lord, I am not proud; my eyes look down.
   I do not strive for greatness, reach for more.

2 I tell my soul to be content. You are
   A child within your mother's arms, no more.

3 Wait, Israel, forever, for the Lord.

THE IMAGE OF THE UNSEEN GOD / COLOSSIANS 1:15-20

First born of all creation.

The image of the unseen God,
   First born of all creation.
All things that are, unseen and seen,
   All powers, dominations,
Were made through him, were made for him,
   The ruler of all nations.

Before all things, in him all things
   Created hold together.
The Body's head, the church's head,
   Is he, and will be, ever.
For he is first, the first to rise,
   In all things first forever.

All fullness will be found in him,
   And reconciliation.
He shed his blood upon the cross
   For us, for our salvation.
To all on earth, in heaven, he
   Brings peace and jubilation.

PSALMS FOR EVERY FRIDAY

MORNING PSALM / Ps. 130

Out of the depths.

1 From depths below I cry to you;
  Lord, hear my plea.
2 Incline your ear to hear my prayer,
  And pity me.

3 If you should keep account of sins,
  Lord, who could live?
4 Love dwells in you to be revered,
  So, Lord, forgive.

5 I look to you, await your word;
  I trust in you.
6 As watchmen wait for dawn, nay more,
  I wait for you.

7 God's faithful love will never fail;
  Wait, Israel.
8 From all your sins, God will redeem
  You, Israel.

EVENING PSALM / Ps. 51

David's prayer for forgiveness.

3 O God, forgive me in your faithful love,
  In your compassion, Lord, blot out my sin.
4 O wash away all my iniquity,
  Go deep, O Lord, to make me pure within.

5 I know my sin, acknowledge my offense;
  I see it constantly before my eyes.
6 Lord, you and you alone I have betrayed,
  Committed what is evil in your eyes.

Whatever be my sentence, you are just,
  And vindicated if you should condemn.
7 Indeed I have been guilty
        from my birth;
  In guilt our parents lived,
        we are like them.

8 You seek in me sincerity of heart.
  Instill in me the wisdom I must know.
9 O sprinkle me with hyssop, make me pure,
  And wash me,
        I shall be as white as snow.

10 Lord, let me hear again
        the sounds of gladness;
  Bones that you have crushed
        shall then rejoice.
11 Lord, turn your face from sin
        and banish sadness,
  Take my guilt away, and hear my voice.

12 Create in me, O God, a faithful heart.
  A steadfast spirit, Lord, instill in me.
13 Lord, cast me not aside, away from you,
  But let your holy spirit dwell in me.

14 Restore in me the joy of being yours.
  Sustain in me a spirit that is true.
15 The fallen I will show your ways, O Lord,
  That sinners all we may return to you.

16 Deliver me, O God, from tears and death.
  My tongue must tell
        how good you were to me.
17 Unseal my lips
        so that my mouth may sing,
  May shout your praise, O Lord, eternally.

18 Our sacrifices give you no delight.
  They neither freedom nor your favor earn.
19 A broken spirit is my sacrifice;
  A humbled heart, O Lord,
        you will not spurn.

20 Be gracious to us,
        bless your people, Lord.
  Rebuild the walls of your Jerusalem,
21 That they may offer
        proper sacrifice,
  A welcome gift to make you
        pleased with them.

CANTICLE OF SIMEON / LUKE 2:29-32

Lord, let me go in peace.

Now let your servant go in peace, O Lord, for what you promised all,
My eyes have seen: salvation Lord, prepared before us all.
A light to guide the Gentiles, and the glory of your Israel.

PSALMS FOR EVERY SATURDAY

MORNING PSALM / PS. 141

Like incense let my prayer arise.

1 Come quickly, Lord, I cry to you,
  Like incense let my prayer arise.
2 Lord, hear my voice, accept my plea,
  My lifted hands, my sacrifice.

3 Lord, set a guard upon my mouth
  To watch the doorway of my lips.
4 Let not my heart to evil turn,
  Nor feet on evil deeds to trip.

  All evildoers' company,
  Their partying, their feasts I flee.
5 The just's rebukes I can accept,
  Their words shall be like oil to me.

  I pray against the wicked, Lord,
6 Let them be judged and see defeat.
  Then all will know my prayers were heard,
  And all will see my words were sweet.

7 Like broken clods when farmers plow,
  Our bones are broken, scattered lie.
8 But still my eyes are fixed on you,
  My hope in you will never die.

9 Lord, free me from the traps they set,
  The snares of those who evil do.
10 Let evildoers fall in them;
  Let me alone, O Lord, come through.

EVENING PSALM / PS. 143

Lord, do not condemn.

1 Lord, you are faithful; hear my plea!
  And in your justice answer me.
2 Your servant, Lord, do not condemn;
  With you no one is innocent.

3 My foe has crushed me to the ground;
  I lie in darkness all around.
4 My spirit faints, my death is near,
  My heart within me numb with fear.

5 But I recall your deeds of old,
  The works that all creation holds.
6 I lift my hands, reach out to you;
  My throat is parched with thirst for you.

7 Lord, come, I can endure no more;
  Hide not or I shall be no more.
8 I seek your faithful love at dawn,
  The road my feet must travel on.

9 Lest I be lost, deliver me,
  My refuge be from enemies.
10 O teach me, Lord, to do your will,
  And guide me with your spirit still.

11 To praise your name, preserve my life.
  As you are just, free me from strife.
12 Destroy my foe for love of me.
  I am your servant, Lord, hear me.

THE SONG OF MOSES AND THE LAMB / REVELATION 15:3-4

They all had harps and sang.

O Lord, our God, Almighty One,
How wonderful, how great your work!
How just and true are all your ways,
O King of Ages and the earth!

Who will not fear and praise your name?
For you alone are holy, true.
They see your saving justice, Lord.
All nations come to worship you.

DAILY PSALMS, READINGS & PRAYERS
FOR THE 13 WEEKS
IN EACH OF
THE 4 SEASONS

WEEK ONE

Week One / SUNDAY
MORNING PRAYER

I. THE PSALMS

MORNING PSALM / PS. 95
O my people, now listen to me.
PAGE 3

PSALM OF THE DAY / PS. 104
Send forth your spirit, Lord.

¹ O BLESS THE LORD, MY SOUL, FOREVERMORE!

For you, O God, are great,
 in glory clothed.
² You made the sky your tent,
 the sun your robe.
³ You stored the waters high
 where you abide;
You made the clouds the chariot you ride.

⁴ The winds your airborne messengers
 became,
The fires you made
 your ministers of flame.
⁵ You laid the earth's foundations,
 steadied her.
⁶ You made the sea a cloak to cover her.

⁷ Your thunder stirred the waters,
 hills emerged;
⁸ The mountains, valleys found their place
 on earth.
⁹ To each you gave its space,
 and promised too:
The waters nevermore shall cover you.

¹⁰ You gave us springs
 to quench your creatures' thirst.
¹¹ The earth is filled with beasts,
 all nature nursed.
¹² The birds have built their nest,
 songs fill the air.
¹³ From heaven you send rain
 to show your care.

¹⁴ You grow the grass
 that gives the cattle feed.
You give us plants that fill our every need;
¹⁵ Our food for strength,
 and bread to make us grow;
And wine for joy, and oil to make us glow.

¹⁶ Our trees grow tall, well watered
 with your care;
In Lebanon you planted cedars there.
¹⁷ The sparrows nest, the stork
 has found her home;
¹⁸ For badgers, crags; for goats,
 the hills to roam.

¹⁹ You mark the seasons, Lord;
 the sun and moon
Know when to rise,
 and where to be at noon.
²⁰ You send the dark of night and light of day.
At night the beasts come out
 to seek their prey.

²¹ The lions roar, they seek their food
 from you.
²² When dawn arrives they know
 their time is due.
²³ They seek their dens,
 and then we hear the call
To rise and go to work till evening falls.

²⁴ How many are your works,
 both great and small!
You fill the earth,
 with wisdom do it all.
²⁵ The vast and mighty sea
 that you create
Is filled with living things,
 both small and great.

²⁶ Leviathan plays there; ships sail on it.
You did it all, much for the fun of it.
²⁷ All look to you for food
 when it comes due.
²⁸ They eat their fill, are filled with gifts
 from you.

29 You hide, they fear;
    if you should take their breath
They all return to dust, and lie in death.
30 But, send your spirit, Lord,
    life starts anew!
Your spirit, Lord,
    shall all the earth renew.

31 Your glory shall endure forevermore.
  Lord, at your glance, all tremble
    and adore.
32 And at your touch volcanoes
    shake the earth.
  O Lord, may you be pleased
    with all your work.

33 As long as I have breath
    my mouth shall sing.
34 My praise, my thoughts, my joy to you
    I bring.
May you be pleased,
    and sinners be no more.
35 O bless the Lord, my soul, forevermore!

II. READINGS & PRAYERS

WINTER

1ST SUNDAY OF ADVENT
Your redemption is at hand:

YEAR A

1. Isaiah 2:1-5.
  Come, let us walk with the Lord.

2. Romans 13:11-14.
  It is time to wake from sleep.

3. Matthew 24:37-44.
  The Son of Man is coming, be prepared.

YEAR B

1 Isaiah 63:17-64:7.
  Rend the heavens, Lord, come down.

2. I Corinthians 1:3-9.
  The revelation we await is Christ.

3. Mark 13:33-7.
  Be on guard; you know not when.

Year C

1. Jeremiah 33:14-16.
  The Lord of justice is coming.

2. I Thessalonians 3:12-4.
  Make still greater progress.

3. Luke 21:25-36.
  There will be signs; be on guard.

REDEEMING LORD,
    STIR UP YOUR MIGHT, AND COME,
To save us from the peril of our sin.
Help us to be on guard and watch for Christ,
That when he comes we may go home
    with him.

SPRING

1ST SUNDAY OF LENT
The Redeemer's work begins:

YEAR A

1. Genesis 2:7-9, 3:1-7.
  Adam and Eve, the serpent, the Fall.

2. Romans 5:12-19.
  Paul on original sin, redeeming grace.

3. Matthew 4:1-11.
  Jesus is tempted by the devil.

YEAR B

1. Genesis 9:8-15.
  The flood, the covenant with Noah.

2. I Peter 3:18-22.
  Salvation in the ark, and by baptism.

3. Mark 1:12-15.
  Jesus' temptation and proclamation.

YEAR C

1. Deuteronomy 26:4-10.
  The Israelite confession of faith.

2. Romans 10-8-13.
  The Christian confession of faith.

3. Luke 4:1-13.
  Another account of Christ's temptation.

O GOD OF STRENGTH,
    AS WE BEGIN THIS LENT,
Help us, the weak, to follow you and fast,
Resist temptation, even to the end,
That we may come to Easter joy at last.

SUMMER
Pentecost Sunday
The coming of the Holy Spirit:

YEARS A, B, & C

*All have the same readings. The Psalm of
the Day (above) is the one used on
Pentecost.*

1. Acts 2:1-11.
   *The Spirit comes in wind and flame;
   all were filled. They boldly spoke
   in foreign tongues; all understood.*

2. I Corinthians 12:3-13.
   *There are different gifts, but one Spirit;
   There is one body, but many members.*

   The Hymn to the Holy Spirit, page
   228, "Come, Holy Spirit, From Above."

3. John 20:19-23.
   *Peace be with you.
   As the Father sent me, I send you:
   Receive the Holy Spirit.*

FALL
22nd Sunday of the Year.
True sacrifice, holiness, and humility:

YEAR A

1. Jeremiah 20:7-9.
   *You duped me Lord;
   you were too strong.*

2. Romans 12:1-2.
   Offer yourself, a living sacrifice.

3. Matthew 16:21-27.
   Take up your cross and follow me.

YEAR B

1. Deuteronomy 4:1-8.
   Keep the commandments of the Lord.

2. James 1:17-27.
   God speaks; be doers of the word.

3. Mark 7:1-23.
   Impurity comes from within, not outside.

YEAR C

1. Sirach 3:17-29.
   The wisdom of humility before the Lord.

2. Hebrews 12:18-24.
   The heavenly Jerusalem, city of God.

3. Luke 14:7-14.
   The humble shall be exalted.

GOD FATHER, JESUS LORD, AND SPIRIT LOVE,
In wind and flame you brought
        your church to birth.
May we, enflamed with heavenly desire,
Go forth to preach the word,
        renew the earth.

LORD, HELP US TO EMBRACE THE CROSS,
To keep your word in heart and deed.
We trust in you to raise us up,
For we are low, and much in need.

Meditation. The Lord's Prayer. Intercessions. Personal Prayers.

EVENING PRAYER

Reflections on the Day. Thanksgiving. Reconciliation.

EVENING PSALM / PS. 23 *The Lord will give me rest.* PAGE 3.

CANTICLE OF MARY / LUKE 1:46-55 *Behold the handmaid of the Lord.* PAGE 3.

Personal Prayers.

Week One / MONDAY

MORNING PRAYER

I. THE PSALMS

MORNING PSALM / PS. 24
Let the King of glory in.
PAGE 4

PSALMS OF THE DAY / PSS. 1 & 7
On the justice of God.

PSALM 1 / *The just shall live, the wicked die.*

1 How blest the just, those who refuse
To listen to the wicked lie,
To walk the way that sinners choose,
To join the scoffers' hue and cry.

2 Their joy, the study of God's law;
They contemplate it day and night.
They are like trees beside the water,
Yielding fruit, escaping blight.

4 Not so the wicked of the land;
The winds blow them like chaff away.
5 At judgment they will never stand,
Among the just they shall not stay.

6 God guards your way, on this rely
The just shall live; the wicked die.

PSALM 7 / *David's plea in his defense.*

2 O Lord, my God, in you I trust.
Preserve me from my enemy,
3 Lest I become the lion's prey,
Be mauled, with none to rescue me.

4 O Lord, if I have done this thing:
Betrayed a friend with treachery;
5 If there is guilt upon my hands,
If I abused my enemy,

6 Then let that enemy arise,
And come to me, as come he must,
And overcome me, trample me,
And lay my honor in the dust.

7 If not, then rise, O Lord, my God!
In fury rise against my foe!
Stand up, O God of majesty;
A judgment for my cause bestow.

8 So let the court of nations meet,
And let the judge of all preside.
9 For God most high is judge of all,
And justice will for me provide.

10 Arrest the guilty, those at fault.
Protect the innocent, the just.
For you who search the mind and heart
Alone are God, who can, and must.

11 My Lord and shield is God most high,
The savior of the upright heart,
12 A judge who justly punishes
Those who from God's commands depart.

13 Unless the wicked change their ways,
Our God will seize a mighty sword,
14 Assemble weapons, bend the bow,
And launch the arrows of the Lord.

15 Those who conceive iniquity,
And who are heavy with its plans,
In time give birth to treachery.
They fail, and fall into God's hands.

16 They dig a pit, and make it deep.
Then fall in it, the pit they made.
17 Upon their heads it all returns:
The evil of the trap they laid.

18 I thank the Lord, the ever just;
All praise God's holy name say I.
Let people sing, let praise arise,
From all on earth to God most high.

II. READINGS & PRAYERS

WINTER
MONDAY: 1ST WEEK OF ADVENT
We walk by faith:

1. (A) Isaiah 4:2-6.
   Let us walk in the light of the Lord.

1. (B,C) Isaiah 2:1-5.
   God's glory will be over all.

2. Matthew 8:5-11.
   Many will come from east and west.

In darkness Lord,
   your light shines through.
We all unworthy trust in you...

SPRING
MONDAY: 1ST WEEK OF LENT
The Lord's criteria for judgment:

1. Leviticus 19:1-18.
   Be holy; keep my commandments.

2. Matthew 25:31-46.
   When I was hungry you gave me food.

You come to us, O Lord, disguised,
We welcome you in any guise...

SUMMER
MONDAY: 9TH WEEK OF THE YEAR.
Persist in doing good:

1a. Tobit 1:1-2, 2:1-9.
   Tobit continues to bury the dead.

1b. II Peter 1:2-7.
   We have all we need to do good.

2. Mark 12:1-12.
   The parable of the wicked tenants.

O God, you are our rock, our cornerstone.
In building we rely on your alone...

FALL
MONDAY: 22ND WEEK OF THE YEAR.
The heart of the good news:

1a. I Thessalonians 4:13-8.
   Fear not for those who have died.

1b. I Corinthians 2:1-5.
   I preach only Christ crucified.

2. Luke 4:16-30.
   Jesus begins his ministry.

Come, let us praise Christ crucified;
For we now live because he died...

Meditation. The Lord's Prayer. Intercessions. Personal Prayers.

EVENING PRAYER

Reflections on the Day. Thanksgiving. Reconciliation.

EVENING PSALM / PS. 4 *I go to sleep in peace.* PAGE 4.

CANTICLE OF ZACHARY / LUKE 1:68-79 *Prepare the way of the Lord.* PAGE 4.

Personal Prayers.

MORNING PRAYER

I. THE PSALMS

MORNING PSALM / PS. 5
At dawn I pray to you.
PAGE 5

PSALMS OF THE DAY / PSS. 3 & 9
Songs of one besieged by enemies.

PSALM 3 / ¹*A psalm of David when he fled from Absalom.*

² O Lord, how many are my enemies!
I see them rise against me,
hear it said:
³ "There is no hope of help from God,
for him."
⁴ But you, O Lord, my shield,
lift up my head.

⁵ When I cry out the Lord will hear
my voice,
And answer from the mount where
God abides.
⁶ When I lie down to sleep
I wake again;
⁷ I do not fear the foes on every side.

⁸ Rise up, O Lord! Deliver me, my God!
And break their jaws and smash
their teeth, O Lord!
⁹ Our safety lies with you alone, O God;
Upon your people breathe your
blessing, Lord.

PSALM 9 / *Rebuke the nations.*

² I thank you, Lord, with all my heart;
I sing your wonders to the sky.
³ I will be glad, I will rejoice
And praise your name, O God most high.

⁴ My foes fall back, they are destroyed,
Defeated by your fury, Lord.
⁵ Now from your throne, O righteous judge,
Defend my cause with justice' sword.

⁶ Rebuke the nations, let them all
Forevermore forgotten be.
⁷ Destroy the wicked and their gods.
A heap of ruins let them be!

⁸ The Lord reigns from eternity,
God's throne of judgment ever stands.
⁹ God rules with justice, equity,
All nations, peoples of all lands.

¹⁰ A tower of strength for the oppressed,
A tower of strength for those in need,
¹¹ Are you for those who trust in you.
Forget us not, your people feed.

¹² I sing your praise, O Zion's King;
To all the world proclaim your deeds.
¹³ You will avenge, will not forget,
But hear the cries of those in need.

¹⁴ Have pity, Lord, behold the wounds
Inflicted by my enemy.
¹⁵ Lord, you alone can raise me up
That songs of praise may rise from me.

¹⁶ The nations sink in pits they dig;
In nets they set their feet are caught;
¹⁷ By snaring evil in its trap,
The judgment of the Lord is wrought.

¹⁸ The wicked perish in Sheol,
The nations, too, who laugh at God.
¹⁹ The needy must not lose their hope;
The poor will never be forgot.

²⁰ Arise, O Lord, and judge the world;
Let mortal nations not prevail.
²¹ Teach all of them to fear the Lord;
Show mortals all that they can fail.

II. Readings & Prayers

WINTER
TUESDAY: 1ST WEEK OF ADVENT
Life on the Lord's mountain:

1. Isaiah 11:1-10.
   A child shall lead the wolf and lamb.

2. Luke 10:21-24.
   You revealed it all to children.

How blest our eyes to see the vision Lord,
May we like children come to our reward...

SUMMER
TUESDAY: 9TH WEEK OF THE YEAR
On staying focused:

1a. Tobit 2:9-14.
   Tobit is blinded, but remains faithful.

1b. II Peter 3:12-8.
   Look forward to the coming of the Lord.

2. Mark 12:13-7.
   Give to God what is God's.

No matter what the future brings,
With you, O Lord, my heart will sing...

SPRING
TUESDAY: 1ST WEEK OF LENT
The power of the word:

1. Isaiah 55:10-11.
   My word shall carry out my will.

2. Matthew 6:7-15.
   Jesus teaches us to pray and forgive.

You spoke, O Lord, and we were made.
Speak on through us, that all be saved...

FALL
TUESDAY: 22ND WEEK OF THE YEAR
Listen to the Lord alone:

1a. I Thessalonians 5:1-11.
   The Lord will come like a thief at night.

1b. I Corinthians 2:10-16.
   Only the Spirit knows the mind of God.

2. Luke 4:31-37.
   Jesus teaches with authority.

Before your word, before your crown,
Let earth and heaven, Lord, bow down...

Meditation. The Lord's Prayer. Intercessions. Personal Prayers.

Evening Prayer

Reflections on the Day. Thanksgiving. Reconciliation.

EVENING PSALM / PS. 6 *My bed is wet with tears.* PAGE 5.

THE CHRIST HYMN / PHILIPPIANS 2:6-11 *The mind of Christ.* PAGE 5.

Personal Prayers.

Week One / WEDNESDAY

MORNING PRAYER

I. THE PSALMS

MORNING PSALM / PS. 101
A royal pledge.
PAGE 6

PSALMS OF THE DAY / PSS. 2, 11 & 14
God's wisdom will prevail.

PSALM 2 / *This day I have begotten you.*

1 Why do nations rage and people protest
  God's appointed?
2 Kings and princes plot against the one
  the Lord anointed.
3 "Let us break these chains," they say,
  "We'll not be disappointed."

4 God, who is enthroned in heaven,
  scoffs, as if to laugh;
5 Then in anger God explodes,
  in terrifying wrath.
6 "I decide who reigns in Zion, guides
  my people's path!"

7 Therefore, I proclaim the word
  which God to me has spoken:
  "You, my son, you are the one I have
  this day begotten.
8 Ask of me and you shall have
  the earth, the land, the ocean.

9 You shall rule the nations,
  you shall shatter them like clay."
10 Listen earthly kings: be warned,
  you rulers-for-a-day:
11 Serve the Lord with reverence,
  in holy fear obey.

12 Lest in anger, suddenly, God's arm be raised to slay,
  Then as mortals all of you shall perish on your way.
  Blest are all who trust the Lord, to God their homage pay.

PSALM 11 / *God's eye still sees.*

1 I take my refuge in the Lord,
  How can you counsel me to fly?
  "Flee like a bird, take to the hills,
  Take refuge there on high.

2 For see, the wicked bend their bows,
  And fit their arrows to the string
  To shoot at those of upright heart
  From darkened shadows where they cling.

3 When all the earth has come unglued
  What else is there the just can do?"

4 The Lord still sits on heaven's throne,
  And dwells within the temple still.
  God's eye still sees, whose searching
  Glance is on us all, for good or ill.

5 God tests the just, and wicked, too,
  Abhors those who love violence,
6 Pours down on them a rain of fire,
  A scorching wind, and heat intense.

7 The Lord loves justice; trust a while.
  The just will see God's face and smile.

PSALM 14 / *Fools say there is no God.*

1 The fools say in their hearts:
  "There is no God."
2 From heaven God looks down on earth
  to see

If even one is wise, keeps God in sight.
3 But no, they all alike have gone astray.
  Not one, not even one,
  does what is right.

4 Will evildoers never understand?
   All those who eat my people up
      like bread,
5 Who never stop to think about
      the Lord.

One day they will be filled with fear
   and dread.
6 For God is with the poor
   whom they would crush.
The Lord, the God of justice is not dead.

7 Lord, come and save us! Hear your people's voice!
   Let Jacob sing, let Israel rejoice!

II. READINGS & PRAYERS

WINTER
WEDNESDAY: 1ST WEEK OF ADVENT
The Messianic banquet:

1. Isaiah 25:6-10.
   A feast, rich food, choice wines.

2. Matthew 15:29-37.
   Moved with pity, Jesus feeds the crowd.

We too are moved, o Lord, by you:
And we are hungry, feed us too...

SPRING
WEDNESDAY: 1ST WEEK OF LENT
Repent or be destroyed:

1. Jonah 3:1-10.
   Jonah preaches, Nineveh repents.

2. Luke 11:29-32.
   One greater than Jonah is here.

O God, our sins fill us with fear.
We too repent, our voices hear...

SUMMER
WEDNESDAY: 9TH WEEK OF THE YEAR
Turn to God in prayer:

1a. Tobit 3:1-11.
   Tobit and Sarah weep and pray.

1b. II Timothy 1:1-12.
   Be strong and wise, I pray for you.

2. Mark 12:18-27.
   You do not know the power of God.

Lord, hear the poor who cry in prayer,
Who trust your faithful love and care...

FALL
WEDNESDAY: 22ND WEEK OF THE YEAR
Bringing the good news to all:

1a. Colossians 1:1-8.
   I thank God for your faith and love.

1b. I Corinthians 3:1-9.
   I planted the seed, God made it grow.

2. Luke 4:38-44.
   Jesus heals and teaches in the towns.

If we would reap, then we must sow.
Lord, let us help; you make it grow...

Meditation. The Lord's Prayer. Intercessions. Personal Prayers.

EVENING PRAYER

Reflections on the Day. Thanksgiving. Reconciliation

EVENING PSALM / PS. 13 *Let me have hope.* PAGE 6.

THE LOVE OF GOD / ROMANS 8:35-39 *Who can be against us?* PAGE 6.

Personal Prayers.

Week One / THURSDAY
MORNING PRAYER

I. THE PSALMS

MORNING PSALM / PS. 100
Praise God from whom all blessings flow.
PAGE 7

PSALMS OF THE DAY / PSS. 8, 15 & 16
Songs of praise, confidence and joy.

PSALM 8 / *How great your name.*

2 O Lord, our Lord, how great your name
throughout the earth!
You are adored, for heaven shows
your boundless worth.

3 Your praises come from children's lips,
from mouths that nurse.
Alone are dumb: your enemies
and ours, the cursed.

4 Above we see the moon and stars
you made for us.
5 Lord, who are we that you should choose
to care for us?

6 You set our place a little space
beneath your throne.
You made our face an earthen
image of your own.

7 You gave us power, put the world
beneath our feet.
8 You made our dower all that lives,
fish, bird, and beast,

9 And all aboard this fragile ark,
our home from birth.
10 O Lord, our Lord, how great your name
throughout the earth!

PSALM 15 / *Who is welcome?*

1 Who is welcome to dwell on your
mountain, O Lord?

2 Those who walk with integrity,
do what is right,
Who speak only the truth,
and who walk by its light.

3 Never those who spread slander,
abusing their friends;
Never those who cast slurs,
and their neighbors condemn.

4 Only those who reject the
contemptible horde,
And who honor the just,
those who honor the Lord.

5 Those who stand by their oaths,
those whose word will endure,
Those who lend interest free,
take no bribe from the poor,

These will never be shaken,
will ever endure.

PSALM 16 / *I live in joy.*

1 Save me, O God, my refuge whom I trust.
2 You are my Lord, for me no one but you.
3 The gods whom I once honored
are but dust.
4 They multiply their pain
who hold them true.

5 O God, you are my portion and my cup.
And you yourself have measured out
the space
Of my inheritance. 6 I like it much.
How lovely are the lines
that you have traced!

I bless the Lord who counsels me by day.
8 Whose heart instructs my conscience
   in the night.
From God's right hand I never more
   shall stray.
The Lord is ever present to my sight.

9 Indeed my heart is glad, I live in joy.
I am at ease,
   you'll not abandon me.
10 You will not let your faithful
   be destroyed.
You ever show the way of life to me.

The pleasures you bestow will never cloy.
Your presence, Lord, to me is perfect joy.

II. READINGS & PRAYERS

WINTER

THURSDAY: 1ST WEEK OF ADVENT
The importance of foundations:

1. Isaiah 26:1-6.
   The Lord is an eternal rock.

2. Matthew 7:21-27.
   The wise will build on rock.

We are God's chosen people and his flock.
Let us, and let our nation build on rock...

SPRING

THURSDAY: 1ST WEEK OF LENT
Prayer for one's people:

1. Esther 12:14-25.
   The Queen prays for her people.

2. Matthew 7:7-12.
   Ask and you shall receive.

Your people and their leaders come to you:
O Father hear us. To your name be true...

SUMMER

THURSDAY: 9TH WEEK OF THE YEAR
The primacy of love:

1a. Tobit 6:11-8:7.
   The wedding of Tobiah and Sarah.

1b. II Timothy 2:8-15.
   If we die with him, we live with him.

2. Mark 12:28-34.
   The two great commandments of love.

O God, your loving children pray,
For love of you, to keep your way...

FALL

THURSDAY: 22ND WEEK OF THE YEAR
The call to discipleship:

1a. Colossians 1:9-14.
   Be worthy of the Lord.

1b. I Corinthians 3:18-23.
   Be fools for Christ.

2. Luke 5:1-11.
   They left all and followed him.

We fear our sin, but hear your call;
To go with you, we leave it all...

Meditation. The Lord's Prayer. Intercessions. Personal Prayers.

EVENING PRAYER

Reflections on the Day. Thanksgiving. Reconciliation.

EVENING PSALM / PS. 131 *A child in your mother's arms.* PAGE 7.

THE UNSEEN GOD / COLOSSIANS 1:15-20 *First born of all creation.* PAGE 7.

Personal Prayers.

Week One / FRIDAY

MORNING PRAYER

I. THE PSALMS

MORNING PSALM / PS. 130
Out of the depths.
PAGE 8

PSALMS OF THE DAY / PSS. 10 & 12
Songs of sorrow.

PSALM 10 / *Lord, why? How long?*

2 Lord, why do you remain aloof?
  And why, in times of trouble, hide?
3 The arrogant pursue the poor.
  O let them fall, be tripped by pride!

4 They boast, they glory in their greed;
  O Lord, they scorn you, they blaspheme!
5 They say that you will not avenge,
  "There is no God!" their cry, their theme.

6 They say, "Our wealth will never fail."
  O God, they sniff at your decrees.
7 They say, "We will not fail, we see
  No end to our prosperity."

8 Their mouths are full of violence;
  Their minds and tongues on evil bent.
9 They lurk in ambush near the towns
  To fall upon the innocent.

10 They sit in secret, keep their watch,
  They wait like lions in their lair
11 To seize some poor afflicted wretch
  To catch him helpless, unaware.

12 They say that you've forgotten us.
  They claim we call on you in vain.
13 Arise, O God, and lift your hand;
  Forget not those who dwell in pain.

14 How long will sinners get away
  With saying, "There's no price to pay"?
15 O God, you see our misery;
  Take up our cause, make them repay!

  The helpless find their help in you;
  The orphan finds an open door.
16 Destroy the wicked of the earth,
  Till wickedness be found no more.

17 The Lord is King forevermore;
  Let pagans perish from the land.
18 You hear the poor who cry to you;
  Your strength be theirs, your mighty hand.

19 If you defend the fatherless,
  Give justice to the poor, oppressed,
  The arrogant will not prevail;
  The poor from all their fears may rest.

PSALM 12 / *The lies of the wicked, the promises of God.*

2 Lord, help! No loyalty is left,
  Good faith and trust are gone.
3 All lie to all. With lying mouths
  And faithless hearts they fawn.

4 They say, "With tongues we shall prevail,
  Our weapon is our mouth."
5 May God cut off their boastful tongue
  And shut their lying mouth.

6 Because they rob the poor who groan,
  God says, "I will arise.
7 And speak to them my saving word;
  I hear my people's cries."

8 The promises of God are true,
  Like silver much refined.
9 O Lord, protect your people from
  The lies of all mankind.

II. Readings & Prayers

WINTER

FRIDAY: 1ST WEEK OF ADVENT
The light of the world:

1. Isaiah 29:17-24.
   On that day the blind shall see.

2. Matthew 9:27-31.
   Jesus touched their eyes; they saw.

All seeing God, O Lord of light,
We long to see, give us your sight...

SPRING

FRIDAY: 1ST WEEK OF LENT
The God of reconciliation:

1. Ezekiel 18:21-28.
   The wicked who repent shall live.

2. Matthew 5:20-26.
   First, be reconciled with your neighbor.

It is God's law by which we live:
Before we come, we must forgive...

SUMMER

FRIDAY: 9TH WEEK OF THE YEAR
Scripture: the lifeline of the faithful:

1a. Tobit 11:5-15.
   Tobiah returns, Tobit is cured.

1b. II Timothy 3:10-17.
   Those who love God will suffer.

2. Mark 12:35-37.
   The Christ is David's son and Lord.

Our life, O Lord, is filled with pain.
God grant we suffer not in vain...

FALL

FRIDAY: 22ND WEEK OF THE YEAR
The primacy of Christ over all:

1a. Colossians 1:15-20.
   Christ is the head of the body.

1b. I Corinthians 4:1-5.
   The Lord alone will judge us.

2. Luke 5:33-39.
   New wine is put in new wineskins.

You are the judge, the groom, new wine;
We are a branch you are the vine...

Meditation. The Lord's Prayer. Intercessions. Personal Prayers.

EVENING PRAYER

Reflections on the Day. Thanksgiving. Reconciliation.

EVENING PSALM / PS. 51 *David's prayer for forgiveness.* PAGE 8.

CANTICLE OF SIMEON / LUKE 2:29-32 *Lord, let me go in peace.* PAGE 8.

Personal Prayers.

Week One / SATURDAY
MORNING PRAYER

I. THE PSALMS

MORNING PSALM / PS. 141
Like incense let my prayer arise.
PAGE 9

PSALMS OF THE DAY / PSS. 17 & 26
Bold pleas for vindication of the just.

PSALM 17 / *Lord, guard me as the apple of your eye.*

1 O hear my plea for justice, Lord;
　O listen to my cry!
　I pray with lips that speak no guile;
　Destroy the lips that lie!

2 Let vindication come from you.
　Your eyes see what is right.
3 For you have tested me, O Lord,
　And searched me in the night.

You tested me with fire, Lord;
　You found no guilty hands.
4 I never spoke against your word;
　I held to your commands.

5 My steps stay firmly in your path;
　My feet will never stray.
6 I call on you, O answer, Lord,
　And hear me as I pray.

7 Lord, demonstrate your faithful love,
　Lift up your mighty arm.
Deliver those who trust in you
　From those who seek their harm.

8 Watch over me, and guard me
　As the apple of your eye.
Beneath the shadow of your wings
　There hidden let me lie.

9 Protect me from the violent,
　The foes that round me dance.
10 Their hearts are filled with hatred, Lord,
　Their mouths with arrogance.

11 My enemies press in on me.
　Eyes fixed to kill have they.
12 Like hungry lions crouched to pounce
　From ambush on their prey.

13 Arise, O Lord, and bring them down,
　In answer to my prayers.
14 Your arm and sword will save my life,
　And make an end of theirs.

Lord, fill your faithful with your gifts;
　Their children, fill them, too.
15 My plea is just; as I arise,
　May I be filled with you.

PSALM 26 / *I walk in my integrity.*

1 Vindicate me, God of justice!
　I have walked with honesty.
　I have kept my faith with you;
　I never lost my loyalty.

2 Look at me, O Lord, and test me.
　Search my heart, and probe my mind.
3 Love for you, my eyes on you,
　And faithfulness are all you'll find.

4 Scoundrels I do not consort with;
　Hypocrites I quickly quit.
5 Evildoers I detest,
　Nor with the wicked will I sit.

6 Innocent, I wash my hands,
　Process about your altar, Lord.
7 I lift my voice in praise to you,
　Rehearsing all your wonders Lord.

8 Lord, I love the house you dwell in,
　Where your majesty resides.
9 Sweep me not away with sinners,
10 Idol makers, rich with bribes.

11 Ransom me; be gracious, Lord,
　I walk in my integrity.
　Standing firm, in front of all,
　I bless you, Lord, eternally.

II. READINGS & PRAYERS

WINTER

SATURDAY: 1ST WEEK OF ADVENT
On that day, when he shall come:

1. Isaiah 13:19-26.
   The Lord will bind your wounds.

2. Matthew 9:35-10:8.
   He pitied them; they were like sheep.

Good Shepherd, send us out today
To bring in the harvest, we pray...

SPRING

SATURDAY: 1ST WEEK OF LENT
The elevation of the covenant:

1. Deuteronomy 26:16-9.
   The ancient covenant with God.

2. Matthew 5:43-8.
   Be more, be children of the Father.

You challenge us, O Lord, to be
Like you, and love our enemy...

SUMMER

SATURDAY: 9TH WEEK OF THE YEAR
The beauty of generosity:

1a. Tobit 12:1-20.
   Raphael explains it all.

1b. II Timothy 4:1-8.
   Preach the word! Stay with the task.

2. Mark 12:38-44.
   Jesus praises a poor widow.

Life's journey is a rocky climb.
May we be generous and kind...

FALL

SATURDAY: 22ND WEEK OF THE YEAR
Christ rules our lives:

1a. Colossians 1:21-23.
   All have been reconciled by Christ.

1b. I Corinthians 4:9-15.
   The apostles seem like fools for Christ.

2. Luke 6:1-5.
   And we are yours in all we do.

We have been purchased, Lord, by you;
And we are yours in all we do...

Meditation. The Lord's Prayer. Intercessions. Personal Prayers.

EVENING PRAYER

Reflections on the Day. Thanksgiving. Reconciliation.

EVENING PSALM / Ps. 143 *Lord, do not condemn.* PAGE 9.

SONG OF MOSES / REVELATION 15:3-4 *They all had harps and sang.* PAGE 9.

Personal Prayers.

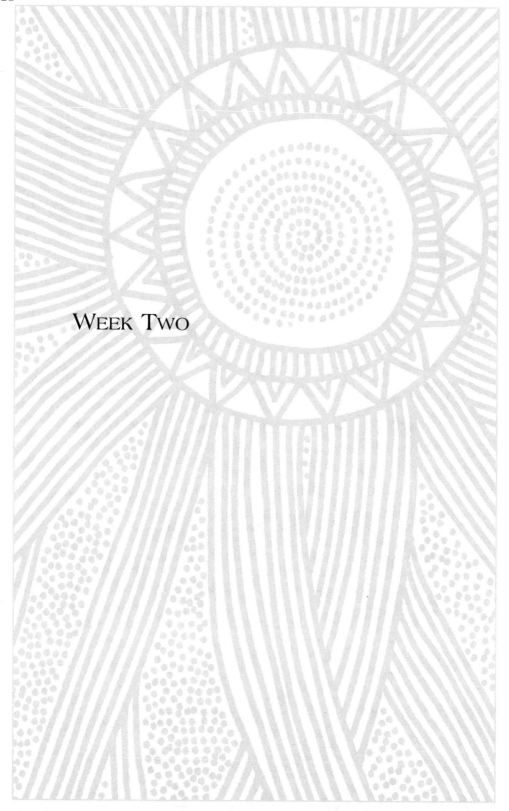

WEEK TWO

MORNING PRAYER

I. THE PSALMS

MORNING PSALM / PS. 95

O my people, now listen to me..

PAGE 3

PSALMS OF THE DAY / PSS. 33 & 126

Today's Lenten And Advent Psalms: Songs of joy and trust.

PSALM 33 / *A new song, for all peoples*

1 Let the just all rejoice in the Lord!
 It is right that the just sing God's praise.
2 Play your harps and give thanks
  to your Lord.
 Play to God on the lyre all your days.

3 Let us sing a new song to the Lord.
 Sing it skillfully, joyfully, too.
4 Every work God has done will endure;
 Every word the Lord spoke
  has come true.

6 At God's word all the heavens were made;
 From the breath of God's mouth
  came its hosts.
7 The Lord gathered the seas in a dish,
 Made the walls of its cellars the coasts.

8 Let the earth, let us all fear the Lord.
 Let all peoples bow down to God's face.
9 The Lord spoke and they all came to be;
 God's command set them all
  in their place.

10 The Lord frustrates
  the plans of the nations;
 The plans of all peoples will fail.
11 But the plans of the Lord stand forever,
 For ages to come will prevail.

5 Lord, you love what is right, what is just;
 Earth is full of your love, yours alone.
12 Blest the nation whose God is the Lord;
 Blest the people you choose
  for your own.

13 From your throne, Lord,
  you watch all below.
14 You see all, every people, all lands.
15 You who made them can look
  in their hearts;
 You see more than the work of their hands.

16 For a king does not win with his army;
17 No soldier is saved by his might.
 All their horses will not give them safety,
 In spite of their strength in a fight.

18 Fear the Lord, trust in God who sees all,
 And bestows faithful love on us first.
19 The Lord rescues our people from death;
 The Lord saves us from hunger
  and thirst.

20 Let us look to the Lord as our shield.
21 Let us trust in God's name and rejoice.
22 Faithful love of the Lord will be ours,
 If we trust in the Lord,
  hear God's voice.

PSALM 126 / *Who sows with tears will reap with joy.*

1 When God restores the lot of Zion,
 Dream though it may be,
2 Our mouths will all be filled with laughter;
 Tongues will shout with glee!

 The nations all will say of us:
 The Lord is on their side!
3 The Lord will do great things for us;
 In joy we shall abide.

4 Restore us, Lord, and bring us back
 As water does for sand.
5 Let those who sow in tears return
 With joy to reap their land.

6 When they go out they go out weeping,
 Scattering their seeds.
 When they return they come back singing,
 Carrying their sheave.

II. READINGS & PRAYERS

WINTER

2ND SUNDAY OF ADVENT
Repent, make straight his path.

YEAR A

1. Isaiah 11:1-10.
   He shall judge the poor with justice.

2. Romans 15:4-9.
   Learn patience from the Scriptures.

3. Matthew 3:1-12.
   John appears to prepare the way.

YEAR B

1. Isaiah 40:1-11.
   Comfort, give comfort to my people

2. II Peter 3: 8-14.
   We see a new heaven, a new earth.

3. Mark 1:1-8.
   John's baptism of repentance.

YEAR C

1. Baruch 5:1-9.
   The glory of Jerusalem will come.

2. Philippians 1:4-11.
   Look for the harvest of justice.

3. Luke 3:1-6.
   All the world shall see salvation.

AWAKEN US, O LORD; PREPARE THE WAY.
And purify our hearts that we may see
The glory of Jerusalem to come.
Your people comfort, Lord,
        and hear their plea.

SPRING

2ND SUNDAY OF LENT
A vision on the mountain top.

YEAR A

1. Genesis 12:1-4.
   The call and promise to Abraham.

2. II Timothy 1:8-10.
   The call of all to holiness.

3. Matthew 17:1-9.
   The transfiguration of Christ.

YEAR B

1. Genesis 22:1-18.
   The call to Abraham to sacrifice his son.

2. Romans 8:31-34.
   God spared not his only son.

3. Mark 9:2-10.
   The transfiguration of Christ.

YEAR C

1. Genesis 15:5-18.
   God's covenant with Abraham.

2. Philippians 3:20-4:1.
   Christ will transfiguration our bodies.

3. Luke 9:28-36.
   The transfiguration of Christ.

O GLORIOUS, O HOLY ONE!
We hear your call, we see your Son,
In nights ahead may we recall
And follow him till day be won.

SUMMER

TRINITY SUNDAY
Praise Father, Son, and Holy Spirit.

YEAR A

1. Exodus 34:1-9.
   Moses talks with God on Sinai.

2. II Corinthians 13:11-13.
   A Trinitarian blessing from Paul.

3. John 3:16-18.
   God sent his son to save, not condemn.

YEAR B

1. Deuteronomy 4:32-40.
   Moses talks to the people about God.

2. Romans 8:14-17.
   The Spirit makes us call God Father.

3. Matthew 28:16-20.
   Baptize them in the name of the Father, and of the Son, and of the Holy Spirit.

YEAR C

1. Proverbs 8:22-31.
   The wisdom of God speaks to us.

2. Romans 5:1-5.
   A Trinitarian explanation of salvation.

3. John 16:12-15.
   The Spirit of Truth will guide you.

BECAUSE YOUR SPIRIT DWELLS IN US,
We call you "Father"; "Jesus", "Lord",
In truth, can call you "Mother" too.
Embrace us all as our reward.

FALL

23RD SUNDAY OF THE YEAR
Reconciliation, healing, and the cross.

YEAR A

1. Ezekiel 33:7-9.
   The prophetic task: correct the wicked.

2. Romans 13:8-10.
   He who loves fulfills the law.

3. Matthew 18:15-20.
   Where two or three gather in my name.

YEAR B

1. Isaiah 35:4-7.
   Fear not, your God will come.

2. James 2:1-5.
   Do not discriminate, God chose the poor.

3. Mark 7:31-37.
   Jesus cures the deaf and dumb.

YEAR C

1. Wisdom 9:13-18.
   Who knows the mind of God?

2. Philemon 9-17.
   Welcome your former slave as me.

3. Luke 14:24-33.
   Consider well the cost; then come.

MYSTERIOUS, ALL KNOWING GOD,
We come to you, the deaf and dumb.
We gather in your holy name,
In answer to your call we come.

Meditation. The Lord's Prayer. Intercessions. Personal Prayers.

EVENING PRAYER

Reflections on the Day. Thanksgiving. Reconciliation

EVENING PSALM / PS. 23 *The Lord will give me rest.* PAGE 3.

CANTICLE OF MARY / LUKE 1:46-55 *Behold the handmaid of the Lord.* PAGE 3.

Personal Prayers.

Week Two / MONDAY

MORNING PRAYER

I. THE PSALMS
MORNING PSALM / PS. 24
Let the King of Glory In.
PAGE 4

PSALMS OF THE DAY / PSS. 20 & 21
Prayers for the king: before battle and after.

PSALM 20 / *We trust in you, O God.*

1 May God be there in time of need;
The God of Jacob be your fort.
2 The sanctuary send its help;
May Zion lend you her support.

3 May God remember all your gifts,
Your sacrifices, holocausts.
4 May you receive your heart's desire,
Your plans fulfilled, no battle lost.

5 May we rejoice; O let us sing,
And let our banners fly in air.
The name of God brings victory!
May God fulfill our every prayer.

6 I know the Lord will answer us,
Will grant this triumph to our king.
From heaven's throne, God's mighty arm
A glorious victory will bring!

7 Some trust in horses, some in arms.
When they collapse we still stand tall.
8 Because we trust your name, O Lord,
9 Grant us this triumph as we call.

PSALM 21 / *You made him glad.*

1 The king rejoices in your strength;
You made him glad in victory.
2 You granted him his heart's desire;
Did not refuse his fervent plea.

3 You set on him a crown of gold;
You blessed him with prosperity
4 He asked for life, for length of days;
You granted him eternity.

5 Through you his glory is complete:
You gave him splendor, majesty.
6 Your presence makes him happy, Lord.
You made him blest eternally.

7 He put his trust in you, O Lord,
Your faithful love, O God most high.
8 He now stands firm, your hand with him;
The hand his enemies defy.

9 When you appear, you will bring fire,
A furnace to consume our foe;
In anger you will swallow them
With fire that ever burns below.

10 Their children, too, will not escape;
You will destroy them and their seed.
11 They plot a war against you, Lord;
They try, but never shall succeed.

12 You put your enemies to flight;
You brandish weapons in their face.
13 That we may sing your praises, Lord,
Bestir your might, bestow your grace.

II. Readings & Prayers

WINTER

Monday: 2nd Week of Advent
Your God will come with vindication:

1. Isaiah 35:1-10.
   Rejoice in song, the land will bloom.

2. Luke 5:17-26.
   Jesus teaches, heals and forgives.

Forgive us, Lord, and make us whole.
Made well by you, in body, soul...

SPRING

Monday: 2nd Week of Lent
Sin and forgiveness:

1. Daniel 9:4-10.
   The people confess their sin to God.

2. Luke 6:36-8.
   Be compassionate, like your Father.

Forgive us Father, we have sinned,
May we by pardon, pardon win...

SUMMER

Monday: 10th Week of the Year
Three new texts; three teachers of the Word:

1a. II Corinthians 1:1-7.
   Words of encouragement from Paul.

1b. I Kings 17:1-6.
   The fiery prophet of the Lord, Elijah.

2. Matthew 5:1-12.
   Jesus begins the sermon on the mount.

You teach us, Lord, and give us ears.;
Unseal our hearts, that we may hear...

FALL

Monday: 23rd Week of the Year
No good deed goes unpunished:

1a. Colossians 1:24-2:3.
   The suffering that I endure for you.

1b. I Corinthians 5:1-8.
   Your boasting is an ugly thing.

2. Luke 6:11-6.
   A miracle incites a frenzy.

O patient God, midst trials of life,
Help us endure in spite of strife...

Meditation. The Lord's Prayer. Intercessions. Personal Prayers.

Evening Prayer

Reflections on the Day. Thanksgiving. Reconciliation.

Evening Psalm / Ps. 4 *I go to sleep in peace.* Page 4.

Canticle of Zachary / Luke 1:68-79 *Prepare the way of the Lord.* Page 4.

Personal Prayers.

MORNING PRAYER

I. THE PSALMS

MORNING PSALM / PS. 5
At dawn I pray to you.
PAGE 5

PSALM OF THE DAY / PS. 25
Lord turn to me and pity me.

1 I lift my heart in hope to you;
  2 O Lord, let me not fail.
Let me not fall into disgrace;
  Let not my foes prevail.

3 No one who looks to you, O God,
  Will be reduced to shame.
The faithless will, the treacherous,
  They have themselves to blame.

4 Make known to me your paths, O Lord;
  Instruct me in your ways.
5 Direct my steps to faithful deeds;
  You are the God who saves.

I look to you forever, Lord.
  6 Remember me and mine.
Your mercy and fidelity
  Will last as long as time.

7 Remember not my youthful sins,
  Consider what is good;
In keeping with your faithful love,
  For you alone are good.

8 The Lord is upright, God is good,
  To sinners shows the way,
9 Will guide the lowly in their path,
  With God they find their way.

10 Those faithful to your covenant
  Receive your faithful love.
11 For all my guilt, for your name's sake,
  Grant pardon from above.

12 Who fear the Lord will learn the way;
  The path for them to choose.
13 Choose well, they and their heirs shall live;
  Choose ill and they shall lose.

14 God counsels those who fear the Lord;
  A covenant they share.
15 My eyes are ever on the Lord
  Who frees my feet from snares.

16 Lord, turn to me and pity me;
  I am alone, depressed.
17 I know your faithfulness, my God.
  Help me in my distress.

The troubles of my heart increase,
  Grow greater day by day.
18 See my affliction, see my pain,
  And take my sins away.

19 How many are my enemies!
  And how they hate me too.
20 Preserve my life from this disgrace.
  21 I wait in hope for you.

Let honesty, integrity,
  Be my protection, Lord.
22 From her distress, redeem as well
  All Israel, O Lord.

II. Readings & Prayers

WINTER
TUESDAY: 2ND WEEK OF ADVENT
The compassion of God:

1. Isaiah 40:1-11.
   Comfort, give comfort to my people.

2. Matthew 18:12-14.
   The search for the lost sheep.

Good shepherd hear your sheep that call;
Fulfill God's plan to save us all...

SPRING
TUESDAY: 2ND WEEK OF LENT
Straight talk from God:

1. Isaiah 1:10,16-20.
   Come. Let us set things right.

2. Matthew 23:1-12.
   Their words are bold, their deeds are few.

O Lord our judge, whom none can fool,
Our scarlet sins white as wool...

SUMMER
TUESDA:, 10TH WEEK OF THE YEAR
The providence of God:

1a. II Corinthians 1:18-22.
   You can rely on the Lord.

1b. I Kings 17:7-16.
   A widow feeds Elijah.

2. Matthew 5:13-16.
   You are the light of the world.

O God, you are the light of day.
We live in night, show us your way...

FALL
TUESDAY: 23RD WEEK OF THE YEAR
Contemplation before action.

1a. Colossians 2:6-15.
   Live in Christ, rooted in him.

1b. I Corinthians 6:1-11.
   Believers will judge the world.

2. Luke 6:12-19.
   Jesus prays, then chooses his apostles.

Your Son, O Father, prayed to you;
As Jesus did, so we would do...

Meditation.   The Lord's Prayer.   Intercessions.   Personal Prayers.

EVENING PRAYER

Reflections on the Day.   Thanksgiving.   Reconciliation.

EVENING PSALM / PS. 6 *Correct me not in anger..* PAGE 5.

THE CHRIST HYMN / PHILIPPIANS 2:6-11 *The mind of Christ.* PAGE 5.

Personal Prayers.

MORNING PRAYER

I. THE PSALMS
MORNING PSALM / PS. 101
A royal pledge.
PAGE 6

PSALM OF THE DAY / PS. 18:1-27
David's epic hymn of praise. Part One: You rescued me.

1 Of David, when God rescued him,
  he said:

2 I love you, Lord, you are my strength,
  my rock.
3 You are my fortress, savior, and my God;
My hideaway, my shield, my source
  of life,
My stronghold. Worthy of all praise is God!

4 I cried to you, you saved me
  from my foe.
5 The waves of death, the mighty seas
  rose high.
6 And I was drowning,
  in a trap enmeshed.
7 I called in anguish: "Lord,
  O hear my cry!"

Far off on high you heard my voice,
  my cry.
8 The mountains trembled
  as your wrath was born.
9 Consuming fire erupted
  from your mouth.
10 Your coming was like lightning in a storm.

11 Atop a cherub, wings outstretched,
  you soared
12 Through darkness, rain and hail,
  upon a cloud.
13 Your voice of thunder shook my enemies;
14 Your shafts of lightning terrorized
  the crowd.

15 The bottom of the sea now lay exposed;
16 The earth's foundation bared by holy ire.
  The mighty Lord of all the world
    came down,
  With roaring voice
    and nostrils breathing fire.

17 You reached down from on high
  and lifted me
18 From drowning, from the clutches
  of my foe.
19 When I was all but lost,
  beyond my strength,
20 You rescued me because
  you love me so.

21 The Lord rewarded me for I was just.
  Because my hands were clean,
    God took my part.
22 God's ways are mine,
  to me the Lord is all.
  To God I have been true
    with all my heart.

23 God's law I ever hold before my eyes.
  The judgments of my Lord
    I keep in sight.
24 And so I shall obtain my just reward
25 For honesty and justice
  in God's sight.

26 With faithful people you are faithful, Lord.
  And with the honest are forever true;
27 Sincere with those who are sincere. But watch,
  You crafty, watch. God can be crafty, too.

II. Readings & Prayers

WINTER
WEDNESDAY: 2ND WEEK OF ADVENT
Incredible extremes combined in God:

1. Isaiah 40:25-31.
   The Lord is awesome over all.

2. Matthew 11:28-30.
   Come to me, you will find rest.

Almighty God, and gentle Lord,
The weary come, your rest implore...

SPRING
WEDNESDAY: 2ND WEEK OF LENT
Trouble ahead for prophets:

1. Jeremiah 18:18-20.
   His enemies plot to bring him down.

2. Matthew 20:17-28.
   Jesus predicts his passion and death.

Like you, O Lord, we are not fooled.
Let all your followers be schooled...

SUMMER
WEDNESDAY: 10TH WEEK OF THE YEAR
The Law and the Spirit:

1a. II Corinthians 3:4-11.
   Law alone kills, the Spirit gives life.

1b. I Kings 18:20-39.
   Elijah versus the priests of Baal.

2. Matthew 5:17-19.
   The Law will all be fulfilled.

You gave us Law, and Spirit too;
May we fulfill them both for you...

FALL
WEDNESDAY: 23ND WEEK OF THE YEAR
Advice from Masters:

1a. Colossians 3:1-11.
   Set your hearts on heaven.

1b. I Corinthians 7:25-31.
   Stay single, time is short.

2. Luke 6:20-26.
   The Lucan beatitudes and woes.

Teach us to listen, Lord, that we
Be quick to hear and slow to speak...

Meditation. The Lord's Prayer. Intercessions. Personal Prayers.

EVENING PRAYER

Reflections on the Day. Thanksgiving. Reconciliation.

EVENING PSALM / PS. 13 *Let me have hope.* PAGE 6.

THE LOVE OF GOD / ROMANS 8:35-39 *Who can be against us?* PAGE 6.

Personal Prayers.

Week Two / THURSDAY
MORNING PRAYER

I. THE PSALMS

MORNING PSALM / PS. 100
Praise God from whom all blessings flow.
PAGE 7

PSALM OF THE DAY / PS. 18:28-51
David's epic hymn of praise. Part Two: You gave me victory.

28 You are the Mighty One
   who saves the poor.
You bring to earth the proud
   who shun your light.
29 You shine for me, you light my lamp,
   O Lord;
You take away the darkness
   of my night.

30 With you I can outdistance anyone,
And with your strength
   climb over any wall.
31 Your way is perfect, Lord,
   your word is pure;
You are a refuge and a shield to all.

32 For who is God besides the Lord
   our God?
Who is a rock for us except our God?
33 You are the one who girded me
   with strength;
The one who kept my way from blame
   is God.

34 You made my feet
   as swift as running deer,
And set me up on high to search below.
35 You trained my hands for battle
   in the wars,
And strengthened them to draw
   the stoutest bow.

36 You gave your shield to me for victory.
You bent down low to lift me
   with your hand.
37 You gave me speed and stamina
   and strength
To catch my foe, so I pursued his band.

38 I never quit the chase,
   I caught my foes.
I struck them down,
   they could no longer stand.
39 They fell to me,
   but you gave me the strength.
40 It was your arm that
   brought them down, your hand.

41 You gave their lives to me, I did the rest.
42 They pleaded but you didn't hear. Nor I.
43 I ground them down like dust,
   and trampled them.
44 You saved me from their spears
   and evil eye.

45 A people I knew not are now my slaves.
   They only hear my voice
   and they obey.
46 Once proud,
   they cringe before me now;
With hearts in anguish,
   vanquished now are they.

47 The Lord lives on!
   Praised be my fort and rock!
48 Exalt the Lord who gave the victory.
49 God made the nations
   bow beneath my knee.
God saved my life
   from every enemy.

50 Before the nations
   I shall praise you, Lord.
I celebrate your name. I shall adore
51 The Lord who gives the king
   his victory,
And all of David's heirs, forevermore.

II. READINGS & PRAYERS

WINTER
THURSDAY: 2ND WEEK OF ADVENT
Help we need, and help is there:

1. Isaiah 41:13-20.
   I am your Lord, I grasp your hand.

2. Matthew 11:11-15.
   The greatness of John, listen to him.

Creator, Lord, be with us, too;
In all we meet may we see you...

SPRING
THURSDAY: 2ND WEEK OF LENT
Blest the one who trusts in God:

1. Jeremiah 17:5-10.
   More tortuous than all, the human heart.

2. Luke 16:19-31.
   The story of Dives and Lazarus.

O Lord, you understand our heart;
We are the poor; show us your heart...

SUMMER
THURSDAY: 10TH WEEK OF THE YEAR
Beyond the law:

1a. II Corinthians 3:15-4:6.
   The Spirit of the Lord gives freedom.

1b. I Kings 18:41-6.
   Elijah foresees the rain and flees.

2. Matthew 5:20-6.
   Your holiness must surpass the law.

The Spirit gives us gifts to use;
We have no freedom to abuse...

FALL
THURSDAY: 23RD WEEK OF THE YEAR
The chosen have responsibilities:

1a. Colossians 3:12-17.
   You are God's chosen, be at peace.

1b. I Corinthians 8:1-17.
   Knowledge inflates, love builds.

2. Luke 6:27-38.
   I say: love your enemies.

To God, not us, is glory due;
To overcome, we must be true...

Meditation. The Lord's Prayer. Intercessions. Personal Prayers.

EVENING PRAYER

Reflections on the Day. Thanksgiving. Reconciliation.

EVENING PSALM / PS. 131 *A child in your mother's arms.* PAGE 7.

THE UNSEEN GOD / COLOSSIANS 1:15-20 *First born of all creation.* PAGE 7.

Personal Prayers.

MORNING PRAYER

I. THE PSALMS

MORNING PSALM / PS. 130
Out of the depths.
PAGE 8

PSALM OF THE DAY / PS. 31
O Lord, you see my misery.

1 In you, O God, I take my refuge;
Let me not be put to shame
For justice' sake deliver me.
2 Come quickly, Lord, to hear my claim.

You are my rock and fortress, Lord,
A citadel where I can hide.
3 For your name's sake be here for me;
You are my leader and my guide

4 To capture me they spread a net;
But you, my savior, set me free.
5 I put my life within your hands;
Be faithful, Lord, deliver me.

6 O God of truth, you hate the lies
Of those who worship worthless gods.
7 I will exult, I will rejoice,
I trust your faithful love, O God.

Lord, you have seen my misery,
And you know well my enemy.
8 Do not abandon me to him,
But set my feet at liberty.

9 Be kind O Lord in my distress,
My eyes grow dim, to darkness doomed.
10 My life is spent in sorrows, sighs;
My strength is wasted, bones consumed.

11 To all my enemies I am
An object of derision, scorn.
To neighbors an embarrassment,
To friends a pity, one to mourn.

When people see me in the street
They shy away, they quickly flee.
12 I am forgotten like the dead,
A broken dish, a useless me.

13 I hear the whispers of the crowd;
I feel the fear that's in the air.
My enemies have hatched their plot
To take my life, make me despair.

14 But I will not! I trust in you;
You are my God, I say it still.
My life is in your hands, O Lord;
15 Save me from those who seek to kill.

16 O turn your face and shine on me,
And in your faithful kindness come.
17 O put me not to shame. Shame them!
18 Let lying lips be stricken dumb.

19 A rich reward you have in store
For those who trust, for all to see.
20 From schemes and plots of lying foes
In your pavilion shelter me.

21 Blest be the Lord whose faithful love
Is ever my security.
22 One time I thought I was forgotten;
Then I called, God heard my plea.

23 So love the Lord, you faithful ones,
Who guards both you and your reward.
24 The arrogant will get their due.
Be stout of heart, and trust the Lord.

II. Readings & Prayers

WINTER

Friday: 2nd Week of Advent
A warning to the petulant:

1. Isaiah 48:17-19.
   I, the Lord, show you the way.

2. Matthew 11:16-9.
   There is no pleasing you.

Lord, we have strayed, make little sense;
Restore to us our innocence...

SPRING

Friday: 2nd Week of Lent
What greed and envy do to us:

1. Genesis 37:3-28.
   Joseph is sold by his brothers.

2. Matthew 21:33-46.
   The parable of the wicked tenants.

We have betrayed you, Lord, our brother.
You tell us now, forgive each other...

SUMMER

Friday: 10th Week of the Year
Appearances are deceiving:

1a. II Corinthians 4:7-15.
   We hold God's glory in earthen vessels.

1b. I Kings 19:9-16.
   Elijah finds God, but not in fire.

2. Matthew 5:27-32.
   Adultery is in the eye and heart.

All seeing God, help us to see
What truly is adultery...

FALL

Friday: 23rd Week of the Year
Know who you are and where you go:

1a. I Timothy 1:1-2,12-14.
   I once was lost, but now am found.

1b. I Corinthians 9:16-27.
   I run and fight with open eyes.

2. Luke 6:39-42.
   Can the blind lead the blind?

O Lord, you hate hypocrisy.
From it the most, deliver me...

Meditation. The Lord's Prayer. Intercessions. Personal Prayers.

Evening Prayer

Reflections on the Day. Thanksgiving. Reconciliation.

Evening Psalm / Ps. 51 *David's prayer for forgiveness.* Page 8.

Canticle of Simeon / Luke 2:29-32 *Lord, let me go in peace.* Page 8.

Personal Prayers.

Week Two / SATURDAY
MORNING PRAYER

I. THE PSALMS

MORNING PSALM / PS. 141
Like incense let my prayer arise.
PAGE 9

PSALM OF THE DAY / PS. 34
Come, glorify the Lord with me.

2 I bless the Lord for all my days;
  In constant praise I raise my voice.
3 My only boast is in the Lord;
  The humble hear, and they rejoice.

4 Come, glorify the Lord with me,
  And sing together, God will hear.
5 I sought the Lord,
    who answered me,
  Delivered me from every fear.

6 Look up to God with joyful eyes
  And you will not be put to shame.
7 A poor man cried, the Lord replied,
  And rescued him from all his pain.

8 The angel of our God is poised
  To rescue those who fear the Lord.
9 Drink deep and see, our God is sweet,
  And blest are those who trust the Lord.

10 So live in awe of God, you saints;
  All those who do shall never want.
11 The rich will thirst, but those who seek
  The Lord have an eternal font.

12 Come children, listen to my words;
  The fear of God is what I teach.
15 Avoid the evil, do the good.
  Let your pursuit and goal be peace.

13 For who among us does not seek
  Long life and peace, prosperity?
14 Then let them keep their tongues
    from sin,
  Speak ever with sincerity.

16 The eyes of God are on the just;
  The ears of God will hear their plea.
18 For when they call God answers them
  And saves them from their enemy.

17 The wicked feel your anger, Lord;
  Their names will be forever lost.
19 The broken hearted feel your love;
  The crushed in spirit are not lost.

20 The trials of the just are many;
  From them all God rescues them,
21 And watches over every bone;
  They shall not break a one of them.

22 Their wickedness destroys the wicked;
  Ruins those who hate the just.
23 The loyal servant God redeems.
  No ruin threatens those who trust.

II. Readings & Prayers

WINTER

SATURDAY: 2ND WEEK OF ADVENT
There is no way to escape the fire:

1. Sirach 48:1-4,9-11.
   Hail Elijah, prophet of fire.

2. Matthew 17:10-13.
   John, the true Elijah, has come and gone.

We have been called with words that burn;
To live and die for you we yearn...

SPRING

SATURDAY: 2ND WEEK OF LENT
The infinite mercy of God:

1. Micah 7:14-20.
   Who is there like you who pardons all?

2. Luke 15:1-3,11-32.
   The prodigal son, the loving father.

Unworthy to be called your child we come,
Forgive us Father, all your daughters, sons...

SUMMER

SATURDAY: 10TH WEEK OF THE YEAR
What God asks is not complicated:

1a. II Corinthians 5:14-21.
   Christ died for you, be reconciled.

1b. I Kings 19:19-21.
   Elisha leaves all to follow Elijah.

2. Matthew 5:33-7.
   Let your yes be yes and no be no.

You give us, Lord, a simple choice;
May we say, "Yes," as with one voice...

FALL

SATURDAY: 23RD WEEK OF THE YEAR
On confidence in God:

1a. I Timothy 1:15-17.
   You can depend on God: I am proof.

1b. I Corinthians 10:14-22.
   Though we are many, we are one body.

2. Luke 6:43-49.
   A good tree bears good fruit.

You are the head, the rock, the vine;
We are the body, house, and wine...

Meditation. The Lord's Prayer. Intercessions. Personal Prayers.

Evening Prayer

Reflections on the Day. Thanksgiving. Reconciliation.

EVENING PSALM / PS. 143 *Lord, do not condemn.* PAGE 9.

SONG OF MOSES / REVELATION 15:3-4 *They all had harps and sang.* PAGE 9.

Personal Prayers.

WEEK THREE

Week Three / SUNDAY
MORNING PRAYER

I. THE PSALMS

MORNING PSALM / PS. 95
O my people, now listen to me.
PAGE 3

PSALMS OF THE DAY / PSS. 19 & 146
In praise of God.

PSALM 19 / *The thoughts of my heart.*

2 The sky tells the story and glory of God;
    Its vault shows the skill
        of God's hands.
3 Each day to the next
      sends the message along,
    Each night to the next it expands.
4 And so without speech, without words,
      even sound,
    5 The message goes out to all lands.

    The message is this: that the sky is a tent
    Pitched on high by the Lord for the sun.
6 Each day, like a bridegroom,
      he comes from his tent
    Like a champion eager to run.
7 His course reaches wide,
      from beginning to end;
    There is nothing can hide from the sun.

8 God's Law is ideal, it refreshes the soul,
    Its decrees are a light to the mind.
9 Its precepts are perfect, rejoicing the heart,
    Its commands are like eyes to the blind.
10 The fear of the Lord is enduring and pure,
    The Lord's judgments are true
      and are kind.

11 I hunger for them more than gold,
      finest gold,
    Than a treasure of gold stored at home.
The words of your mouth
    are far sweeter to me
Than the honey
    that drips from the comb.
12 Your servants find light in the law
    they obey;
    Great rewards come with your words
    alone.

13 Lord, who are aware
    of their unconscious sins?
    O my God, from my guilt set me free.
14 From conscious sin
    guard and protect me, O Lord;
    May it gain no control over me.
I seek to be blameless of grievous offense,
    Wholly yours, free of sin would I be.

15 May the words of my mouth
    and the thoughts of my heart
    All be yours my redeemer and rock.

PSALM 146 / *Forever faithful is the Lord.*

1 Sing alleluia, praise the Lord!
O praise the Lord, my soul, give praise.
2 Forever sing to God your hymn.
As long as you shall live sing praise.

3 Put not your trust in mortal kings
Who cannot save, whose breath will fail.
4 The day that they return to dust
The plans they made will not prevail.

5 All those who trust the Lord are blest,
The God of Jacob is their aid.
6 The Lord created heaven, earth,
The sea and all in it God made.

Forever faithful is the Lord.
7 Who feeds the poor, sets captives free,
Who renders justice to the wronged,
8 Who opens eyes so blind can see.

The Lord will make the crooked straight.
9 God loves the just; the stranger, guards.
To widows, orphans, God gives hope;
But makes the path of evil hard.

10 The Lord shall reign forevermore,
Your God, O Zion, and your Lord.
From age to age let everyone
Sing alleluia, praise the Lord!

II. READINGS & PRAYERS

WINTER

3RD SUNDAY OF ADVENT
Rejoice and hope, prepare the way:

YEAR A

1. Isaiah 35:1-6,10.
   Fear not, your God will come to save.

2. James 5:7-10.
   Be patient, like the prophets.

3. Matthew 11:2-11.
   Jesus and John identify each other.

YEAR B

1. Isaiah 61:1-2,10-11.
   "The spirit of God is upon me."

2. 1 Thessalonians 5:16-24.
   Rejoice, the Lord will come.

3. John 1:6-8,19-28.
   John identifies who he is.

YEAR C

1. Zephaniah 3:14-18.
   The Lord your God is in your midst.

2. Philippians 4:4-7.
   The Lord is near, rejoice in him.

3. Luke 3:10-18.
   John tells the people what to do.

O FAITHFUL GOD,
   YOU GIVE US HOPE
Because your promises are true.
O Master, tell us who we are,
That we may do our work for you.

SPRING

3RD SUNDAY OF LENT
God requires fidelity and fruitfulness:

YEAR A

1. Exodus 17:3-7.
   Moses strikes the rock for water.

2. Romans 5:1-2,5-8.
   The love of God has been poured out.

3. John 4:5-42.
   Jesus and the woman at the well.

YEAR B

1. Exodus 20:1-17.
   Moses gives the commandants.

2. I Corinthians 1:22-25.
   "We preach Christ crucified."

3. John 2:13-25.
   Jesus cleanses the temple.

YEAR C

1. Exodus 3:1-15.
   Moses and the burning bush.

2. I Corinthians 10:1-12.
   The example of Moses and the people.

3. Luke 13:1-9.
   The barren tree shall be cut down.

REDEEMING LORD,
   NEW MOSES FOR THE WORLD,
We ask of you that by our Lenten works
You prune us, cleanse us of our sin.
Lord, with your living water
   quench our thirst.

SUMMER
CORPUS CHRISTI
The feast of the Body of Christ.

YEAR A

1. Deuteronomy 8:2-3, 4-16.
   God feeds the people in the desert.

2. I Corinthians 10:16-17.
   Is not the bread we break the Christ?

3. John 6:51-58.
   I am the living bread.

YEAR B

1. Exodus 24:3-8.
   This is the blood of the covenant.

2. Hebrews 9:11-15.
   The blood of Christ cleanses our souls.

3. Mark 14:12-16, 22-26.
   This is my body: this is my blood.

YEAR C

1. Genesis 14:18-20.
   The king brought bread and wine to bless.

2. I Corinthians 11:23-26.
   When you eat this bread...

3. Luke 9:11-17.
   They all ate and were filled.

YOU ALWAYS FED YOUR PEOPLE, LORD,
And now your body, blood you give;
We hunger for this food, O Lord.
Feed on, we eat that we may live.

FALL
24TH SUNDAY OF THE YEAR
How God forgives.

YEAR A

1. Sirach 27:30-28:7.
   You must forgive to be forgiven.

2. Romans 14:7-9.
   In life and death we are the Lord's.

3. Matthew 18:21-35.
   "How often must we forgive?"

YEAR B

1. Isaiah 50:4-9.
   "I have set my face like flint."

2. James 2:14-18.
   "Faith without works is dead."

3. Mark 8:27-35.
   Peter's faith, and a warning to all.

YEAR C

1. Exodus 32:7-14.
   Moses fends off God's wrath.

2. I Timothy 1: 12-17.
   Christ came to save sinners.

3. Luke 15:1-32.
   The prodigal son and loving father.

FORGIVING FATHER, WE YOUR CHILDREN
Come to you defiled by sin.
We promise we shall follow Christ,
Forgive each other, die with him.

Meditation. The Lord's Prayer. Intercessions. Personal Prayers.

EVENING PRAYER

Reflections on the Day. Thanksgiving. Reconciliation.

EVENING PSALM / PS. 23 *The Lord will give me rest.* PAGE 3.

CANTICLE OF MARY / LUKE 1:46-55 *Behold the handmaid of the Lord.* PAGE 3.

Personal Prayers.

Week Three / MONDAY
MORNING PRAYER

I. THE PSALMS

MORNING PSALM / PS. 24
Let the King of glory in.
PAGE 4

PSALMS OF THE DAY / PSS. 36 & 41
Songs of fidelity midst enemies.

PSALM 36 / *How precious is your faithful love.*

2 Sin dominates the wicked heart.
  They see no need to fear the Lord.
3 Deluded by their flattery,
  They think they can escape the sword.

4 Their words are mischievous and false.
  On wisdom they have turned their back.
5 At night they hatch their evil plots;
  By day, pursue their wicked track.

  No evil is too great for them;
6 But greater is your faithful love.
7 For mountain high and ocean deep,
  It touches all below, above.

8 How precious is your faithful love!
  Beneath the shadow of your wing
9 We hide, we feast and taste the stream
  Of your delights, and there we sing:

10 "You are the fountain of our life.
  You are the light by which we see.
11 O Lord, bestow your faithful love
  On those who serve you faithfully."

12 Let not proud feet descend on me;
  Let not rough hands drive me away.
13 Let evildoers bite the dust,
  And thrust to earth, there let them stay.

PSALM 41 / *Support me in the way of truth.*

2 Bless those whose words are ever true.
  At testing time the Lord will be
3 Their way to life; salvation from
  The lying tongues of enemies.

4 Support them, Lord, when they are ill;
  Sustain them, take their pain away.
5 Have pity, Lord, upon us all,
  And heal us, we have gone astray.

6 My enemies speak ill of me.
  "Let that one die and be no more."
7 They only come to tell me lies,
  And then go out to tell still more.

8 They whisper, plot to take my life.
9 "Try poison, that should do the job."
10 Yes, even those who were my friends
  Have joined my enemies, O God.

11 Have pity on me, Lord, once more;
  Let me arise to strike my foe.
12 That you still love me I will know,
  When I see all of them brought low.

13 Support me in the way of truth;
  Forever keep me in your grace.
14 Praised be the God of Israel!
  Forevermore! In every place!

II. Readings & Prayers

WINTER
Monday: 3rd Week of Advent[*]
Listen to the prophets:

1. Numbers 24:2-7, 15-17.
   A star from Jacob will arise.

2. Matthew 21:23-27.
   The priests question Jesus' authority.

All seeing God, your word is true;
We question not, we follow you...

SPRING
Monday: 3rd week of Lent
Where will God find faith?

1. II Kings 5:1-15.
   Naaman is cured of leprosy.

2. Luke 4:24-30.
   No prophet is accepted at home.

Give us the faith of pagans, Lord,
That we to health may be restored...

SUMMER
Monday: 11th week of the Year
There are bad people out there:

1a. II Corinthians 6:1-10.
   Now is the acceptable time!

1b. I Kings 21:1-16.
   Ahab and Jezebel plot against Naboth.

2. Matthew 5:38-42.
   Turn the other cheek.

When foes appear, help us to turn
Our cheek to them, our hearts to you...

FALL
Monday: 24th week of the Year
Some passages with surprises:

1a. I Timothy 2:1-8.
   Pray for those in authority.

1b. I Corinthians 11:17-26.
   When you gather for the Lord's supper.

2. Luke 7:1-10.
   Jesus cures the centurion's servant.

Like you we marvel at his simple faith.
May you find faith in us like his...

Meditation. The Lord's Prayer. Intercessions. Personal Prayers.

Evening Prayer

Reflections on the Day. Thanksgiving. Reconciliation.

Evening Psalm / Ps. 4 *I go to sleep in peace.* Page 4.

Canticle of Zachary / Luke 1:68-79 *Prepare the way of the Lord.* Page 4.

Personal Prayers.

[*]Note: December 17 will fall on one of the weekdays this week. On that day use the Psalms and Readings on Pages 58-59, omitting the rest of this week's days. Thereafter, for the rest of the Christmas season (till the feast of the Baptism of Christ), follow the numbered calendar dates, not the days of the week, whatever day of the week those dates fall on. The one exception: the 4th Sunday of Advent always falls on Week Four/Sunday and replaces the calendar day on which it falls.

Week Three / TUESDAY
MORNING PRAYER

I. THE PSALMS

MORNING PSALM / PS. 5
At dawn I pray to you.
PAGE 5

PSALM OF THE DAY / PS. 35
The cry of one besieged by enemies.

PSALM 35 / *My God, do not be far from me.*

1 Attack, O Lord, my enemies;
  Make war on those at war with me.
2 Take up the sword against my foe,
3 And say, "I am your victory!"

4 Frustration and disgrace be theirs
  Who seek my life, who plan my end.
5 Drive them like chaff before the wind,
  Your angel driving after them.

6 Their way be dark and slippery,
  Your angel, Lord, in hot pursuit.
7 Without a cause they spread a net,
  A trap to leave me destitute.

8 Disaster take them unaware.
  The snare they set catch them instead.
9 Then I shall sing, rejoice in God,
  The Lord who saved me from the dead.

10 My bones cry out: "Lord, who but you
  Can help the weak, put down the strong?
  You save the poor, and the oppressed,
  From those who prey,
      who do them wrong.

11 Malicious witnesses have come
  With accusations new to me.
12 My love with hatred they repay.
  I stand alone, Lord, hear my plea.

13 When they were ill I prayed for them;
  I put on sackcloth, fasted too.
14 Like one who mourned a mother lost,
  I was their brother, loving, true.

15 When I fell ill they came to jeer.
  Some whom I did not know or see
16 Lit into me, tore me apart,
  And mocked and gnashed their teeth
      at me.

17 How long, O Lord, will you look on?
  Come save me from these savage beasts.
18 Then I shall thank you in the throng
  Of those whose praise will never cease.

19 My enemies, the treacherous,
  Rejoice; they wink the eye and vow
20 Not peace, but war on the oppressed.
21 They cry, "Aha, we have him now!"

22 O Lord, you see! No silence now!
  My God, do not be far from me.
23 Awake and come to my defense,
  My Lord and God, O hear my plea!

24 And vindicate me, Lord, my God,
  For justice's sake do not let them
  Rejoice and gloat at me and say:
25 "We got our wish, we swallowed him!"

26 Let them be filled with shame, disgrace,
  Who find their joy in my dismay.
27 Let those who seek my vindication
  Shout for joy, be glad and say:

  "How great is God, how good to us!
  The Lord rejoices in our song."
28 My tongue shall tell your justice, Lord,
  Shall sing your praises all day long.

II. Readings & Prayers

WINTER

Tuesday: 3rd Week of Advent

The Lord hears the cry of the poor:

1. Zephaniah 3:1-2, 9-13.
   Woe to the proud; peace to the poor.

2. Matthew 21:28-32
   Sinners believed in John.

We are not proud, rebellious;
We come repentant, Lord; save us...

SUMMER

Tuesday, 11th Week of the Year

The standard Christ lays down for us:

1a. II Corinthians 8:1-9.
   Christ was poor; be kind to them.

1b. I Kings 21:17-29.
   Elijah curses Ahab and Jezebel.

2. Matthew 5:43-48.
   Be perfect: love your enemies

Forgiving all, forever true,
we would be perfect, Lord, like you...

SPRING

Tuesday, 1st Week of Lent

How our heavenly Father will treat us:

1. Daniel 3:25,34-43.
   We come with humble hearts, O Lord.

2. Matthew 18:21-35.
   How many times we must forgive.

Forgive us, Lord, for we have sinned;
May we by pardon, pardon win...

FALL

Tuesday, 24th Week of the Year

The compassion of Jesus:

1a. I Timothy 3:13.
   Qualifications for church office:

1b. I Corinthians 12:12-14, 27-31.
   You are the body of Christ.

2. Luke 7:11-17.
   Jesus raises the widow's son.

We are your body, Lord,
Show us compassion, too...

Meditation. The Lord's Prayer. Intercessions. Personal Prayers.

Evening Prayer

Reflections on the Day. Thanksgiving. Reconciliation.

Evening Psalm / Ps. 6 *My bed is wet with tears.* Page 5.

The Christ Hymn / Philippians 2:6-11 *The mind of Christ.* Page 5.

Personal Prayers.

Week Three / WEDNESDAY
MORNING PRAYER

I. THE PSALMS

MORNING PSALM / PS. 101
A royal pledge.
PAGE 6

PSALM OF THE DAY / PS. 37
Reassurance for the just.

PSALM. 37 / *Your enemies will not survive.*

1 Be not upset at wickedness,
  At those who practice wrong.
2 Like grass they quickly fade away,
  Do not stay green for long.

3 Trust God, do good, and dwell secure
  On land bequeathed to you.
4 Delight in God who then will make
  Your heart's desire come true.

5 Commit to God your destiny.
  The Lord will act, and soon.
6 Your vindication will break through
  As sunshine does at noon.

7 Await and trust the Lord. Do not
  Begrudge the prosperous.
8 Abandon anger, give up wrath;
  It injures only us.

9 Soon you will see the wicked fall.
  Yes, one day you will see.
10 The faithful will inherit all;
  The wicked cease to be.

11 The humble will inherit all,
  Enjoy prosperity.
12 The wicked plot against the just,
  In fury grind their teeth..

13 In heaven, Lord, you laugh at them.
  You know their day will come.
22 Those blessed by you inherit all;
  Those cursed by you get none.

14 They draw their swords and bend their bows
  To slay the poor and just.
15 Their swords will turn upon themselves;
  Their bows will lie in dust.

16 The little that the just possess
  Exceeds the wicked's gold.
17 Lord, you will break the wicked's arms;
  The just you will uphold.

18 You guard the just, their days, their needs;
  Their portion will survive.
19 When famine strikes you give them food;
  In drought you save their lives.

20 Our enemies will not survive;
  Like smoke they blow away.
21 The just will give with open hearts;
  The wicked won't repay.

23 The Lord delights in helping us;
  God firms our step, we stand.
24 Though we may trip, we shall not fall;
  God takes us by the hand.

25 I once was young and now am old,
  But never did I see
  The just bereft, their children left
  To beg their bread from me.

26 The just are ever generous;
  Their children will be blest.
28b They lend. The wicked never do.
  Their children are distressed.

27 So turn from evil and do good
  To live eternally.
28a God loves the just, will not forsake
  But guard them faithfully.

II. Readings & Prayers

WINTER
WEDNESDAY: 3RD WEEK OF ADVENT
See the signs of God:

1. Isaiah 45:6-8, 18-25.
Let justice come like gentle rain.

2. Luke 7:18-23.
Tell John what you have seen and heard.

We long for you, O Lord, be near;
Come down that we may see and hear...

SUMMER
WEDNESDAY: 11TH WEEK OF THE YEAR
Attitudes and motives are important:

1a. II Corinthians 9:6-11.
God loves a cheerful giver.

1b. II Kings 2:1, 6-14.
Elijah goes to heaven in a whirlwind.

2. Matthew 6:1-6,16-18.
Do not behave like hypocrites.

Great God, purge our hypocrisy.
Give us your generosity...

SPRING
WEDNESDAY: 3RD WEEK OF LENT
Commandments for God's people:

1. Deuteronomy 4:1, 5-9.
Moses lays down the law.

2. Matthew 5:17-19.
Jesus: the law will be fulfilled.

Lord, you have blessed us with your law;
May we fulfill and teach it all...

FALL
WEDNESDAY: 24TH WEEK OF THE YEAR
Contrasts between the love of God and ours:

1a. I Timothy 3:14-16.
The mystery of faith is wonderful.

1b. I Corinthians 12:31-13:13.
The qualities of love.

2. Luke 7:31-35.
A generation of spoiled children.

Lord, you are patient, you are kind;
No greater love shall any find...

Meditation. The Lord's Prayer. Intercessions. Personal Prayers.

EVENING PRAYER

Reflections on the Day. Thanksgiving. Reconciliation.

EVENING PSALM / PS. 13 *Let me have hope.* PAGE 6.

THE LOVE OF GOD / ROMANS 8:35-39 *Who can be against us?* PAGE 6.

Personal Prayers.

Week Three / THURSDAY
MORNING PRAYER

I. THE PSALMS

MORNING PSALM / PS. 100
Praise God from whom all blessings flow.
PAGE 7

PSALMS OF THE DAY / PSS. 37:29-40 & 39
Reassurance and a plea for light.

PSALM 37:29-40 / *Salvation for the just will come.*

²⁹ The just are heirs, the land is theirs
 To keep eternally.
³⁴ We look to you, Lord, keep your ways
 That we your heirs may be.

³⁰ The mouth speaks wisdom in the just;
 Their tongues will never trip.
³¹ Their hearts hold fast the law of God;
 Their feet will never slip.

³² The wicked spy upon the just,
 To kill is their intent.
³³ But God will not abandon them,
 Nor let them be condemned.

³⁵ Yes, I have seen the wicked thrive
 And flourish like a tree.
³⁶ I looked again and they were gone.
 There was no one to see.

³⁷ Observe the honest, mark the good;
 Their future is secure.
³⁸ But not the wicked. Lord, for them
 Destruction is assured.

³⁹ Salvation for the just will come
 From you, O Lord, alone.
In time of trouble you will be
 Their fortress built on stone.

⁴⁰ You rescue them from wicked hands,
And bring them back to you.
Lord, you deliver them because
They put their trust in you.

PSALM 39 / *Lord, let me know my end.*

² I swore to watch my tongue,
 to keep my mouth from sin;
To muzzle it, keep all within.

³ The wicked came, and I was dumb,
 said not a word.
It only made the pain grow worse.

⁴ It smoldered in my heart,
 it flamed within my brain,
I broke and spoke, could not refrain:

⁵ Lord, let me know my end,
 the number of my days.
How frail I am, unsure my ways.

⁶ How short the span of life!
 How close to us our death!
To you we all are but a breath.

⁷ Like breath we disappear,
 like shadows we pursue.
We scrimp and save, for what? For whom?

⁸ What lies ahead? You are my hope,
 and all I want.
⁹ Free me from sin, and fools who taunt.

¹⁰ I will be dumb again,
 not say another word,
And trust in you to do your work.

¹¹ Yet, Lord, one prayer I make:
    to lift this plague from me.
    Your heavy hand has ravaged me.

¹² You chasten us for sin,
    consume what we desire.
    A breath are we, and you a fire.

¹³ But hear the prayer we breathe;
    turn not aside in ire;
    And let our tears put out your fire.

I walk with you,
    a stranger in your house, a guest;
    And like my fathers I request:

¹⁴ Avert your gaze, O Lord,
    that I may smile once more
    Before I go, to be no more.

II. READINGS & PRAYERS

WINTER
THURSDAY: 3RD WEEK OF ADVENT
Listen to a loving God:

1. Isaiah 54:1-10.
    The Lord will take you back.

2. Luke 7:24-30.
    Jesus talks about John the Baptizer.

The prophets speak for God above;
We hear their words, they come with love...

SPRING
THURSDAY: 3RD WEEK OF LENT
Whose side will we be on?

1. Jeremiah 7:23-28.
    This nation does not listen.

2. Luke 11:14-23.
    The one not with me is against me.

You chose us, Lord, and we choose you;
We are with you in all we do...

SUMMER
THURSDAY: 11TH WEEK OF THE YEAR
Jesus teaches prayer, forgiveness:

1a. II Corinthians 11:1-11.
    Put up with my jealousy for you.

1b. Sirach 48:1-14.
    In praise of Elijah.

2. Matthew 6:7-15.
    The Lord's prayer.

"Our Father," we presume to say,
For Jesus taught us so to pray...

FALL
THURSDAY: 24TH WEEK OF THE YEAR
The importance of Scripture and Love:

1a. I Timothy 4:12-16.
    Read Scripture, preach and teach.

1b. I Corinthians 15:1-11.
    Remember the gospel I preached.

2. Luke 7:36-50.
    Those who love much are forgiven.

O Word of God, we love your words,
Especially of mercy, Lord...

Meditation. The Lord's Prayer. Intercessions. Personal Prayers.

EVENING PRAYER

Reflections on the Day. Thanksgiving. Reconciliation.

EVENING PSALM / PS. 131 *A child in your mother's arms.* PAGE 7.

THE UNSEEN GOD / COLOSSIANS 1:15-20 *First born of all creation.* PAGE 7.

Personal Prayers.

Week Three / FRIDAY

MORNING PRAYER

I. THE PSALMS

MORNING PSALM / PS. 130
Out of the depths.
PAGE 8

PSALM OF THE DAY / PS. 38
The prayer of one gravely ill.

PSALM 38 / *Do not abandon me, O God.*

2 Rebuke me not in anger, Lord,
  Nor punish me in wrath.
3 Your arrows have sunk deep in me.
  Your hand has crossed my path.

4 No part of me was left unscathed;
  No soundness lies within;
Because of you, your anger Lord,
  Because of me, my sin.

5 My many sins hang over me;
  They weigh me down with shame.
6 My wounds are festering and foul;
  My folly is to blame.

7 Bent over, prostrate on the ground;
  My day is filled with groans.
8 My body hot with fever burns;
  No health is in my bones.

9 My life is spent, crushed utterly;
  My heart in anguish moans.
10 You see it all, my sighs, my pleas,
  Not hid from you my groans.

11 My heart is throbbing, strength is gone;
  Now everything looks gray.
12 Companions, friends, they all have left.
  My neighbors stay away.

13 The foes who seek my life are here,
  Who aim to do me wrong.
  They set their traps and tell their lies;
  They do it all day long.

14 But I am deaf, I hear them not,
  Their lies and treachery.
15 And I am dumb, my mouth is shut;
  No answer comes from me.

16 I wait for you, for you, O Lord,
  To answer them for me.
17 I only pray that when I fall,
  They shall not gloat in glee.

18 I know that I am on the edge;
  My pain is that intense.
19 I do confess my sin to you;
  I grieve for my offense.

20 How many are the enemies
  Who hate me without cause!
21 The good I do is paid with ill,
  Because I love your laws.

22 Do not abandon me, O God;
  Be near, be my reward.
23 Come quickly now, it is my hour;
  Be my salvation, Lord.

II. READINGS & PRAYERS

WINTER

Friday: 3rd Week of Advent
An invitation from the Lord:

1. Isaiah 56:1-3, 6-8.
   My house shall be a house of prayer.

2. John 5:33-36.
   John was a lamp, my work is light..

Show us your light, your work, your way,
That we may follow you today...

SUMMER

FRIDAY: 11TH WEEK OF THE YEAR
The feast of the Sacred Heart of Jesus:

A 1. Deuteronomy 7:6-11.
   The Lord set his heart on you.

2. I John 4:7-16.
   God loved us first.

3. Matthew 11:25-30.
   I am gentle and humble of heart.

B 1. Hosea 11:1-9.
   When Israel was a child I loved him.

2. Ephesians 3:8-19.
   The love of Christ surpasses all.

3. John 19:31-37.
   They pierced his side; blood poured out.

C 1. Ezekiel 34:11-16.
   I will tend my sheep.

2. Romans 5:5-11.
   The love of God has been poured out.

3. Luke 15:3-7.
   Rejoice, I have found my lost sheep.

Good Shepherd, Lord, whose Sacred Heart
    rejoiced with all who dwell above,
When you brought back the sheep you lost,
    We trust in you, your faithful love.

SPRING

FRIDAY: 3RD WEEK OF LENT
What is truly important:

1. Hosea 14:2-10.
   Forsake your idols; God will heal.

2. Mark 12:28-34.
   The two great commandants.

For us, O Lord, no god but you;
And we shall love our neighbor, too...

FALL

FRIDAY: 24TH WEEK OF THE YEAR
In the vineyard of the Lord:

1a. I Timothy 6:2-12.
   Be content, fight the good fight.

1b. I Corinthians 15:12-20.
   Christ lives; our faith is not in vain.

2. Luke 8:1-3.
   Many women assisted Jesus.

You seek the help of all
    to spread your word.
May all with faith cooperate, O Lord...

Meditation. The Lord's Prayer. Intercessions. Personal Prayers.

EVENING PRAYER

Reflections on the Day. Thanksgiving. Reconciliation.

EVENING PSALM / PS. 51 *David's prayer for forgiveness.* PAGE 8.

CANTICLE OF SIMEON / LUKE 2:29-32 *Lord, let me go in peace.* PAGE 8.

Personal Prayers.

Week Three / SATURDAY
MORNING PRAYER

I. THE PSALMS

MORNING PSALM / PS. 141
Like incense let my prayer arise.
PAGE 9

PSALMS OF THE DAY / PSS. 29 & 40
Praise, gratitude, promises, and pleas.

PSALM 29 / *The voice of God!*

1 Give God the glory, all you lords on high.
  Pay homage to the Lord, the royal crown.
2 Come glorify the name of God most high.
  Before the glory of the Lord bow down.

3 Across the waters rolls the voice of God.
  The God of glory thunders o'er the sea.
4 How awesome in its strength
    the voice of God;
  How glorious, how filled with majesty!

5,7 The voice of God like fire
      from heaven springs;
  Engulfs the mighty cedars in its flame.
6 Makes Lebanon to skip, a calf in spring;
  Makes Sirion to roar, an ox untamed.

8 The voice of God convulses all the earth;
  It shakes the wilderness, it strips the trees.
9 It terrifies the beasts to giving birth;
  And in the temple all cry, "Glory be!"

10 Above the storm the Lord, enthroned in light
  Serenely reigns forevermore in peace.
11 May God bestow upon the people might,
  And graciously bestow on them God's peace.

Psalm 40 / *I come to do your will.*

2 I called and called to God,
    Who stooped to hear my plea.
3 And raised me from this pit of death,
    This bog surrounding me.

My feet were set on solid rock;
    My steps made firm by God.
4 A song was placed upon my lips,
    A hymn of praise to God.

5 That all in awe might see and hear,
    And come to trust the Lord.
  Trust not the proud, nor those who lie;
    Bless those who trust the Lord.

6 Lord, you have done great things for us,
    None can compare with you.
  Were I to try to tell them all,
    I never would get through.

7 You do not seek our sacrifice;
    Obedience you ask.
8 Burnt offerings you do not need;
    Your will will be my task.

9 Lord, "Here am I," to do your will;
    It is my joy, my part.
  As it is written in the scroll:
    "Your law is in my heart."

10 I sang it in the great assembly:
    How you saved me, Lord;
  Proclaimed your righteousness to all;
    You know it well, my Lord.

11 I did not keep it to myself;
    I spread it everywhere.
  I did not hide your faithful love
    From those who gathered there.

12 Do not withhold from me, O Lord,
    Your tender care for me.
Let your enduring faithful love
    Be ever there for me.

13 For countless evils circle me;
    My sins have followed me.
I have more ills than I have hair.
    My heart is failing me.

14 O favor me and save me, Lord;
    Come quickly with your arm.
15 Frustration and disgrace inflict
    On those who do me harm.

16 Let them turn back and be disgraced
    Who wish to see me dead.
Let all who cry "Aha!" at me
    Be shamed themselves instead.

17 Let all who seek you, Lord, be glad;
    Let them rejoice in God.
Let those who love salvation cry
    Forever: "Great is God!"

18 Lord, I am poor and much in need;
    But you will find a way
To help me and deliver me.
    O Lord, do not delay.

II. READINGS & PRAYERS

WINTER
ADVENT: DECEMBER 17*
Where does Jesus come from?

1. Genesis 49:2, 8-10.
    The scepter shall not pass from Judah.

2. Matthew 1:1-17.
    The genealogy of Jesus Christ.

O faithful God, your word is true.
We trust the Word that comes from you...

SPRING
SATURDAY: 3RD WEEK OF LENT
What God asks of us:

1. Hosea 6:1-6.
    The Lord seeks love not sacrifice.

2. Luke 18:9-14.
    The prayers of the pharisee & publican.

O Lord, you seek no gift from me,
Except my heart's humility...

SUMMER
SATURDAY: 11TH WEEK OF THE YEAR
God will take care of you:

1a. II Corinthians 12:1-10.
    I boast only of my weakness.

1b. II Chronicles 24:17-25.
    Zechariah prophecies, and is killed.

2. Matthew 6:24-34.
    Do not worry about tomorrow.

Though I am weak and foes are strong,
My trust in you, O Lord, lives on...

FALL
SATURDAY: 24TH WEEK OF THE YEAR
The seed is the word of God:

1a. I Timothy 6:13-16.
    Keep at the task until he comes.

1b. I Corinthians 15:35-37, 42-49.
    Our natural bodies will become spiritual.

2. Luke 8:4-15.
    The parable of the sower and the seed.

Great harvester, great sower of the Word,
Transform your seed to fruit, O Lord...

Meditation. The Lord's Prayer. Intercessions. Personal Prayers.

EVENING PRAYER

Reflections on the Day. Thanksgiving. Reconciliation.

EVENING PSALM / PS. 143 *Lord, do not condemn.* PAGE 9.

SONG OF MOSES / REVELATION 15:3-4 *They all had harps and sang.* PAGE 9.

Personal Prayers.

*NOTE: The Psalms and Readings for December 18, when it falls on a weekday, are found on page 223. For December 19 and the following dates, return to pages 64 and following.

Week Four

Week Four / SUNDAY
MORNING PRAYER

I. THE PSALMS

MORNING PSALM / PS. 95
O my people, now listen to me.
PAGE 3

PSALM OF THE DAY / PS. 89:2-19 & 20-28
PART I. A Hymn of Praise. PART II. The Covenant with David.

PSALM 89:2-19 / *Your faithful love shines out in all you do.*

2 Forever will I sing your love, O Lord,
To every age your faithfulness confirm.
3 I said: "Your faithful love will never end.
As fixed and sure as heaven, it is firm."

4 God said: "I have a covenant with them:
My servant David is my chosen one.
5 And I have sworn to him:
Upon your throne
Your sons shall sit as long as shines
the sun."

6 Let heaven praise the wonders
of our God!
Let its assembly sing with one accord.
7 For who on high can be compared
to God?
Or who among the lords
is like our Lord?

8 One held in awe by all the holy ones,
Our God is awesome,
great beyond compare.
9 O mighty God, who is like you, O Lord?
Your strength and faithfulness
are everywhere.

10 You rule the surging seas,
you still the waves.
11 You crushed the monster Rahab
with a blow.
12 The heavens and the earth belong to you.
Your mighty arm has scattered every foe.

You set in place the world and all it holds.
The mountains, north and south,
your might proclaim.
Mount Tabor, Hermon, you created all.
13 They sing for you and echo back
your name.

14 You have a mighty arm,
your hand is strong.
Your right hand raised on high is ever true.
15 Your throne, O Lord, is founded on the right,
Your faithful love shines out in all you do.

16 The people who rejoice in you are blest.
They walk in light that shines
on all from you.
17 Your saving justice, Lord, will lift them up,
To praise the name of God
the whole day through.

18 You are the strength your people glory in,
And by your grace our victory you bring.
19 Indeed you are a shield to us, O Lord,
The holy one of Israel, our King.

PSALM 89:20-28 / *I chose my servant, David, I swore to him.*

20 You told your faithful in a vision once:
I chose a youth,
no soldier for my king.
21 My servant, David, from my people took,
And with my holy oil anointed him.

22 My strength of hand
shall be in David's hand;
My arm sustain the power in his arm.
23 The wicked shall not trip my chosen one;
No foe shall overcome nor do him harm.

62

²⁴ His foes, and those who hate him,
     I will crush.
²⁵ Fidelity and faithful love I give.
   My name will bring a victory to him.
²⁶ His hand shall rule the sea,
     and he shall live.

²⁷ Then he shall say to me:
     "You are my God,
   My father, and my rock of refuge, Lord,"
²⁸ To him I will reply: "You are my son,
   First born, the kings of earth
     be your reward."

II. READINGS & PRAYERS

WINTER

4TH SUNDAY OF ADVENT
The conception of Christ.

YEAR A

1. Isaiah 7:10-14.
   A virgin shall conceive a son.
2. Romans 1:1-7.
   Jesus, son of David, Son of God.
3. Matthew 1:18-24.
   He is Emmanuel, God with us.

YEAR B

1. II Samuel 7:1-16.
   David's house will last forever.
2. Romans 16:25-27.
   The mystery is now revealed.
3. Luke 1:26-38.
   The Annunciation of the Lord.

YEAR C

1. Micah 5:1-4.
   He shall come from Bethlehem.
2. Hebrews 10:5-10.
   He brings a new covenant.
3. Luke 1:39-45.
   Mary visits Elizabeth.

IN MARY, HIDDEN, YOU BEGAN
The work of saving us from sin.
O Father, now begin again
Within our hearts; we wait for him.

SPRING

4TH SUNDAY OF LENT
Jesus, Son of Mercy, Son of Light.

YEAR A

1. I Samuel 16:1-13.
   David is anointed king.
2. Ephesians 5:8-14.
   Flee darkness; seek the light.
3. John 9:1-41.
   Jesus gives sight to the blind.

YEAR B

1. II Chronicles 36:14-23.
   God's people prove unfaithful.
2. Ephesians 2:4-10.
   But God proves merciful.
3. John 3:14-21.
   God sent his Son to save.

YEAR C

1. Joshua 5:9-12.
   The people celebrated passover.
2. II Corinthians 5:17-21.
   God has reconciled us.
3. Luke 15:1-32.
   The merciful father and prodigal son.

O FATHER, WE WERE BLIND, WERE LOST.
You rescued us, you gave us sight.
But we in darkness wander still,
And still we seek your Son, our Light.

SUMMER

12TH SUNDAY OF THE YEAR
God rules the world; believe in him.

YEAR A
1. Jeremiah 20:10-13.
   The prophet prays for vengeance.
2. Romans 5:12-15.
   Grace overcomes the offense.
3. Matthew 10:26-33.
   Be not afraid; your father reigns.

YEAR B
1. Job 28:8-11.
   I set the limits of the seas.
2. II Corinthians 5:14-17.
   God makes all things new.
3. Mark 4:35-41.
   The wind and sea obey him.

YEAR C
1. Zechariah 12:10-11.
   They shall mourn as for an only son.
2. Galatians 3:26-29.
   By faith you all belong to Christ.
3. Luke 9:18-24.
   Peter's confession of faith.

GOD, FATHER, SON, YOU RULE THE WAVES.
The seas obey; the winds do, too.
Midst enemies and stormy seas,
Increase our faith, our trust in you.

FALL

25TH SUNDAY OF THE YEAR
About money, and the goodness of God.

YEAR A
1. Isaiah 55:6-9.
   My ways are high above your ways.
2. Philippians 1:20-27.
   Alive or dead, my life is Christ.
3. Matthew 20:1-16.
   The workers all are paid the same.

YEAR B
1. Wisdom 2:12,17-20.
   The wicked plot against the just.
2. James 3:16-4:3.
   Conflicts come from envy and greed.
3. Mark 9:30-37.
   The first must serve the least of all.

YEAR C
1. Amos 8:4-7.
   The Lord condemns cheating the poor.
2. I Timothy 2:1-8.
   Pray for leaders and be at peace.
3. Luke 16:1-13.
   You cannot serve God and money.

LORD, YOU ARE JUST AND GENEROUS
To all your children in their need.
We pray for all, our leaders, too.
Let envy cease, dispel our greed.

Meditation. The Lord's Prayer. Intercessions. Personal Prayers.

EVENING PRAYER

Reflections on the Day. Thanksgiving. Reconciliation.

EVENING PSALM / PS. 23 *The Lord will give me rest.* PAGE 3.

CANTICLE OF MARY / LUKE 1:46-55 *Behold the handmaid of the Lord.* PAGE 3.

Personal Prayers.

Week Four / MONDAY
MORNING PRAYER

I. THE PSALMS

MORNING PSALM / PS. 24
Let the King of glory in.
PAGE 4

PSALM OF THE DAY / PS. 89:29-38 & 39-53
The Covenant with David continued. Part III: The King's Lament.

PSALM 89:29-38 / *I will not violate my covenant.*

29 Forever will he have my faithful love;
My covenant with him will never pass.
30 His royal line shall last forevermore.
His throne endure as long as heaven lasts.

31 But if his children should forsake my law,
Refuse to follow my decrees, my way;
32 If they should not observe
what I command,
And from my statutes choose
to ever stray;

33 Their sins will I then punish
with my rod;
Iniquity with plagues will I repay.
34 But never will I stop my faithful love;
Fidelity I never will betray.

35 I will not violate my covenant,
Nor will I ever change
what you have heard.
36 I swore to David on my holiness;
I cannot lie, forever true my word.

37 The sun shall set, shall cease to shine, to be,
Before this throne, this dynasty shall die.
38 The moon will die, but David's seed live on.
His throne is firmer, higher than the sky.

PSALM 89:39-53 / *Have you created us in vain?*

39 But lo, in anger
you have spurned him, Lord,
In rage have turned
from your anointed one,
40 Your covenant, your servant you forgot,
Defiled in dust the crown of David's son.

41 You breached the walls
that had protected him.
Reduced his fortress to a pile of stone.
42 As every passerby takes more away,
He hears the taunts of all
and stands alone.

43 You lifted high the hands of all his foes.
You made his enemies rejoice, O Lord.
44 In anger you deflected all his blows;
In battle you did not sustain his sword.

45 You took the royal scepter
from his hand.
46 You cast his throne to earth;
cut short his days.
47 And covered him with shame.
O Lord, how long
Will you be turned away,
and anger blaze?

48 Remember me, how short
   my span of life.
49 O Lord, have you created us in vain?
   Can anyone escape from death alone?
50 Will not your faithful love of old
   remain?

You promised David your fidelity.
51 O Lord, see what abuse
   they fling at me.
Your servant, I have borne
   the nations' lies.
52 Your foes' abuse of your anointed see!

At every step I am abused by them.
53 But you are ever blessed, O Lord. Amen.

II. Readings & Prayers

WINTER
Advent: December 19
God makes the barren fruitful:

1. Judges 13:2-7, 24-25.
   The promised birth of Samuel.

2. Luke 1:5-25.
   The promised birth of John.

Lord, nothing is impossible with you.
Our lives are barren, make them fruitful, too...

SPRING
Monday: 4th Week of Lent
The will of God is clear:

1. Isaiah 65:17-21.
   God will create a world of joy.

2. John 4:43-54.
   Jesus heals an official's son.

You want to heal us, calm our fears;
Lord, give us faith, and wipe our tears...

SUMMER
Monday: 12th Week of the Year
Obedience rewarded, hypocrisy scorned:

1a. Genesis 12:1-9.
   Abraham went as God told him.

1b. II Kings 17:5-8, 13-15.
   Israel is rejected, Judah chosen.

2. Matthew 7:1-5.
   Remove the beam from your eye first.

Just Lord, you give to all their due;
May we prove faithful, true to you...

FALL
Monday: 25th Week of the Year
How to work with one's neighbor:

1a. Ezra 1:1-6.
   The return to rebuild Jerusalem.

1b. Proverbs 3:27-34.
   Be just; quarrel not.

2. Luke 8:16-18.
   Let your light shine for all to see.

To build your kingdom, Lord, we must
Cooperate, shed light, and trust...

Meditation. The Lord's Prayer. Intercessions. Personal Prayers.

Evening Prayer

Reflections on the Day. Thanksgiving. Reconciliation.

Evening Psalm / Ps. 4 *I go to sleep in peace.* Page 4.

Canticle of Zachary / Luke 1:68-79 *Prepare the way of the Lord.* Page 4.

Personal Prayers.

Week Four / TUESDAY
MORNING PRAYER

I. THE PSALMS

MORNING PSALM / PS. 5
At dawn I pray to you.
PAGE 5

PSALMS OF THE DAY / PSS. 42 & 43
A song of sorrow in captivity.

PSALM 42:2-6 / *I thirst for you, O God*

2 Like deer that thirst for running water,
  So my soul seeks you, O God.
3 I thirst for you, my living Lord.
  When shall I see the face of God?

4 My tears have been my steady diet.
  Day and night they ask of me:
  "This god, your god, where is he now?"
3 Continually taunting me.

As I pour out my soul in tears
5 I still recall those happy days
  When in procession to the temple
  We would march with shouts of praise.

6 O why are you so sad my spirit?
  Why the sighs, why groan and mope?
  For God is still your Lord and savior.
  Praise the Lord! Keep up your hope!

PSALM 42:7-12 / *Have you forgotten me?*

7 My soul is sad for I recall
  The land where I knew liberty.
8 For here the depths cry out to depths,
  And torrents, waves sweep over me.

9 Each day, Lord, send your faithful love;
  Each night your praise will be with me.
10 I pray to you, the God of life;
  My rock have you forgotten me?

Why must I walk so mournfully?
  My enemies oppress me, God.
11 They crush my bones; they taunt, I hear
  Their constant cry: "Where is your God?"

12 O why are you so sad my spirit?
  Why the sighs, why groan and mope?
  For God is still your Lord and savior.
  Praise the Lord! Keep up your hope!

PSALM 43 / *Send forth your light and truth.*

1 Defend me God, my cause is just.
  From faithless people rescue me.
2 You are my God, you are my refuge.
  Why have you rejected me?

My enemies harass me, Lord;
  O why must I go through this hell?
3 Send forth your light and truth to lead me
  To the mountain where you dwell.

4 Then I shall come before your altar
  Full of joy in you, my God.
  And I will praise you on my harp,
  Forever praise you, Lord my God!

5 O why are you so sad my spirit?
  Why the sighs, why groan and mope?
  For God is still your Lord and savior.
  Praise the Lord! Keep up your hope!

II. READINGS & PRAYERS

WINTER
ADVENT: DECEMBER 20
The incarnation of the Son of God:

1. Isaiah 7:10-14.
   A virgin shall be with child.

2. Luke 1:26-38.
   The annunciation to Mary.

Like Mary, we would servants be,
And say, "Your will be done in me..."

SUMMER
TUESDAY: 12TH WEEK OF THE YEAR
The way of the Lord:

1a. Genesis 13:2, 5-18.
   Abram, Lot divide the land.

1b. II Kings 19:9-36.
   Jerusalem is saved by prayer.

2. Matthew 7:6, 12-14.
   The golden rule.

Your way, O Lord, leads to success,
We put our faith in nothing less...

SPRING
TUESDAY: 4TH WEEK OF LENT
Water as a symbol of healing and life:

1. Ezekiel 47:1-9, 12.
   The miraculous river of God.

2. John 5:1-3, 5-16.
   The miraculous pool of Bethesda.

We thirst for you as you do us.
Our health, O Lord, restore to us...

FALL
TUESDAY: 25TH WEEK OF THE YEAR
God's work and word:

1a. Ezra 6:7-20
   Rebuilding the Temple.

1b. Proverbs 21:1-6, 10-13.
   The Lord looks at the heart.

2. Luke 8:19-21.
   My family are those who keep my word.

Examine me, the work I do;
I seek your word and trust in you...

Meditation. The Lord's Prayer. Intercessions. Personal Prayers.

EVENING PRAYER

Reflections on the Day. Thanksgiving. Reconciliation.

EVENING PSALM / PS. 6 *My bed is wet with tears.* PAGE 5.

THE CHRIST HYMN / PHILIPPIANS 2:6-11 *The mind of Christ.* PAGE 5.

Personal Prayers.

Week Four / WEDNESDAY
MORNING PRAYER

I. THE PSALMS

MORNING PSALM / PS. 101
A royal pledge.
PAGE 6

PSALMS OF THE DAY / PSS. 49 & 52

Two wisdom psalms directed at the wealthy and powerful.

PSALM 49 / *All shall die and leave their wealth behind.*

2 Hear this, all you people, listen
    All who live on earth,
3 Whether you be rich or poor,
    Of low or noble birth.

4 Words of wisdom I shall utter,
    Insights from the heart.
5 Listen; you will hear a proverb
    Sung upon the harp.

6 Why should I be fearful, sad,
    When foes encircle me:
7 Those who trust in wealth and boast
    Of their sufficiency?

8 No one can redeem one's life,
    Pay off one's debt on high.
9 Far too costly is the ransom.
    10 All will surely die.

11 All can see, the wisest die,
    The rich and foolish, too.
All must leave their wealth behind;
    12 Their home will be their tomb.

There they shall forever stay,
    Though they on earth rose high.
13 No one can retain one's wealth;
    They all, like beasts, will die.

14 Such the fate of all the proud,
    Contented with their lot,
15 Headed for Sheol like sheep;
    Death shepherding the flock.

Down they go, Sheol their home,
    Their bodies waste away.
16 God will save me from Sheol;
    Will snatch my soul away.

17 Envy not the prosperous
    Whose riches ever grow.
18 Death will take their wealth away;
    With them it will not go.

19 Living they are quite content;
    They think they did all right.
20 Dying as their parents died,
    To never see the light.

21 Wealthy people fail to see
They all, like beasts, will die.

PSALM 52 / *One day the Lord will bring you down.*

3 Why boast of wickedness,
    you powerful,
Of victories against the commonweal?
4 Your tongues are razor sharp,
    all day you plan
To pull off still another shady deal.

5 Your hateful tongues love evil
    more than good,
6 Love lying more than truth,
    and words that kill.
7 One day the Lord will break you,
    bring you down,
Uproot you from the land, one day God will.

8 The just in awe will see, will laugh and say:
9 "Behold the one who had no use
    for God;
Who trusted more in power
    and in wealth,
Relied on evil plots instead of God."

10 But I, an olive tree in heaven's court,
Will trust your faithful love
    for all my days.
Will give you thanks
    for all that you have done,
11 Will glorify your name
    and give you praise.

II. READINGS & PRAYERS

WINTER

ADVENT: DECEMBER 21
Mary visits her cousin Elizabeth:

1. Songs 2:8-14.
   Arise my love, my dove, and come.
2. Luke 1:39-45.
   Elizabeth's inspired greeting.

"Hail Mary, full of grace," we say.
Your children greet you; for us pray...

SPRING

WEDNESDAY: 4TH WEEK OF LENT
God is like a mother, father to us:

1. Isaiah 49:8-15.
   Can a mother forget her child?
2. John 5:17-30.
   Jesus calls God his father.

O loving God, a mother mild;
I trust in you, I am your child...

SUMMER

WEDNESDAY: 12TH WEEK OF THE YEAR
How God rewards fidelity:

1a. Genesis 15:1-12,17-18.
    Abram is justified by faith.
1b. II Kings 22:8-13, 23:1-3.
    The covenant is renewed.
2.   Matthew 7:15-20.
    By their fruits you will know them.

With land, redemption, fruit, O Lord;
You grant your people their reward...

FALL

WEDNESDAY: 25TH WEEK OF THE YEAR
Our God has work for us to do:

1a. Ezra 9:5-9.
    The Lord has not forgotten us.
1b. Proverbs 30:5-9.
    Ask only for what you need.
2.   Luke 9:1-6.
    He sent them out to spread the news.

Lord, give us work, and all we need
To spread your word, to sow your seed...

Meditation. The Lord's Prayer. Intercessions. Personal Prayers.

EVENING PRAYER

Reflections on the Day. Thanksgiving. Reconciliation.

EVENING PSALM / PS. 13 *Let me have hope.* PAGE 6.

THE LOVE OF GOD / ROMANS 8:35-39 *Who can be against us?* PAGE 6.

Personal Prayers.

Week Four / THURSDAY
MORNING PRAYER

I. THE PSALMS

MORNING PSALM / PS. 100

Praise God from whom all blessings flow.

PAGE 7

PSALM OF THE DAY / PS. 50

An indictment of superficial religion.

PSALM 50 / *Make grateful praise your sacrifice.*

1 The God of gods, the Lord now speaks.
From east to west, God summons all.
2 From Zion's hill of perfect beauty
God appears and sounds the call.

3 The Lord who comes will not be mute.
Preceded by consuming flame,
4 Surrounded by a raging storm,
God calls to judgment those to blame.

5 "First bring my faithful, those who kept
My covenant and sacrifice.
6 That I alone am judge and just
You soon shall see in paradise.

7 But you, my people Israel:
Against you I will testify.
I speak to you, so pay me heed;
I am your Lord, your God am I.

8 I censure not your sacrifice,
Your daily offerings to me.
9 I claim no bull or goat from you,
10 For all the beasts belong to me.

11 The cattle on a thousand hills,
The forest dwellers too are mine.
I know each bird that flies above,
For all that moves on earth is mine.

12 If I were hungry, why tell you?
The world is mine and all it holds.
13 Do I need meat to eat to live?
Do I need blood so I won't scold?

14 Make grateful praise your sacrifice;
Fulfill your promises to me.
15 Then call on me in time of need
To rescue you, to honor me."

16 But, to the wicked God will say:
"You speak of covenant. Absurd!
17 How dare you talk about my law?
You hate my rules, ignore my word.

18 You meet a thief, make him your friend;
Keep company with those who lust.
19 You say whatever comes to mouth,
Become a person none can trust.

20 You sit and slander family,
Your mother's child. When you do this
21 Shall I be dumb? Am I like you?
I lay the charge, you answer it.

22 Mark this, you who forget your God,
Lest I destroy, abandon you.
23 To honor me give thanks and praise.
When you obey, I shall be true."

II. READINGS & PRAYERS

WINTER
ADVENT: DECEMBER 22
The generosity of two women:

1. I Samuel 1:24-28.
   Hannah gives Samuel to the Lord.

2. Luke 1:46-56.
   The Canticle of Mary.

Like Mary, Hannah, Lord, we give
Ourselves, our all, that all may live...

SPRING
THURSDAY: 4TH WEEK OF LENT
The people's lack of faith in Christ:

1. Exodus 32:7-14.
   Moses fends off God's anger.

2. John 5:31-47.
   Even Moses will condemn them.

We do believe your works and word;
Increase our faith in you, O Lord...

SUMMER
THURSDAY: 12TH WEEK OF THE YEAR
Build your house on rock:

1a. Genesis 16:6-16.
   Sarah & Hagar; Isaac & Ishmael.

1b. II Kings 24:8-17.
   Jerusalem falls to Babylon.

2. Matthew 7:21-29.
   Jesus teaches with authority.

You show us, Lord, your way, your path;
We follow to escape your wrath...

FALL
THURSDAY: 25TH WEEK OF THE YEAR
God's work never ends:

1a. Haggai 1:1-8.
   Rebuild my temple says the Lord.

1b. Ecclesiastes 1:2-11.
   Nothing is new under the sun.

2. Luke 9:7-9.
   Herod is curious about Jesus.

Rebuild, renew, and persevere;
O patient Lord, be with us here...

Meditation. The Lord's Prayer. Intercessions. Personal Prayers.

EVENING PRAYER

Reflections on the Day. Thanksgiving. Reconciliation.

EVENING PSALM / PS. 131 *A child in your mother's arms.* PAGE 7.

THE UNSEEN GOD / COLOSSIANS 1:15-20 *First born of all creation* PAGE 7.

Personal Prayers.

Week Four / FRIDAY

MORNING PRAYER

I. THE PSALMS

MORNING PSALM / PS. 130
Out of the depths.
PAGE 8

PSALM OF THE DAY / PS. 44
An aggressive national lament.

PSALM 44 / *Arise, O God, and save!*

2 Our ears have heard the tales, O Lord.
　　For ages we've been told:
　The wonders that your hands performed,
　　Your deeds in days of old.

3 The nations that you harried out
　　To pave the way for us.
4 No sword gave us the victory;
　　It was your love for us.

5 You are our King, O God: command!
　　Give Jacob victory.
6 Through you, your name, we conquer all.
　　We crush our enemy.

7 No sword will give us victory;
　　We do not trust in bows.
8 You put to shame our enemy;
　　You conquer all our foes.

9 We glory in the Lord our God,
　　In you forevermore.
　We praise your name unceasingly;
　　We praise and we adore.

10 But now you have rejected us.
　　We fight alone until,
11 When forced to flee, our enemy
　　Can plunder us at will.

12 Like sheep for slaughter we've become
　　Dispersed throughout the land.
13 You sold us for a trifle, Lord;
　　Got little back in hand.

14 The butt of nations we've become;
　　Our failure all discuss.
15 A byword for defeat are we;
　　They shake their heads at us.

16 The sight of spiteful enemies
　　Brings shame into our face.
17 The sound of taunts reviling us
　　Adds gall to our disgrace.

18 All this though we forgot you not;
　　Your covenant we kept.
19 Our heart did not turn back from you;
　　Your way we never left.

20 Yet you have left us crushed, we lie
　　In shadows dark and deep.
21 Had we forgot the name of God,
　　To pagans sold our hearts,

22 Would not God know, who always knows
　　The secrets of the heart?
23 Because of you each day anew
　　They slaughter us like sheep.

24 Awake, O Lord, why do you sleep?
　　Do not reject us still.
25 Why do you hide your face from us,
　　Ignoring all our ills?

26 We are bowed down to earth, O Lord,
　　Yes, even to the grave.
27 As love demands, your faithful love,
　　Arise, O God, and save!

II. Readings & Prayers

WINTER
ADVENT: DECEMBER 23
John is the Elijah who was to come:

1. Malachi 3:1-4, 23-24.
   I send my messenger.

2. Luke 1: 57-66.
   Zachary names his son John.

As we revere the messenger,
So may the message find our ear...

SPRING
FRIDAY: 4TH WEEK OF LENT
The mystery of hatred and evil:

1. Wisdom 2:1,12-22.
   The wicked plan to kill the just.

2. John 7:1-2,10,25-30.
   The leaders plan to kill Jesus.

O God, you know our enemy,
Save us from their iniquity...

SUMMER
FRIDAY: 12TH WEEK OF THE YEAR
God's people have to suffer much:

1a. Genesis 17:9-10,15-22.
   God's covenant with Abraham.

1b. II Kings 25:1-12.
   The Babylonian captivity begins.

2. Matthew 8:1-4.
   Jesus cures a leper.

From illness and captivity,
We trust you, Lord, to set us free...

FALL
FRIDAY: 25TH WEEK OF THE YEAR
God's promises will be fulfilled:

1a. Haggai 1:15-2:9.
   A little while and I shall come.

1b. Ecclesiastes 3:1-11.
   There is a time for everything.

2. Luke 9:18-22.
   Jesus contemplates his future.

With you, O Lord, we look ahead:
For light we seek, your cross we dread...

Meditation. The Lord's Prayer. Intercessions. Personal Prayers.

EVENING PRAYER

Reflections on the Day. Thanksgiving. Reconciliation.

EVENING PSALM / PS. 51 *David's prayer for forgiveness.* PAGE 8.

CANTICLE OF SIMEON / LUKE 2:29-32 *Lord, let me go in peace.* PAGE 8.

Personal Prayers.

Week Four / SATURDAY
MORNING PRAYER

I. THE PSALMS

MORNING PSALM / PS. 141
Like incense let my prayer arise.
PAGE 9

PSALMS OF THE DAY / PSS. 45 & 46
Two songs filled with joy and confidence.

PSALM 45 / *A wedding song for King & Queen.*

2 A noble theme has stirred my heart:
  A royal wedding song I sing.
  Be swift my tongue, be skilled my pen,
  For I must play before the king.

3 You are the handsomest of men;
  And charm has graced your royal lips.
  You have been blessed eternally.
4 Take up the sword that rides your hip.

5 Advance in majesty, proceed
  Triumphantly, O mighty king.
  For truth and justice fight the fight,
  And may your arm the battle win.

6 Your arrows pierce your enemies;
  Beneath your feet they find their fate.
7 Your throne endures; your scepter rules.
  You love the good, and evil hate.

8 For this the Lord anointed you
  With oil of gladness over all.
9 You smell of aloe, cassia, myrrh;
  Their fragrance from your garments falls.

From ivory paneled palaces
Comes music played to make you glad.
10 The daughters of the kings, your court;
  Your queen in gold of Ophir clad.

11 O daughter listen, understand,
  And heed my words for they are true.
  Forget your people and your home.
12 Fair one, the king has chosen you.

He is your Lord, so honor him,
13 O daughter brought to us from Tyre.
  Our people shall pay court to you;
  Rich gifts from them you shall acquire.

14 The bride, adorned in gold and gems,
15 Is led in splendor to the king.
  Her maidens too go in with her,
16 And filled with joy, they too shall sing.

17 Your sons shall sit upon his throne,
  Become the princes of the land.
18 Your name will be forever known.
  This song be sung throughout the land.

PSALM 46 / *Be still and know that I am God.*

2 Our refuge and our strength is God,
  Who, ever near, will hear our plea.
3 The earth may reel, the mountains fall,
  The waters rage upon the sea;
4 But through it all we shall not fear
  The mountain's crash, the roaring tide,
  For God, the Lord of hosts, is here;
  The God of Jacob at our side.
5 A river makes the city glad,
  The dwelling place of God most high.
6 She shall not fall, for God will come,
  At dawn will come to hear her cry.
7 The nations rage and kingdoms fall,

And earth itself shall not abide.
8 But God, the Lord of hosts is here;
  The God of Jacob at our side.
9 O come and see what God had done:
  The desolation of the earth.
10 The Lord breaks bows,
    and shatters spears,
  Makes wars to cease,
    brings peace on earth.
11 "Be still, and know that I am God;
  And over all I still preside."
12 Yes, God, the Lord of hosts, is here;
  The God of Jacob at our side.

II. Readings & Prayers

WINTER
ADVENT: DECEMBER 24
Prophetic words:

1. II Samuel 7:1-5, 8-11, 16
   Your throne shall stand forever.

2. Luke 1:67-69.
   The Canticle of Zachary.

The day arrives, the Lord is due;
The way prepared, we wait for you...

SPRING
SATURDAY: 4TH WEEK OF LENT
The opposition grows:

1. Jeremiah 11:18-20.
   They hatch their plots against me.

2. John 7:40-53.
   Can the Messiah be from Galilee?

Lord, we are frightened easily;
O God of strength, our refuge be...

SUMMER
SATURDAY: 12TH WEEK OF THE YEAR
God's children live by faith:

1a. Genesis 18:1-15.
   God promises Abraham a son.

1b. Lamentations 2:2, 10-14, 18-19.
   My eyes worn out from tears.

2. Matthew 8:5-17.
   Jesus cures the centurion's son.

God knows how fathers love their sons;
Lord, care for all your little ones...

FALL
SATURDAY: 25TH WEEK OF THE YEAR
Death and glory lie ahead:

1a. Zechariah 2:5-9, 14-15.
   For Jerusalem, a promise of greatness.

1b. Ecclesiastes 11:9-12:8.
   To the young: remember God.

2. Luke 9:43-45.
   The disciples do not understand.

What lies ahead we do not see.
No matter, Lord, we follow thee...

Meditation. The Lord's Prayer. Intercessions. Personal Prayers.

EVENING PRAYER

Reflections on the Day. Thanksgiving. Reconciliation.

EVENING PSALM / PS. 143 *Lord, do not condemn.* PAGE 9.

SONG OF MOSES / REVELATION 15:3-4 *They had harps and sang.* PAGE 9.

Personal Prayers.

Week Five

Week Five / SUNDAY

MORNING PRAYER

I. THE PSALMS

MORNING PSALM / PS. 95

O my people, now listen to me.

PAGE 3

PSALMS OF THE DAY / PSS. 96 & 97

New universal songs for all peoples, all creation.

PSALM 96 / *All you peoples, give glory to God.*

1 Let us sing a new song to the Lord.
2 All the earth render praise to God's name;
3 Day by day tell the story, the deeds;
   To nations God's glory proclaim.

4 God is great, and should greatly be praised
   Beyond all other lords and above.
5 For the lords of the nations wear rags,
   But the Lord wears the heavens above.

6 Robed in glory and honor is God,
   Strength and majesty also abide.
7 All you peoples give glory to God;
   The Lord's name be your honor and pride.

8 Bring and enter God's courts,
   Before majesty, holiness bow.
9 Let earth tremble, but ever stand firm.
10 Tell the nations God reigns even now.

   God will judge all the nations with truth.
11 Earth and heaven exult with one voice.
   Let the sea and all in it resound;
12 Let the land and all on it rejoice.

   Let the trees of the forests be glad
13 When the Lord shall descend upon earth;
   Who will govern the nations with justice,
   Who judges all peoples with truth.

PSALM 97 / *The Lord is King, let earth rejoice.*

1 The Lord is King, let earth rejoice,
   The many isles be glad.
2 Enthroned on justice, based on right,
   In clouds the Lord is clad.

3 A fire precedes, and it consumes
   The foes on every side.
4 God's lighting flashes light the world,
   Earth trembles, seeks to hide.

5 Before the Lord of all the earth
   The mountains melt like wax.
6 The heavens shine God's justice forth;
   All see the light shine back.

7 Idolaters are put to shame;
   To God their gods must bow.
8 And Zion, Judah, both rejoice:
   The Lord will judge them now.

9 You are supreme, above the earth;
   Above the gods your throne.
10 You love all those who evil hate.
   You guard and save your own.

11 A light will dawn upon the just,
   And joy their hearts can claim.
12 Be glad you just, in God rejoice,
   And praise the holy name.

II. READINGS & PRAYERS

WINTER

DECEMBER 25TH: CHRISTMAS DAY[*]

A child is born for us.

AT MIDNIGHT:

1. Isaiah 9:1-6.
   A Son is given us.

2. Titus 2:11-14
   The grace of God has appeared.

3. Luke 2:1-14
   Angels sing, "Glory to God."

AT DAWN:

1. Isaiah 62:11-12.
   See, your Savior comes.

2 Titus 3:4-7.
   He saved us because of his mercy

3. Luke 2:15-20.
   Shepherds find the child.

THE DAY:

1. Isaiah 52:7-10.
   All the earth shall see.

2. Hebrews 1:1-6
   The Father speaks through the Son.

3. John 1:1-18.
   In the beginning was the Word.

LET ALL NOW JOIN THE ANGELS' HYMN,
And glory sing to God on high.
Like shepherds we still search for him.
Bring peace to earth, your people cry.

SPRING

5TH SUNDAY OF LENT

Through death to life.

YEAR A

1. Ezekiel 37:12-14.
   I will put my Spirit in you.

2. Romans 8:8-11.
   The Spirit of God dwells in you.

3. John 11:1-45.
   I am the resurrection and the life.

YEAR B

1. Jeremiah 3:31-34.
   I will make a new covenant.

2. Hebrews 5:7-9.
   The Son learned obedience.

3. John 12:20-33.
   If it dies it yields much fruit.

YEAR C

1. Isaiah 43:16-21.
   See, I am doing something new.

2. Philippians 3:8-14.
   For Christ I have left everything.

3. John 8:1-11.
   Who has no sin, cast the first stone.

NEW LIFE, O GOD, WE SEEK FROM YOU.
Lord, send your Spirit from on high.
We need forgiveness, we have sinned.
To calvary we go to die.

[*]NOTE: During the WINTER-Christmas Season only, we follow the numbered days on the calendar, not the days of the week. So today, on Christmas Day, whatever day of the week it may be, use the Sunday Psalms on the previous page. Tomorrow, on December 26, use the Monday Psalms on the facing page, and so on, till the feast of the Baptism of Christ.

SUMMER

13TH SUNDAY OF THE YEAR
How prophets are treated.

YEAR A

1. II Kings 4:8-11,14-16.
   Elisha's promise of a son.

2. Romans 6:3-4,8-11.
   To live with Christ, we die with him.

3. Matthew 10:37-42.
   To live with me take up the cross.

YEAR B

1. Wisdom 1;13-15; 2:23-24.
   Death comes from Satan, not God.

2. II Corinthians 8:7-15.
   Let your abundance full their need.

3. Mark 5:21-43.
   Little girl, get up.

YEAR C

1. I Kings 19:16-21.
   Elisha succeeds Elijah.

2. Galatians 5:13-18.
   Love your neighbor as yourself.

3. Luke 9:51-62.
   Jesus sets his face for Jerusalem.

THERE IS NO TURNING BACK, O LORD;
I go with you to Calvary.
To share with you a prophet's lot,
To die with you is life to me.

FALL

26TH SUNDAY OF THE YEAR.
The rich are lost, poor sinners saved.

Year A

1. Ezekiel 18:25-28.
   He who repents shall live.

2. Philippians 2:1-5.
   He emptied self, became a slave.

3. Matthew 21:28-32.
   The prostitutes believed in him.

YEAR B

1. Numbers 11:25-29.
   Would that all were prophets!

2. James 5:1-6.
   Your wealth will rot.

3. Mark 9:38-48.
   The one not against us is with us.

YEAR C

1. Amos 6:4-7.
   Woe the complacent rich.

2. I Timothy 6:11-16.
   Fight the good fight of faith.

3. Luke 16:19-31.
   Dives and Lazarus.

WILL ANYTHING AWAKE THE RICH?
Not even if one from the grave
Should come to warn them: they are dead.
From such a death, may we be saved.

Meditation. The Lord's Prayer. Intercessions. Personal Prayers.

EVENING PRAYER

Reflections on the Day. Thanksgiving. Reconciliation.

EVENING PSALM / PS. 23 *The Lord will give me rest.* PAGE 3.

CANTICLE OF MARY / LUKE 1:46-55 *Behold the handmaid of the Lord.* PAGE 3.

Personal Prayers.

Week Five / MONDAY
MORNING PRAYER

I. THE PSALMS

MORNING PSALM / PS. 24
Let the King of glory in.
PAGE 4

PSALMS OF THE DAY / PSS. 57 & 60
Amidst disaster, songs of hope and gratitude.

PSALM 57 / *Your faithful love from heaven bring.*

2 Have mercy on me, mercy, God most high!
 Conceal me in the shadow of your wing.
 Protect me there till dangers pass me by.

3 I cry to you who give me everything.
 Reach down, save me from taunting
  enemies.
4 Your faithful love for me from heaven bring.

5 For here I lie among devouring beasts,
 Their lion tongues are like
  a sharpened sword;
 Like arrows, spears, their rows
  of sharpened teeth.

7 To capture me they spread a net, O Lord.
 They dug a pit; before my face it yawned.
 But they themselves fell in as their reward.

8 My heart is firm, O God; I sing this song,
 My heart is firm, I chant this hymn to you.
9 Awake my heart and harp,
  awake the dawn!

10 Among the people
  I give thanks to you.
 I sing your praise
  among the nations all:
 "The Lord above us, all is faithful, true."

6,12 Your faithful love for us is heaven tall.
 Above the heavens be exalted, Lord!
 On earth your glory reaches over all.

PSALM 60 / *Let those you love be saved by you.*

3 O Lord, our God, you have rejected us;
 You turned away, and you are angry still.
 No more, O Lord! Restore;
  come back to us.

4 You shook the earth, split wide
  the valleys, hills.
 It totters still. Repair, extend its days.
5 Your people suffer hardship, every ill.

 You made them drink your wine;
  they stagger, dazed.
6 They seek your safety, out of range,
  O Lord.
 For those who fear the Lord a banner raise.

7 Let those you love be saved by you,
  O Lord.
 Let your right hand deliver those you own.
 O answer me; bring victory, O Lord!

8 The Lord has spoken
  from the holy throne:
 "I portion out the valley of Succoth;
 In triumph I take Schechem for my own.

9 Manasseh, Gilead, I take them both.
 My helmet Ephraim,
  Moab is my bowl.
 My scepter will be Judah,
  so my oath.

¹⁰ On Edom I shall plant my sandals sole.
 Philistia shall see my victory.
¹¹ Now who will give me Edom's throne,
 my goal?"

¹² Have you rejected us? Lord,
 march with me
¹³ Against our foe, no human help will do.
¹⁴ Lord, trample them; give us the victory.

II. READINGS & PRAYERS

WINTER

DECEMBER 26: SECOND DAY OF CHRISTMAS
The Feast of St. Stephen, first martyr:

1. Acts 6:8-10, 7:54-59.
 I see the Son at God's right hand.

2. Matthew 10:17-22.
 The Spirit will be speaking in you.

In words and blood, you speak through us
Your courage too, Lord, give to us...

SPRING

MONDAY: 5TH WEEK OF LENT
Two witnesses prove false, two prove true:

1. Daniel 13:41-62.
 Daniel saves Susanna from death.

2. John 8:12-20.
 I am the light of the world.

Your testimony, Lord, is true
We put our trust in it, in you...

SUMMER

MONDAY: 13TH WEEK OF THE YEAR
On bargaining with God:

1a. Genesis 18:16-33.
 For ten good men I will forbear.

1b. Amos 2:6-16.
 The swift of foot will not escape.

2. Matthew 8:18-22.
 Let the dead bury the dead.

There is no bargaining with you.
We must risk all to follow you...

FALL

MONDAY: 26TH WEEK OF THE YEAR
How differently God sees the world:

1a. Zechariah 8:1-8.
 I will restore my people.

1b. Job 1:6-22.
 The Lord gives, and takes away.

2. Luke 9:46-50.
 The least among you is the greatest.

Lord, help us see what will abide,
For you, our God, are on our side...

Meditation. The Lord's Prayer. Intercessions. Personal Prayers.

EVENING PRAYER

Reflections on the Day. Thanksgiving. Reconciliation.

EVENING PSALM / PS. 4 *I go to sleep in peace.* PAGE 4.

CANTICLE OF ZACHARY / LUKE 1:68-79 *Prepare the way of the Lord.* PAGE 4.

Personal Prayers.

Week Five / TUESDAY
MORNING PRAYER

I. THE PSALMS

MORNING PSALM / PS. 5
At dawn I pray to you.
PAGE 5

PSALM OF THE DAY / PS. 55
A lament over treacherous friends.

PSALM 55 / *Cast your burdens on the Lord.*

2 Lord, hear my prayer, hide not your face,
3 And answer me, I have no peace.
4 The hostile cries of enemies
  Have shaken me, and they increase.

5 My heart is torn and pounds within;
  Death's terrors launch attacks without.
6 With terror, trembling I am struck.
  I shudder, overwhelmed, in doubt.

7 Had I but wings, how I would fly
  Away from here and be at rest.
8 The wilderness would be my nest;
9 Find shelter from the raging storm.

10 O Lord, confuse their wicked tongues.
11 How violent their city is!
12 Within its walls dwells every sin.
  Oppression there forever lives.

13 It is not just my enemies
  Who pile on me the woes I bear;
  I could have hid myself from them.
14 But those, my friends for whom I cared,

15 My peers, those who were close to me,
  I walked the house of God with them.
16 Let death now come upon them all,
  For where they dwell sin lives with them.

17 I call on God to save me now.
18 At dawn and dusk, at noon I pray.
  I utter my complaints and moan,
  For God to hear my voice today.

19 The Lord will save me from my foes,
  The many who are gathered here.
20 The God of old who does not change
  Will humble those who do not fear.

21 My friends betrayed, laid hands on me;
  Their broken word was my reward.
22 With speech like cream, and hearts for war,
  Their words like oil, in fact were swords

23 O cast your burdens on the Lord,
  For God will help, not be remiss;
  Will not allow the just to fall,
  To be destroyed in the abyss.

24 The Lord will cast the wicked down,
  The violent, the treacherous.
  They shall not live out half their days.
  We trust you, Lord, to care for us.

II. Readings & Prayers

WINTER

December 27, the 3rd Day of Christmas
The feast of St. John, evangelist:

1. I John 1:1-4.
   We write what we have seen.

2. John 20:2-8.
   The "other" disciple ran ahead.

And, like an eagle soared above,
We honor, Lord, the one you loved...

SUMMER

Tuesday: 13th Week of the Year
Warnings we should heed:

1a. Genesis 19:15-29.
   Flee, and don't look back.

1b. Amos 3:1-8; 4:11-12.
   Prepare to meet your God.

2. Matthew 8:23-27.
   The winds and sea obeyed him.

Yes, they obeyed, though we do not,
So often, like the wife of Lot...

SPRING

Tuesday: 5th Week of Lent
Look up for your salvation:

1. Numbers 21:4-9.
   Those bitten looked and lived.

2. John 8:21-30.
   When I am lifted up, then you will see.

You are the Lord, the great I AM.
We look to you, you are the lamb...

FALL

Tuesday: 26th Week of the Year
The patience of God with people:

1a. Zechariah 8:20-23.
   Come, let us go seek the Lord.

1b. Job 3:1-23.
   Perish the day that I was born.

2. Luke 9:51-56.
   Jesus resolves to proceed.

Lord, we are up and we are down.
Give us the grace to carry on...

Meditation. The Lord's Prayer. Intercessions. Personal Prayers.

EVENING PRAYER

Reflections on the Day. Thanksgiving. Reconciliation.

Evening Psalm / Ps. 6 *My bed is wet with tears.* Page 5.

The Christ Hymn / Philippians 2:6-11 *The mind of Christ.* Page 5.

Personal Prayers.

Week Five / WEDNESDAY
MORNING PRAYER

I. THE PSALMS

MORNING PSALM / PS. 101
A royal pledge.
PAGE 6

PSALMS OF THE DAY / PSS. 47, 53, & 54
Three songs in praise of God, and condemnation of the enemy.

PSALM 47 / *Let trumpets blast for God, our King.*

2 Clap hands! Praise God with shouts of joy,
You kings of earth applaud your Lord.
3 For God is awesome over all,
The King of kings and Lord of lords.

4 All peoples have been given us;
God put the nations at our feet.
5 God chose our heritage for us,
The pride of Jacob, God's elite.

6 Lord, mount your throne to shouts of joy;
Let trumpets blast for God, our King!
7 You lords, sing praise, a song of praise,
To God, our King, your praises sing!

8 The Lord is King of all the earth.
You kings sing hymns to God alone,
9 Who is the king of all your lands,
And sits on heaven's holy throne.

10 The lords of all the peoples come
Before the God of Abraham.
For all of them belong to God,
The Lord most high, the great I AM.

PSALM 53 / *They all have gone astray.*

2 Fools say within their hearts:
"There is no God."
They are corrupt, depraved,
not one does right.
3 From heaven's throne,
the Lord looks down to see
If even one is wise, keeps God in sight.

4 But no, they all alike have gone astray.
Not one, not even one,
does what is right.
5 Will evildoers never understand?
They eat my people,
swallow them like bread.

They never stop to think about the Lord.
One day they will be filled with fear
and dread.
6 The Lord will scatter all their
wicked bones;
Reject, put them to shame.
God is not dead.

7 If only our deliverance would come!
From Zion's hill, O Lord,
renew your choice.
When God restores our people
to their place,
Let Jacob sing, let Israel rejoice.

PSALM 54 / *The Lord will be my help.*

3 Lord, save me by the power of your name.
And vindicate me with your might, O Lord.
4 Give ear and hear the words
that stake my claim.

5 For aliens have lifted up their sword;
Barbarians who seek to take my life.
They give no thought to you
who are the Lord.

6 The Lord will be my helper in this strife.
7 God will support me, will repay my foe;
In faithful love for me
will take their life.

8 Because you rescued me from every woe,
I praise your name and offer sacrifice.
9 My eyes look down in triumph
on my foe.

II. READINGS & PRAYERS

WINTER
DECEMBER 28: 4TH DAY OF CHRISTMAS
Feast of the Holy Innocents:

1. I John 1:5-2:2.
   The blood of Christ rids all of sin.

2. Matthew 2:13-18.
   Herod kills the children.

We praise the innocents, O Lord;
Give them, and Herod, their reward...

SPRING
WEDNESDAY: 5TH WEEK OF LENT
Opposition to God's Son heats up:

1. Daniel 3:14-20,91-95.
   The three men in the fiery furnace.

2. John 8:31-42.
   I come from God and do his will.

The rage of enemies we hear:
Lord, steady us, and calm our fear...

SUMMER
WEDNESDAY: 13TH WEEK OF THE YEAR
The ways of God are often strange:

1a. Genesis 21:5,8-20.
   God cared for Ishmael too.

1b. Amos 5:14-15, 21-24.
   Let justice surge like water.

2. Matthew 8:28-34.
   Jesus casts the demons into swine.

Your ways, O God, are ever new;
May we not fear, but trust in you...

FALL
WEDNESDAY: 26TH WEEK OF THE YEAR
God's people have work to do:

1a. Nehemiah 2:1-8.
   Send me to rebuild the city.

1b. Job 9:1-16.
   No man is just before the Lord.

2. Luke 9:57-62.
   Whoever keeps looking back is unfit.

Your follower, Lord, I would be;
The future, not the past, for me...

Meditation. The Lord's Prayer. Intercessions. Personal Prayers.

EVENING PRAYER

Reflections on the Day. Thanksgiving. Reconciliation.

EVENING PSALM / PS. 13 *Let me have hope.* PAGE 6.

THE LOVE OF GOD / ROMANS 8:35-39 *Who can be against us?* PAGE 6.

Personal Prayers.

Week Five / THURSDAY
MORNING PRAYER

I. THE PSALMS

MORNING PSALM / PS. 100
Praise God from whom all blessings flow.
PAGE 7

PSALMS OF THE DAY / PSS. 56 & 58
Confidence in God, and vengeance on my foe.

PSALM 56 / *When fear comes near I trust in you.*

2 Have pity on me, Lord,
  they do me wrong.
3 My enemies, and they are many too,
  Harass me and oppress me
    all day long.

4 O God, when fear comes near
  I trust in you.
5 I praise your word, and fear
    then disappears.
  For they are only flesh, what can they do?

6 All day in my affairs they interfere.
7 They plot against me,
    lie in ambush, Lord,
8 In hope of killing me, lurk ever near.

9 Repay them for their crimes.
    Be angry, Lord!
10 My wanderings my griefs are known to you.
  My tears you store, and all my deeds
    record.

11 My foes will flee the day I call on you.
12 For this I know: that you are
    on my side.
13 I trust in you, what can mere mortals do.

14 I shall give thanks and keep my vows
    in sight.
15 You saved my life,
    my feet from stumbling, Lord.
  When God is at my side I walk in light.

PSALM 58 / *Let them vanish like the mist.*

2 You lords of power: are you just?
  Do you judge others honestly?
3 No, crime is ever on your mind,
  And ever dealing lawlessly.
4 From birth the wicked go astray;
  From womb to tomb, lie constantly.

5 They have the venom of a snake,
  A viper that can stop its ear,
6 And so not heed the charmer's voice;
  His words and spells it will not hear.
7 Lord, smash the teeth, destroy the fangs
  Of our oppressors, far and near.

8 Lord, let them vanish like the mist;
  Be trodden under like the grass,
9 To disappear like snails in slime;
  Or like the stillborn, let them pass.
10 Before they know it, in the wind,
  Like brambles, thistles, let them pass.

11 The just will be avenged, rejoice
  As they see justice win the day.
12 And they will bathe their feet in blood,
  In wicked blood, and all will say:
  The just indeed have their reward.
  The justice of the Lord holds sway.

II. READINGS & PRAYERS

WINTER
DECEMBER 29: 5TH DAY OF CHRISTMAS
Light and glory:

1. I John 2:3-11.
   Who loves his brother lives in light.

2. Luke 2:22-35.
   The Canticle of Simeon.

Lord, shine on us the light of truth,
That we may share your glory, too...

SPRING
THURSDAY: 5TH WEEK OF LENT
Jesus and his enemies dispute:

1. Genesis 17:3-9.
   Abraham is promised posterity.

2. John 8:51-59
   Before Abraham came to be, I AM.

Lord, we rejoice with Abraham
We bow to you, the great I AM...

SUMMER
THURSDAY: 13TH WEEK OF THE YEAR
Fearful commands, awesome power:

1a. Genesis 22:1-19.
   God tests the faith of Abraham.

1b. Amos 7:10-17.
   Go, prophecy to Israel.

2. Matthew 9:1-8.
   Jesus forgives sin, heals paralysis

We praise you, God, for all you do;
Forever say our "yes" to you...

FALL
THURSDAY: 26TH WEEK OF THE YEAR
Workers needed, who have love and trust:

1a. Nehemiah 8:1-12.
   The people heard the law and wept.

1b. Job 19:21-7.
   I know that my Redeemer lives.

2. Luke 10:1-12.
   The harvest is rich, the workers few.

We love you, Lord, in you we trust;
And we are ready; Lord, send us...

Meditation. The Lord's Prayer. Intercessions. Personal Prayers.

EVENING PRAYER

Reflections on the Day. Thanksgiving. Reconciliation.

EVENING PSALM / PS. 131 *A child in your mother's arms.* PAGE 7.

THE UNSEEN GOD / COLOSSIANS 1:15-20 *First born of all creation.* PAGE 7.

Personal Prayers.

Week Five / FRIDAY
MORNING PRAYER

I. THE PSALMS

MORNING PSALM / PS. 130
Out of the depths.
PAGE 8

PSALMS OF THE DAY / PSS. 59 & 61
Cries for help from one in peril.

PSALM 59 / *Like dogs, they come at night and howl.*

2 Lord, save me from my enemies;
Against my foe a fortress be.
3 From evildoers save me, Lord;
From murderers come rescue me.

4 To take my life the violent
Have hatched a plot and lie in wait.
5 For no offense of mine, O Lord,
They have no reason for their hate.

Bestir yourself on my behalf,
6 O God of Israel, O Lord!
Awake! Bring nations to account.
No mercy for the traitor's sword.

7 Like dogs they come at night to howl;
They prowl the city spreading fear.
8 They bark their insults, bare their fangs,
With evil tongues say, "Who will hear?"

9 But you, O Lord, you laugh at them.
You hold the nations in contempt.
10 You are my refuge, God, my rock.
I wait for you, you are my strength.

11 My faithful God will come to me,
That I may gloat upon my foe.
12 But let them live, lest we forget;
Lord, let them wander, bring them low.

13 Their sinful mouths, their lying lips
Have trapped them in their foolish pride.
14 In anger put an end to them
To show the world that you abide.

15 Like dogs they come at night, each night,
To prowl the city, roam and howl;
16 Like scavengers they search for food;
Unsatisfied, they snarl and growl.

17 At dawn I praise your faithful love.
You were my refuge in distress.
18 I sing my hymn to you, O Lord,
My strength will be your faithfulness.

PSALM 61 / *I stand upon the edge of an abyss.*

2 O God, I cry to you; Lord, hear my prayer.
3 I stand upon the edge of an abyss.
I call to you,
my heart grows faint with care.

Lord, lead me from this fearful precipice,
4 To rock on high, a refuge from my foe.
5 Beneath your wing, inside your tent,
my bliss.

6 The vows I daily keep, O Lord, you know.
Grant this request from one
who fears your name.
7 God save the king! Long life on him bestow.

8 Your faithful love forever may he claim.
That he may be enthroned
before you, God.
9 I vow, O Lord, to ever praise your name.

II. READINGS & PRAYERS

WINTER

DECEMBER 30: 6TH DAY OF CHRISTMAS.
Instructions for little ones:

1. I John 2:12-17.
   Have no love for the world.

2. Luke 2:36-40.
   The child grew in wisdom and grace.

We marvel, Lord, at how you grew,
Teach us each day to grow anew...

SUMMER

FRIDAY: 13TH WEEK OF THE YEAR
Matthew is called from tax collecting:

1a. Genesis 23:1-4, 24:1-8, 62-67.
   Sarah dies, Isaac marries Rebekah.

1b. Amos 8:4-6, 9-12.
   Let us fix our scales for cheating.

2. Matthew 9:9-13.
   I have come to call sinners.

The world will give no true reward;
So call us to your service, Lord...

SPRING

FRIDAY: 5TH WEEK OF LENT
The wicked rise against the just:

1. Jeremiah 20:10-13.
   The Lord is with me; in God I trust.

2. John 10:31-42.
   *For which good deed would you
   stone me?*

O Lord, they rail against us, too;
Give us your strength, we trust in you...

FALL

FRIDAY: 26TH WEEK OF THE YEAR
Confess and hear the words of God:

1a. Baruch 1:15-22.
   *Lord we have sinned,
   are filled with shame.*

1b. Job 38:12-21, 40:3-5.
   The Lord replies, Job is silent.

2. Luke 10:13-16.
   Those who hear you, hear me.

How terrible the curse of God
For those who spurn the Word of God...

Meditation. The Lord's Prayer. Intercessions. Personal Prayers.

EVENING PRAYER

Reflections on the Day. Thanksgiving. Reconciliation.

EVENING PSALM / PS. 51 *David's prayer for forgiveness.* PAGE 8.

CANTICLE OF SIMEON / LUKE 2:29-32 *Lord, let me go in peace.* PAGE 8.

Personal Prayers.

Week Five / SATURDAY
MORNING PRAYER

I. THE PSALMS

MORNING PSALM / PS. 141
Like incense let my prayer arise.
PAGE 9

PSALMS OF THE DAY / PSS. 62 & 63
Songs of longing and trust.

PSALM 62 / *My soul in silence waits.*

2 My soul in silence waits for God alone,
From whom my help will come.
   I shall not fall.
3 God is my rock, my fort, salvation's throne.

4 How long will this go on? Will you, will all,
Keep beating on the just
   to bring them down,
As on a sagging fence, a leaning wall?

5 Their only goal: to bring the just one down.
They take delight in lies,
   make them their own.
Inside they curse, while outwardly
   they fawn.

6 My soul in silence waits for God alone.
I shall not fall, my help will come
   from God,
6 Who is my rock, my fort, salvation's throne.

8 My safety and my glory rest with God.
9 You too must give your hearts,
   must trust till death;
Our mighty rock, our refuge is our God.

10 The lowliest of us is but a breath.
The high born are no more, illusions all.
All weigh no more than air,
   and end in death.

11 Be sure of this: extortioners will fall.
Think not of robbery, crime doesn't pay.
Should wealth increase,
   pay it no heed at all.

12 The Lord once spoke:
   two things I heard God say:
13 That strength and faithful love
   belong to God,
And all will get their due; God will repay.

PSALM 63 / *Like dry and lifeless land, I thirst for you.*

2 O God, you are my God, I long for you.
My soul and body hunger for your love.
Like dry and lifeless land I thirst for you.

3 In temple, Lord, I look to you above,
To see your strength and glory all my days.
4 More dear to me than life, your faithful love.

5 My lips shall praise and bless you
   all my days.
I lift my hands and call upon your name.
6 My hunger satisfied, I sing your praise.

7 At night in bed,
   I pray and praise your name.
8 For you have hidden me
   beneath your wing.
9 I cling to you, your hand supports
   my frame.

10 May those who seek my life
   lose everything;
Be given to the power of the sword;
11 Become the food of jackals,
   while I sing.

12 The king will find delight in God, his Lord,
And all who swear by God, rejoice with him;
While liars are struck dumb as their reward.

II. Readings & Prayers

WINTER

DECEMBER 31: 7TH DAY OF CHRISTMAS
Christ and the anti-Christs:

1. I John 2:18-21.
   Children, it is the final hour.

2. John 1:1-18.
   The word was made flesh.

The anti-Christs who love the night
Are vanquished by the Lord of light...

SPRING

SATURDAY: 5TH WEEK OF LENT
God's will for his faithful ones:

1. Ezekiel 37:21-28.
   I will bring my people back.

2. John 11:45-57.
   One man must die that all be one.

To make us one, that none be lost,
Such is God's will, but at what cost?

SUMMER

SATURDAY: 13TH WEEK OF THE YEAR
God is always starting new:

1a. Genesis 27:1-5,15-29.
   The story of Jacob and Esau.

1b. Amos 9:11-15.
   I will restore my people.

2. Matthew 9:14-17.
   New wine for new wineskins.

Lord, ever ancient, ever new,
The time is now to start anew...

FALL

SATURDAY: 26TH WEEK OF THE YEAR
Through works and pain we come to joy:

1a. Baruch 4:5-12, 27-29.
   God punished you to bring you back.

1b. Job 42:1-16.
   I repent what I have said.

2. Luke 10:17-24.
   The disciples and Jesus rejoice.

How good it is to see their joy;
Let all who share the cross, enjoy!

Meditation. The Lord's Prayer. Intercessions. Personal Prayers.

Evening Prayer

Reflections on the Day. Thanksgiving. Reconciliation.

EVENING PSALM / PS. 143 *Lord, do not condemn.* PAGE 9.

SONG OF MOSES / REVELATION 15:3-5 *They all had harps and sang.* PAGE 9.

Personal Prayers.

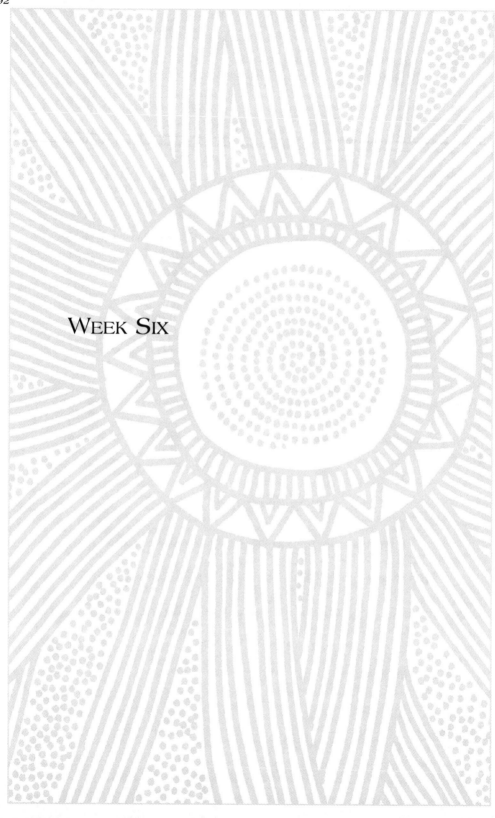

WEEK SIX

Week Six / SUNDAY

MORNING PRAYER

I. THE PSALMS

MORNING PSALM / PS. 95

O my people, now listen to me.

PAGE 3

PSALM OF THE DAY / PS. 72

A prayer for the king.

PSALM 72 / *Let kings, and nations, too, their tributes pay.*

1 O God, endow the king with your decrees.
  Give David's son your sense of right
      and wrong.
2 That he may govern us with justice, Lord,
  And give the poor the rights for which
      they long.

3 Let mountains yield prosperity and peace.
  May hills bring yields of plenty,
      justly shared.
4 Let him take up the causes of the poor;
  May their oppressors fall
      and not be spared.

5 Let him live on as long as sun shall shine,
  As long as moon endures,
      through every age.
6 Let him descend like rain upon the grass;
  And for this arid land its thirst assuage.

7 The just will thrive as long as he shall live.
  His peace abound until the moon be gone.
8 From sea to sea, his reign extend to all;
  To him the ends of all the earth belong.

9 Let even desert tribes be brought to him.
  And let his enemies be cast adrift.
10 Let kings and nations too their tribute pay;
11 From Tarshish, Sheba, Saba, all bring gifts.

12 Because he saves the poor
      who cry to him,
  The lowly who have nowhere else
      to turn;
13 Because he has compassion on them all,
  Delivers them, their cries
      he does not spurn;

14 Because he saves their lives
      from violence,
  And holds their blood as precious as
      his own,
15 Long may he live! Give Sheba's gold
      to him.
  His people's prayers and blessings
      he shall own.

16 Let mountain tops be blanketed
      with wheat.
  Let fruit abound like grass in Lebanon.
17 Let all be blest in him and call him blest;
  His name be blest, enduring as the sun!

18 Blest be the Lord, the God of Israel;
  For God alone does wondrous things.
      Amen!
19 Blest be God's glorious name
      forevermore;
  And may that glory fill the earth. Amen!

II. READINGS & PRAYERS

WINTER

JANUARY 1: 8TH DAY OF CHRISTMAS
Feast of Mary, Mother of God.

YEARS A, B, & C

1. Numbers 6:22-27.
   The Lord bless you and keep you.

2. Galatians 4:4-7.
   God sent his Son, born of woman.

3. Luke 2:16-21.
   Mary treasured all these things.

HAIL MARY, MOTHER OF THE LORD!
God made you mother of us, too.
Your heart is great, immaculate,
With joy we sing our songs to you.

SPRING

PALM SUNDAY
Hosanna to the Son of David.

YEARS A, B, & C

1. Isaiah 50:4-7.
   I give my back to those who beat me.

2. Philippians 2:6-11.
   Accepting death upon a cross.

3A. Matthew 27:11-54.
   The Passion and Death of Christ.

3B. Mark 15:1-39.
   The Passion and Death of Christ.

3C. Luke 23:1-49.
   The Passion and Death of Christ.

OUR MIND SHOULD BE THE MIND OF CHRIST,
Who died for us upon the tree.
God raised him up, so at his name,
Let all adore and bend the knee.

SUMMER

14TH SUNDAY OF THE YEAR
The virtue of humility.

YEAR A

1. Zechariah 9:9-10.
   Your king comes meekly on an ass.

2. Romans 8:9-13.
   Live in the Spirit of Christ.

3. Matthew 11:25-30.
   I am gentle and humble of heart.

YEAR B

1. Ezekiel 2:2-5.
   I send you to a rebel race.

2. II Corinthians 12:7-10.
   I glory in my weakness.

3. Mark 6:1-6.
   A prophet is despised at home.

YEAR C

1. Isaiah 66:10-14
   I will send peace like a river.

2. Galatians 6:14-18.
   I boast only of the cross of Christ.

3. Luke 10:1-9.
   Wherever you go, bring peace.

O GENTLE LORD, WITH HUMBLE HEART,
You enter meekly, bringing peace.
Give us your Spirit and your strength
To conquer fear, make conflict cease.

FALL

27TH SUNDAY OF THE YEAR.
Of vineyards, marriage, and faith.

YEAR A

1. Isaiah 5:1-7.
   The vineyards that gave sour grapes.

2. Philippians 4:6-9.
   Dismiss anxiety, be at peace.

3. Matthew 21:33-43.
   A man leased out his vineyard.

YEAR B

1. Genesis 2:18-24.
   It is not good for man to be alone.

2. Hebrews 2:9-11.
   Christ is our brother, God our father.

3. Mark 10:2-12.
   What God has joined we must not divide.

YEAR C

1. Habakkuk 1:2-3, 2:2-4.
   The rash have no integrity.

2. II Timothy 1:6-8, 13-14.
   The Spirit of God makes us strong.

3. Luke 17:5-10.
   If you had faith you could do anything.

YOUR SERVANTS TEND YOUR VINEYARD, LORD,
Together, male and female, too.
O Lord, increase our faith and love
That we may bear good fruit for you.

Meditation. The Lord's Prayer. Intercessions. Personal Prayers.

EVENING PRAYER

Reflections on the Day. Thanksgiving. Reconciliation.

EVENING PSALM / PS. 23 *The Lord will give me rest.* PAGE 3.

CANTICLE OF MARY / LUKE 1:46-55 *Behold the handmaid of the Lord.* PAGE 3.

Personal Prayers.

Week Six / MONDAY

MORNING PRAYER

I. THE PSALMS

MORNING PSALM / PS. 24
Let the King of glory in.
PAGE 4

PSALMS OF THE DAY / PSS. 66 & 67

Two hymns of praise.

PSALM 66 / *Proclaim the glory of God's name.*

2 Let all the earth cry out to God with joy!
  Proclaim the glory of God's name always.
3 Say to the Lord:
  "How awesome are your deeds!
  Your strength is great;
    your foes are on their knees.
4 And all are at your feet
    with hymns of praise."

5 O come and see the awesome deeds
    of God.
6a Who turned the sea to land
    to let them pass;
7 Who ever rules with might,
    whose searching eyes
  Are on the nations lest the rebels rise.
6b Let us rejoice in God while ages last.

8 All people, join with us
    to praise the Lord
9 Who gave us life, set us on solid ground.
10 Who tested us as silver is refined;
11 Led us through snares and ills
    of every kind,
12 Till we through fire and water
    freedom found.

13 I bring my offerings
    and pay my vows,
14 The promises I made in my travail.
15 A holocaust and incense offer you,
  A sacrifice of bulls
    and goats for you.
16 All you who fear the Lord
    come hear my tale.

17 I cried aloud, God's praise upon my tongue.
19 I raised my voice; my prayers were heard above.
18 If I had harbored evil in my heart,
  The Lord would not have taken up my part.
20 Praise God who heard and came with faithful love.

PSALM 67 / *Let all the nations ever praise.*

6 LET ALL THE PEOPLES PRAISE YOU, LORD.
  LET ALL THE NATIONS EVER PRAISE!

2 O God be gracious to us, bless us,
  Make your face to shine on all.
3 So may your way be known on earth,
  Your saving strength to nations all.

4a Let all the peoples praise you, Lord;
5a You govern them with equity.
4b Let all the nations ever praise;
5b You guide them to their destiny.

7 Let all the earth produce its fruit;
  And may the Lord bless one and all.
8 May God go on to ever bless.
  Let all the earth hold God in awe.

II. READINGS & PRAYERS

WINTER
JANUARY 2: 9TH DAY OF CHRISTMAS
John points to Jesus:

1. I John 2:22-28.
   What you have heard from me hold fast.

2. John 1:19-28.
   I am not the one who is to come.

Not one of us is worthy, Lord;
Yet, you we seek, and your reward...

SPRING
MONDAY OF HOLY WEEK
The 1st Servant Song; the gentle Lord:

1. Isaiah 42:1-7.
   A bruised reed he shall not break.

2. John 12:1-11.
   Jesus defends Mary from Judas.

The bruised you do not break, O Lord.
The generous get their reward...

SUMMER
MONDAY: 14TH WEEK OF THE YEAR
The love of God for God's people:

1a. Genesis 28:10-22.
   Jacob's ladder and talk with God.

1b. Hosea 2:16-22.
   God betroths his people.

2. Matthew 9:18-26.
   Jesus restores a little girl's life.

We are betrothed, you call us wife,
Through us, O Lord, beget new life...

FALL
MONDAY: 27TH WEEK OF THE YEAR
Compassion as the test of love:

1a. Jonah 1:1-2:1-11.
   Jonah tries to run from God.

1b. Galatians 1:6-12.
   Paul reproaches his people.

2. Luke 10:25-37.
   The good Samaritan.

Not words, but deeds of love you seek;
They come from gentle hearts, the meek...

Meditation. The Lord's Prayer. Intercessions. Personal Prayers.

EVENING PRAYER

Reflections on the Day. Thanksgiving. Reconciliation.

EVENING PSALM / PS. 4 *I go to sleep in peace.* PAGE 4.

CANTICLE OF ZACHARY / LUKE 1:68-79 *Prepare the way of the Lord.* PAGE 4.

Personal Prayers.

Week Six / TUESDAY
MORNING PRAYER

I. THE PSALMS

MORNING PSALM / PS. 5
At dawn I pray to you.
PAGE 5

PSALM OF THE DAY / PS. 68
In praise of Zion, where God chose to dwell.

PSALM 68 / *How awesome in this holy place is God.*

2 Arise, O God, disperse your enemy,
3 Like drifting smoke, like melting wax in fire.
 Before the Lord the wicked all shall flee.

4 The just rejoice, are jubilant, lift high
5 Their voice in joyful song;
    they bless the Lord,
 Whose name is God,
    who rides the clouds and sky.

6 The orphan finds a parent in the Lord,
 The widow a defender for her home.
 Their refuge is the temple of the Lord.

7 The desolate will not be left alone.
 God sets the captive free,
    in peace to dwell;
 While rebels are cast out and deserts roam.

8 You led us, Lord, through wilderness
    as well.
9 Because of you earth quaked,
    and heaven rained
 Before the Lord, the God of Israel.

10 Upon your flock, O Lord,
    you showered rain,
11 Upon your thirsty land abundantly.
 The poor a kindly God did not disdain.

12 The Lord announced the news of victory,
 To all the people, so they all might know:
13 "The armies of your enemies now flee"

14 Now ours the silver, gold left by the foe.
15 When God caused all our enemies to flee,
 The spoils were scattered everywhere
    like snow.

16 The mighty mountain Bashan,
    many-peaked,
17 Is filled with envy of this hill, O Lord,
 On which you chose to dwell, Lord,
    why this peak?

18 You have a thousand chariots and swords;
 Nay twice ten thousand
    serve before your face.
 But you came here from there
    to be adored.

19 You chose this hill, O Lord,
    to be your place.
 You led the captives back,
    here made them stay.
 They fought your dwelling
    in this holy place.

20 Blest be the Lord who carries us each day,
21 Who is our God, the God who sets us free;
 In whom we find our way: the only way.

22 The Lord will split the skulls of enemies:
23 "From Bashan and the sea,
    all these I bring,
24 That in their blood you all may
    wash your feet."

25 I see the entry of my God and King:
26 The great parade now enters
    sacred space;
 The singers first, musicians last, all sing:

27 "O Israel, bow down before God's face!"
28 The vast assembly cries,
    "O bless the Lord!"
 Here Benjamin, there Judah, all in place.

29 Show all, O God, the power
  of your sword.
30 Their kings will bring you gifts
  and pay you heed,
  Here, in Jerusalem, where you are Lord.

31 Rebuke the beasts
  that lurk amid the reeds,
32 The bulls that prey, the warlike; scatter all.
  Let Egypt come to God upon her knees.

33 O praise the Lord, sing hymns,
  you kingdoms all,
34 To God who rides the clouds,
  the ancient skies,
  Who thunders with a mighty voice to all.

35 Confess the strength of God
  who dwells on high.
  In Israel the majesty of God
  Rules over all and reaches to the sky.

36 How awesome in this holy place is God!
  From here the Lord of Israel bestows
  Strength, power to the people. Blest be God!

II. READINGS & PRAYERS

WINTER
JANUARY 3: 10TH DAY OF CHRISTMAS
We are given names:

1. I John 2:29-3:6.
  We are called God's children.

2. John 1:29-34.
  John cries "Behold: the lamb of God."

We are the children of the Lord,
He is the lamb whom we adore...

SPRING
TUESDAY OF HOLY WEEK
The mission of Christ and Christians:

1. Isaiah 49:1-6. The 2nd Servant Song.
  "You are my servant," says the Lord.

2. John 13:21-38.
  Jesus predicts Peter's denial.

You know our human weakness, Lord;
Yet love us still, and send us forth...

SUMMER
TUESDAY: 14TH WEEK OF THE YEAR
The Lord seeks help from those who care:

1a. Genesis 32:23-33.
  God calls Jacob Israel.

1b. Hosea 8:4-13.
  Who sows the wind reaps a whirlwind.

2. Matthew 9:32-38.
  The harvest rich, but laborers are few.

Great harvester, you sow the seed;
Let us supply the help you need...

FALL
TUESDAY: 27TH WEEK OF THE YEAR
What God is doing is what counts:

1a. Jonah 3:1-10.
  Jonah preaches, Nineveh repents.

1b. Galatians 1:13-24.
  Paul tells his story.

2. Luke 10:38-42.
  Mary chose the better part.

Like Martha, we becoame upset.
Like Mary, teach us not to fret...

Meditation. The Lord's Prayer. Intercessions. Personal Prayers.

EVENING PRAYER

Reflections on the Day. Thanksgiving. Reconciliation.

EVENING PSALM / PS. 6 *My bed is wet with tears.* PAGE 5.

THE CHRIST HYMN / PHILIPPIANS 2:6-11 *The mind of Christ.* PAGE 5.

Personal Prayers.

Week Six / WEDNESDAY
MORNING PRAYER

I. THE PSALMS

MORNING PSALM / PS. 101
A royal pledge.
PAGE 6

PSALM OF THE DAY / PS. 69
The ballad prayer of an afflicted one.

PSALM 69 / *From the waters of affliction, save me, Lord.*

2 Save me, O God!
  The waters of affliction now abound.
3 The slimy bog
  In which I sink provides no solid ground.
The fearful flood
  Has overcome; I am about to drown.

4 O Lord, hear me:
  My throat is parched, eyes dim,
      and near despair.
5 My enemy?
  I have more enemies than I have hair.
And wrongfully:
  The loss I did not cause must I repair?

6 O Lord, you see.
  From you I cannot hide my foolish deeds.
7 Let those who seek
  The Lord of hosts not fall because of me.
Let those who seek
  You, Lord, our God, not come to shame
      through me.

8 For you alone
  I bear the insults, and accept disgrace.
9 I have become
  An outcast and a stranger to my race.
10 My zeal I own;
  But all the insults meant for you, I face.

11 I kept a fast;
  They laughed and jeered at my humility.
12 In sackcloth dressed;
  It didn't suit and they made fun of me.
13 I am depressed,
  The butt of jokes,
      the sport of drunkards' glee.

14 I make this plea:
  Your faithful love, I need it now, O God.
15 Lord, answer me!
  Come rescue me from sinking in this bog.
From enemies,
  And from the waters, save me, O my God.

16 O Lord, let not
  The waters of this sea sweep over me.
Let not the pit
  Close over me, O Lord, and swallow me.
17 Despise me not;
  Your faithful love is great; Lord, turn to me.

18 Hide not your face!
  In my distress make haste to answer me.
19 Draw near this place
  Where enemies abound, and set me free
20 From my disgrace.
  You know my shame,
      you know my enemy.

21 They broke my heart;
  I looked for sympathy,
      but there was none.
Things fell apart.
  I looked for comforters; I found not one.
22 O cruel hearts,
  To slake my thirst with vinegar, for fun.

23 A curse on them!
  Let friends betray, their table be a trap.
24 A curse on them!
  And let their eyes grow dim,
      their legs collapse.
25 Pour out on them
  Your anger, Lord; and may it never lapse.

26 Lord, punish them;
    Their camps be desolate,
        their people gone.
27 They hounded him
    On whom you laid your hand;
        they poured it on.
28 Pour guilt on them
    O God, and let them never see the dawn.

29 Erase them, Lord,
    From heaven's book,
        the page of those who live.
30 And save me, Lord;
    I am afflicted, and in pain I live.
31 But to you, Lord,
    My songs of praise and gratitude
        I give.

32 To please God more,
    We do not need more oxen, bulls,
        and tears.
33 Rejoice you poor
    Who seek the Lord; be glad
        and calm your fears.
34 God hears the poor;
    To those in bondage, God is ever near.

35 So praise the Lord
    You heavens, and the earth
        and waters, too.
36 Rebuild, O Lord,
    The cities in the land you loved, and do.
37 We praise you, Lord.
    Your servants dwell in them;
        their lives renew.

II. READINGS & PRAYERS

WINTER

JANUARY 4: 11TH DAY OF CHRISTMAS
To whom shall we belong?

1. I John 3:7-10
    The one who sins belongs to Satan.

2. John I:35-42.
    The Lord said, "Come and see."

O Lord, you have invited us;
And we accept; in you we trust...

SPRING

WEDNESDAY OF HOLY WEEK
The fidelity of Christ:

1. Isaiah 50:4-9. The 3rd Servant Song.
    My face I did not shield.

2. Matthew 26:14-25.
    Judas plots Jesus' betrayal.

Lord, how you loved your enemy!
Love conquers even treachery...

SUMMER

WEDNESDAY: 14TH WEEK OF THE YEAR
In time of need we look for help:

1a. Genesis 41:55-42:24.
    His brothers come to Joseph.

1b. Hosea 10:1-12.
    It is time to seek the Lord.

2. Matthew 10:1-7.
    The reign of God is at hand.

Indeed it is time, for one and all;
To seek the Lord and heed God's call...

FALL

WEDNESDAY: 27TH WEEK OF THE YEAR
The myopia of people:

1a. Jonah 4:1-11.
    Jonah is unhappy and wants to die.

1b. Galatians 2:1-14.
    Paul withstands Peter.

2. Luke 11:1-4.
    Jesus teaches us how to pray.

We see so little; think so small.
Teach us to pray, that we grow tall...

Meditation. The Lord's Prayer. Intercessions. Personal Prayers.

EVENING PRAYER

Reflections on the Day. Thanksgiving. Reconciliation.

EVENING PSALM / PS. 13 *Let me have hope.* PAGE 6.

THE LOVE OF GOD / ROMANS 8:35-39 *Who can be against us?* PAGE 6.

Personal Prayers.

Week Six / THURSDAY
MORNING PRAYER

I. THE PSALMS

MORNING PSALM / PS. 100
Praise God from whom all blessings flow.
PAGE 7

PSALMS OF THE DAY / PSS. 64 & 65
Songs of confidence in the triumph of God and a rich harvest.

PSALM 64 / *The Lord has arrows, too.*

2 Lord, hear my voice, I plead with you;
  Preserve me from the foes I fear.
3 And hide me from their hidden plots.
  Their wicked mob is very near.

4 They whet their tongues
    like sharpened swords;
  Their cruel words like arrows fly
5 From ambush at the innocent,
  Without a warning, from the sky.

6 They make their plans, they lay their snares,
  And cunningly they bide their time.
7 They say in secret, "Who can see?"
  Or "Who could solve our perfect crime?"

But there is one who reads the mind;
  Who knows the depths of human hearts.
8 The Lord most high has arrows, too;
  And suddenly they find their marks.

9 All those who see recoil in fear.
  All those who lie shall be undone.
10 And everyone will stand in awe,
  And tell the world
    what God has done.

And as they ponder what was done,
11 The just shall all rejoice in praise,
  Shall take their refuge in the Lord,
  Exult in God for all their days!

PSALM 65 / *Lord, visit earth and bring us rain.*

2 O God of Zion, praise to you!
3 You hear our prayers; our vows we pay.
4 To you all flesh must bring its sins;
  They cover us; forgive, we pray.

5 How blest are those whom you invite
  To dwell with you in heaven's court!
  You fill us there with all the gifts
  That fill your house, your temple, Lord.

6 O God, our savior, answer us
  With mighty deeds and victory
  We trust in you, you are the hope
  Of all the earth, the distant sea.

7 You fixed the mountains with your hand;
  A mighty hand belongs to you.
8 You calmed the roaring of the waves;
  The tumult of the peoples, too.

9 The ends of earth are awed by you;
  They see your signs and hear your voice.
  The twinkling stars of dawn and dusk
  All shout for joy; in you rejoice.

10 Lord, visit earth, the earth you made.
  Fill her with joy; bring us your rain.
  The rivers of our God must come
  To make us fruitful, give us grain.

11 Lord, bless the earth with gentle rain.
  Make soft the furrows of our fields,
12 That harvest wagon tracks be deep,
  To crown our year with heavy yields.

13 Let endless fields be filled with grain.
  Let every hill be clothed with joy.
14 Let hills have flocks and valleys wheat.
  Let all the earth sing songs of joy!

II. Readings & Prayers

WINTER

JANUARY 5: 12TH DAY OF CHRISTMAS
The simple faith of the first disciples:

1. I John 3:11-21.
   We live because we love.

2. John 1:43-51
   New disciples follow Jesus.

Love is catching, new loves come,
Let us so love that all be won...

SUMMER

THURSDAY: 14TH WEEK OF THE YEAR
The ties that bind:

1a. Genesis 44:18-45:5.
   Joseph reveals himself.

1b. Hosea 11:1-9.
   My heart is overwhelmed.

2. Matthew 10:7-15.
   What you were given, freely give.

Lord, we are bound in love to you,
And to each other: keep us true...

SPRING

HOLY THURSDAY
Easter Triduum begins; The Last Supper:

1. Exodus 12:1-8, 11-14
   The Passover of the Lord.

2. I Corinthians 11:23-26.
   Eat this bread and drink this cup.

3. John 13:1-15.
   Jesus washes the disciples feet.

Lord, wash our feet, our hands, head, too;
You teach us, Lord, in all you do...

FALL

THURSDAY: 27TH WEEK OF THE YEAR
Get serious:

1a. Malachi 3:13-20.
   Judgement will come like fire.

1b. Galatians 3:1-5.
   Have you lost your minds?

2. Luke 11:5-13.
   Persistence pays off.

So much of life we throw away;
Lord, help us truly find your way...

Meditation. The Lord's Prayer. Intercessions. Personal Prayers.

EVENING PRAYER

Reflections on the Day. Thanksgiving. Reconciliation.

EVENING PSALM / PS. 131 *A child in your mother's arms.* PAGE 7.

THE UNSEEN GOD / COLOSSIANS 1:15-20 *First born of all creation.* PAGE 7.

Personal Prayers.

Week Six / FRIDAY
MORNING PRAYER

I. THE PSALMS

MORNING PSALM / PS. 130
Out of the depths.
PAGE 8

PSALM OF THE DAY / PS. 22

The Good Friday Psalm: The ultimate hymn of desolation and trust.

PSALM 22 / *My God, have you forsaken me?*

2 My God, my God, have you forsaken me?
 So far away, so silent to my plea.
3 I cry to you by day; you answer not.
 I cry all night; no respite is my lot.

4 You are the holy one of Israel.
5 Of old our people looked to you for help.
6 You saved them when they trusted
 in your name.
 You did not fail, did not put them to shame.

7 But me, I am a worm,
 one whom they scorn.
8 They mock and shake their heads;
 I am forlorn.
9 "He trusted God; let God deliver him,"
 they say.
 "If God loves him,
 let God come down today."

10 From mother's womb
 you were my place of rest.
11 You brought me out; you laid me
 on her breast.
12 Do not desert me now; my hour is near.
 There is no one to help; my foes are here.

13 I am surrounded by a herd of beasts.
14 They circle, mouths agape,
 as for a feast.
15 As weak as water, all my bones
 are racked;
 My heart dissolves; it drips away like wax.

16 My mouth is dry; tongue parched,
 I lie in dust.
17 A pack of wicked dogs surround the just.
18 My hands and feet so thin I count
 each bone.
19 They stare, divide my clothes,
 one wins my robe.

20 Be not far off! You are my help, O Lord.
21 Give back my life and save me
 from the sword.
22 From howling dogs,
 from roaring lions' mouths,
 From raging bulls, from all,
 Lord, lead me out.

23 Then I shall sing to brothers, sisters, all;
 In the assembly, sing your praise with all.
24 O you who fear the Lord, of Jacob's race,
 O Israel, give praise before God's face.

25 The Lord will not despise the poor
 at prayer,
 Not turn away, but show them loving care.
26 A hundred times I sing this song and pray.
 With those who fear the Lord my vows
 I pay.

27 The poor will eat their fill
 and praise the Lord.
 Forever lift your hearts and seek the Lord.
28 One day the nations all will come to God,
29 Will bend the knee, and all be ruled by God.

30 And all who sleep below shall bend the knee,
 And bow to God. So shall it be with me.
31 My children, too, in ages yet to come,
32 The yet unborn shall tell what God has done.

II. READINGS & PRAYERS

WINTER

JANUARY 6: EPIPHANY.
We have seen his star:

1. Isaiah 60:1-6.
   The glory of the Lord shines on you.

2. Ephesians 3:2-6.
   God's secret plan is now revealed.

3. Matthew 2:1-12.
   We come to worship the king.

As with gladness men of old
Did the guiding star behold.
As with joy they hailed its light,
Leading onward, beaming bright.
So, most gracious Lord, may we
Evermore be led by thee.

SUMMER

FRIDAY: 14TH WEEK OF THE YEAR
There is danger in the world:

1a. Genesis 46:1-7, 28-30.
    Jacob comes to Joseph.

1b. Hosea 14:2-10.
    Return to God, who heals.

2. Matthew 10:16-23.
   I send you out like sheep.

We know that you have trials for us.
We trust in you to speak for us...

SPRING

GOOD FRIDAY: THE PASSION OF THE LORD.
Father, I put my life in your hands:

1. Isaiah 52:13-53:12. Final Servant Song.
   Like a lamb led to slaughter.

2. Hebrews 4:14-16,5:7-9.
   *The great high priest who never sinned,
   but cried with tears to God.*

3. John 18:1-19:42.
   The Passion and Death of Christ.

O sinless Savior, loving Lord,
We heard your cry, we saw you pray.
Obedient to God like you,
To win salvation we obey.

FALL

FRIDAY: 27TH WEEK OF THE YEAR
Faith is the critical choice:

1a. Joel 1:13-2:2.
    The day of the Lord is coming.

1b. Galatians 3:7-14.
    Believers, the true children of Abraham.

2. Luke 11:15-26.
   A house divided cannot stand.

Lord, we believe; have chosen you;
Now strengthen us to keep us true...

Meditation.   The Lord's Prayer.   Intercessions.   Personal Prayers.

EVENING PRAYER

Reflections on the Day.   Thanksgiving.   Reconciliation.

EVENING PSALM / PS. 51 *David's prayer for forgiveness.*   PAGE 8.

CANTICLE OF SIMEON / LUKE 2:29-32 *Lord, let me go in peace.*   PAGE 8.

Personal Prayers.

Week Six / SATURDAY

MORNING PRAYER

I. THE PSALMS

MORNING PSALM / PS. 141
Like incense let my prayer arise.
PAGE 9

PSALM OF THE DAY / PS. 71
An old man still singing God's praise.

PSALM 71 / *Let me not prove a fool.*

1 I put my trust in you, O Lord;
    Let me not prove a fool.
2 In your fidelity, O Lord,
    Save me from ridicule.

3 A rock and refuge from my foe,
    A fortress be for me.
4 From wicked hands, the cruel grasp
    Of violence, save me.

5 Since I was but a child, O Lord,
    I put my trust in you.
6 You brought me from my mother's womb;
    From birth I leaned on you.

7 I praise you yet, show many, too:
    You are my refuge still.
8 All day my mouth will sing your praise,
    And, Lord, it always will.

9 As I grow old and lose my strength,
    In age forsake me not.
10 My enemies are watching me;
    They seek my life, they plot.

11 "God doesn't care whom we ensnare;
    We have no need to fear."
12 You do care Lord! Take up your sword;
    Do not delay; be near!

13 Let my accusers be disgraced,
    All those who seek my life.
Put all the slanderers to shame,
    Who fill my days with strife.

14 Whatever comes, I still will hope,
    And praise you all my days.
15 How good you are, how much you save;
    I cannot count the ways.

16 I come into your temple, Lord,
    To make your praises known;
To celebrate the goodness that
    Is yours and yours alone.

17 Lord, you have taught me from my youth.
    I still proclaim your deeds.
18 And now that I am old and gray,
    Do not forsake my needs.

I need to tell the things you've done
    To every age anew.
19 Your strength and power reach the sky.
    Who is there, God, like you?

20 You gave me hardship; but you will
    Restore my life to me.
21 From depths below will lift me high,
    Where you will comfort me.

22 On lyre and harp your faithful love
    I praise the whole day long.
O holy one of Israel,
    To you I sing my song.

23 My lips will shout, my tongue will tell
    With joy your saving grace.
24 While those who try to do me harm
    But buy their own disgrace.

II. Readings & Prayers

WINTER

JANUARY 7: 1ST DAY AFTER EPIPHANY
Calls to attention:
(Note: if today is Sunday, begin Week 7, page 109.)

1. I John 3:22-4:6.
   Put every spirit to a test.

2. Matthew 4:12-17,23-25.
   The kingdom is close at hand.

Help us discern the good, O Lord,
We won't succeed without your word...

SPRING

HOLY SATURDAY: THE EASTER VIGIL
This is the night:

1. Genesis 1:1,26-31.
   God looked at all that he had made.

2. Exodus 14:15-15:1.
   I will sing to the Lord triumphant.

3. Romans 6:3-11.
   Christ, raised, will never die again.

4A. Matthew 28:1-10.
   He is not here. He has been raised.

4B. Mark 16:1-8.
   He is going ahead of you.

4C. Luke 24:1-12.
   Remember what he said to you.

The Easter Proclamation, page 227.

SUMMER

SATURDAY: 14TH WEEK OF THE YEAR
Counsels for discipline:

1a. Genesis 49:29-33,50:15-24.
   The final days of Jacob and Joseph.

1b. Isaiah 6:1-8.
   The call to be a prophet.

2. Matthew 10:24-33.
   Do not be afraid.

We hear the call to live your word
And eagerly accept, O Lord...

FALL

SATURDAY: 27TH WEEK OF THE YEAR
By faith we enter a new world:

1a. Joel 4:12-21.
   It is harvest time for God.

1b. Galatians 3:22-29.
   We are children of God by faith.

2. Luke 11:27-28.
   Not family ties, but living faith.

How deep the bond of faith, O Lord;
With Mary, we believe your word...

Meditation. The Lord's Prayer. Intercessions. Personal Prayers.

EVENING PRAYER

Reflections on the Day. Thanksgiving. Reconciliation.

EVENING PSALM / PS. 143 *Lord, do not condemn.* PAGE 9.

SONG OF MOSES / REVELATION 15:3-4 *They all had harps and sang.* PAGE 9.

Personal Prayers.

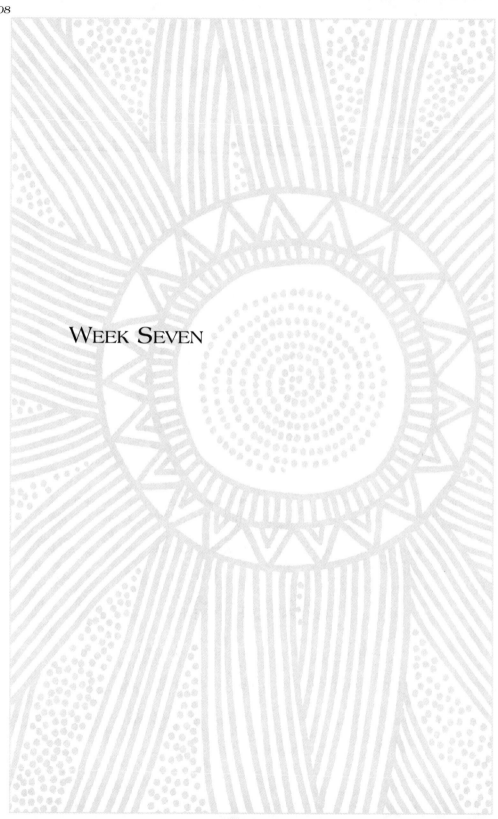

WEEK SEVEN

Week Seven / SUNDAY
MORNING PRAYER

I. THE PSALMS

MORNING PSALM / PS. 95
O my people, now listen to me.
PAGE 3

PSALM OF THE DAY / PS. 118
The Easter Psalm: a royal hymn of thanksgiving.

PSALM 118 / *God's faithful love will never end.*

1 Give thanks, give praise, the Lord is good.
  God's faithful love will never end.
2 O house of Israel, sing out:
  God's faithful love will never end!

3 O house of Aaron, too, sing out:
  God's faithful love will never end!
4 Let all who fear the Lord cry out:
  God's faithful love will never end!

5 In my distress I called on God,
  Who answered me, who set me free.
6 I have no fear, the Lord is here;
  So what can mortals do to me?

7 With God to help me, at my side,
  My foes shall fall, do what they can.
8 To take our refuge in the Lord
  Is better than to trust in man.

9 To take our refuge in you, Lord,
  Is better than to trust in kings.
10 The nations came to hem me in;
  But in your name I clipped their wings.

11 They hemmed me in on every side;
  But in your name I cut them off.
12 They swarmed like bees,
    like burning thorns;
  But in your name I cut them off.

13 They pressed me hard, I nearly fell;
  But with your help I overcame.
14 You, Lord, are my deliverer;
  My strength and might are in your name.

15 Our tents resound with shouts of joy;
  Victorious, the just are free!
16 The Lord's right hand is raised on high.
  To that right hand all glory be!

17 I shall not die, but live to sing
  The wondrous works of God most high.
18 Though you severely punished me,
  O Lord, you did not let me die.

19 O gates of justice, open wide,
  That I may enter, praise the Lord.
20 They are the gates, O Lord,
      through which
  The just go in to their reward.

21 I praise you for you answered me;
  You are my savior, you alone.
22 The stone the builders cast aside
  Has now become the cornerstone!

23 The Lord, our God, accomplished this;
  And marvelous it is to see.
24 This is the day the Lord has made;
  Let us rejoice, be filled with glee.

25 O save us, we beseech you, Lord;
  And grant us your prosperity.
26 Whoever comes in your name, Lord,
  Is blest, and by us blest will be.

27 The Lord is God, who gave us light;
  So let us join to praise the Lord.
  With branches in our hands we come
  Before the altar of the Lord.

28 You are my God, the God I praise;
  You are the one to whom I bend.
29 Give thanks and praise, the Lord is good;
  God's faithful love will never end!

II. Readings & Prayers

WINTER

The Baptism of Christ

This is my beloved Son; hear him.

Years A, B, & C

1. Isaiah 42:1-7.
   My servant shall bring justice.

2. Acts 10:34-38.
   Peter preaches to Gentiles too.

Year A

3. Matthew 3:13-17.
   We must fulfill what God demands.

Year B

3. Mark 1:7-11.
   Jesus was baptized by John.

Year C

3. Luke 3:15-16,21-22.
   You are my beloved son.

God, Father, we have seen your Son
Baptized with water, Spirit, too.
May we who have been christened, Lord,
Be like your Son in all we do.

SPRING

Easter Sunday

The Resurrection of the Lord.

Years A, B, & C

1. Acts 10:34, 37-43.
   Peter proclaims the risen Christ.

2a. Colossians 3:1-4.
   Out with the old, in with the new!

2b. I Corinthians 5:6-8.
   You have been raised with Christ.

The Easter Hymn: Page 227.

3. John 20:1-9.
   Peter and John run to the empty tomb.

The Lord is risen! Alleluia!
Christians, it is really true!
He brings us peace, and says to us:
Behold, I shall make all things new.

SUMMER

15TH SUNDAY OF THE YEAR
God sends us out to sow the Word.

YEAR A

1. Isaiah 55:10-11.
   Rain makes the earth fruitful.

2. Romans 8:18-23.
   All creation wants to be redeemed.

3. Matthew 13:1-9 or 23.
   A sower went out to sow his seed.

YEAR B

1. Amos 7:12-15.
   Go shepherd, prophecy to Israel.

2. Ephesians 1:3-10.
   God predestined us through Christ.

3. Mark 6:7-13.
   He called the twelve and sent them out.

YEAR C

1. Deuteronomy 30:10-14.
   The love of God is near to you.

2. Colossians 1:15-20.
   Through Christ all things were made.

3. Luke 10:25-37.
   Who is my neighbor?

WE GO, WE SOW, WE PREACH THE WORD;
We try to love and die for it.
But you alone can make it grow;
O Lord, rain down your grace on it.

FALL

28TH SUNDAY OF THE YEAR
God's invitations, our ingratitude.

YEAR A

1. Isaiah 25:6-10.
   The heavenly banquet.

2. Philippians 4:12-14, 19-20.
   With God I can do anything.

3. Matthew 22:1-14.
   Invite them all to the wedding.

YEAR B

1. Wisdom 7:7-11.
   Wisdom is better than wealth.

2. Hebrews 4:12-13.
   The word of God is powerful.

3. Mark 10: 17-27.
   Sell what you have, and follow me.

YEAR C

1. II Kings 5:14-17.
   Naaman is cured of leprosy.

2. II Timothy 2:8-13.
   If we die with him, we live with him.

3. Luke 17:11-19.
   Where are the other nine?

LORD, YOU INVITE US TO A FEAST;
To follow you; you cure our ills.
May we be grateful for your gifts,
Accept your word, and do your will.

Meditation. The Lord's Prayer. Intercessions. Personal Prayers.

EVENING PRAYER

Reflections on the Day. Thanksgiving. Reconciliation.

EVENING PSALM / PS. 23 *The Lord will give me rest.* PAGE 3.

CANTICLE OF MARY / LUKE 1:46-55 *Behold the handmaid of the Lord.* PAGE 3.

Personal Prayers.

Week Seven / MONDAY

MORNING PRAYER

I. THE PSALMS

MORNING PSALM / PS. 24

Let the King of glory in.

PAGE 4

PSALMS OF THE DAY / PSS. 75 & 76

Two hymns exalting the power of God over God's enemies.

PSALM 75 / *The Lord will cast the wicked down.*

2 WE THANK YOU, GOD, FOR YOU ARE NEAR,
  YOUR WONDROUS DEEDS THE WORLD SHALL HEAR!

3 "I choose the time when I shall come
  To judge the world with equity.
4 The earth will shake and people fear,
  But I will bring security."

5 Let not the boastful carry on;
  Let not the wicked scorn and mock.
6 Their voices full of arrogance,
  They rail against the Ancient Rock.

7 What lifts a man will never come
  From east or west or wilderness,
8 But from the Lord, who casts some down;
  Lifts others up to happiness.

9 The hand of God holds out a cup,
  The wine of wrath, and from it pours;
  And all the wicked of the earth
  Shall drink until there be no more.

10 The God of Jacob I shall praise;
  My joyful songs to heaven fly.
11 The Lord will cast the wicked down;
  Our God will lift the just on high.

PSALM 76 / *When you are angry, who can stand?*

2 You showed your love in Judah, Lord;
  Your name is great in Israel.
3 In Salem where you pitched your tent;
  On Zion's hill you chose to dwell.
4 You broke the fiery arrows there;
  The swords and shields of war dispelled.

5 You were resplendent, glorious,
  Above the mountains' majesty.
6 Your bravest foes were stupefied.
  They could not lift a hand or flee.
7 O God of Jacob, at your blast
  They fainted, chariot and steed.

8 For you are awesome, Lord, our God.
  When you are angry, who can stand?
9 In heaven you pronounce the sentence.
  Earth in fear and silence stands,
10 When you arise in judgment, Lord,
  To save the lowly of the land.

11 Before the anger of the Lord
  Let human anger bow in awe.
12 Renew and keep the vows you made;
  Then bring your gifts and tributes all.
13 God curbs the spirit of the princes,
  Fills the kings of earth with awe.

II. Readings & Prayers

WINTER
Monday: 1st Week of the Year
Three new books, three new stories:

1. Hebrews 1:1-6.
   God has spoken through his Son.

1a. I Samuel 1:1-8.
   The barren Hannah weeps.

1b. Mark 1:14-20
   The reign of God is at hand.

We shall repent, we do believe,
That we God's blessing may receive...

SUMMER
Monday: 15th week of the Year
We must decide whose side we are on:

1a. Exodus 1:8-14,22.
   Egypt comes to hate Israel.

1b. Isaiah 1:10-17.
   Wash yourselves; aim for justice.

2. Matthew 10:34-11:1.
   I come not for peace, but division.

We cast our lot with you, O Lord.
We seek a holy one's reward...

SPRING
Monday of Easter Week
Early witnesses of the the resurrection:

1. Acts 2:14,22-32.
   Peter witnesses to the resurrection.

2. Matthew 28:8-15.
   Jesus appears to the women.

Let joy outstrip our fear, O Lord.
Send us, like them, to spread the word...

FALL
Monday: 28th week of the Year
Against slavery, of body and soul:

1a. Romans 1:1-7.
   Paul prays for grace and peace in Rome.

1b. Galatians 4:22-5:1.
   We are not slaves, but free.

2. Luke 11:29-32.
   It is an evil age that seeks a sign.

Lord, break the chains of humankind;
We pray for open hearts and minds...

Meditation. The Lord's Prayer. Intercessions. Personal Prayers.

Evening Prayer

Reflections on the Day. Thanksgiving. Reconciliation.

Evening Psalm / Ps. 4 *I go to sleep in peace.* Page 4.

Canticle of Zachary / Luke 1:68-79 *Prepare the way of the Lord.* Page 4.

Personal Prayers.

MORNING PRAYER

I. THE PSALMS

MORNING PSALM / PS. 5
At dawn I pray to you.
PAGE 5

PSALMS OF THE DAY / PSS. 70 & 77
Two prayers of one in deep distress.

PSALM 70 / *Make haste, do not delay.*

2 Be gracious, God; deliver me.
  Make haste to help me, Lord.
3 Confusion, shame inflict on them
  Who seek my ruin, Lord.

4 Let them turn back and be disgraced
  Who wish to see me dead.
Let all who cry, "Hah hah," at me,
  Be shamed themselves instead.

5 Let all who seek you, Lord, be glad;
  May they rejoice in God.
Let those who love salvation cry
  Forever, "Great is God!"

6 Lord, I am poor and much in need;
  But you will find a way
To help me and deliver me.
  O Lord, do not delay.

PSALM 77 / *Has God forgotten us?*

2 I cry aloud to God to hear;
I seek the Lord in my distress.
3 At night I lift my hands to pray,
But still remain the comfortless.
4 I think of God, I cry and groan;
I meditate, become depressed.

5 I close my eyes,
    but cannot sleep.
I cannot speak, am troubled so.
6 I think of days gone by, of old,
Remembering years long ago.
7 Communing with my heart
    at night,
I pray, and so my questions grow:

8 Will God our people ever spurn,
And never turn again to us?
9 What happened to
    God's faithful love,
And all the promises to us?
10 Has God forgotten how to pity,
Turned in wrath away from us?

11 And then I said: "Is it my fault
The hand of God has changed,
    grown cold?"
12 But then I thought of all your works,
The wondrous deeds performed of old.
13 I still remember them, O Lord,
Am still convinced they must be told.

14 Your way is holy after all.
O God, there is no god but you.
15 You are the God of miracles;
You show your might in all you do.
16 With your strong arm you saved us all,
The tribes of Jacob, Joseph, too.

17 The waters saw your hand, O Lord.
They trembled and drew back in fear.
18 The clouds poured down their rain
    in floods.
Skies rumbled, bolts of light appeared.
19 A crash was heard, a mighty wind,
Earth quaked and shook,
    knew God was near.

20 You made a pathway through the sea
   That mighty waters could not block.
   Without a trace on ocean's floor,
21 You led your people like a flock
   With Moses, Aaron in the lead,
   You were their shepherd and their rock.

II. READINGS & PRAYERS

WINTER
TUESDAY: 1ST WEEK OF THE YEAR
God's promises come true:

1a. Hebrews 2:5-12.
    Through suffering, Christ reigns.

1b. I Samuel 1:9-20.
    The promised birth of Samuel.

2. Mark 1:21-28.
    Jesus teaches with authority.

O Holy One of God, O Lord,
You speak, we hear and trust your word...

SPRING
TUESDAY: 1ST WEEK OF EASTER
Witnessing to Christ; a labor of love:

1. Acts 2:36-41.
    Peter tells the people what to do.

2. John 20:11-18.
    Jesus appears to Mary Magdalene.

O Teacher, tell us what to do,
For we, like Mary, love you, too...

SUMMER
TUESDAY: 15TH WEEK OF THE YEAR
Pagans have more faith than the chosen:

1a. Exodus 2:1-15.
    The early life of Moses.

1b. Isaiah 7:1-9.
    Isaiah tells Ahaz not to fear.

2. Matthew 11:20-24.
    Capernaum is condemned.

The more you do, the less they trust;
Lord, let it not be so with us...

FALL
TUESDAY: 28TH WEEK OF THE YEAR
On living faith and active love:

1a. Romans 1:16-25.
    The just shall live by faith.

1b. Galatians 5:1-6.
    Do not go back to slavery.

2. Luke 11:37-41.
    Give alms, and you will be healed.

It is our faith that makes us whole,
That speaks with love, restores the soul...

Meditation. The Lord's Prayer. Intercessions. Personal Prayers.

EVENING PRAYER

Reflections on the Day. Thanksgiving. Reconciliation.

EVENING PSALM / PS. 6 *My bed is wet with tears.* PAGE 5.

THE CHRIST HYMN / PHILIPPIANS 2:6-11 *The mind of Christ.* PAGE 5.

Personal Prayers.

Week Seven / WEDNESDAY
MORNING PRAYER

I. THE PSALMS

MORNING PSALM / PS. 101
A royal pledge.
PAGE 6

PSALM OF THE DAY / PS. 78:1-33
Lessons from the past: I. In the desert.

PSALM 78:1-33 / *In spite of all, they still went on to sin.*

1 My people give me ear
  and hear my words.
2 My theme will be:
  the lessons of the past.
3 Things we have known
  and heard our parents tell;
The mighty deeds of God,
  the truths that last.

4 We must not keep them
  from our children's ears,
But speak to generations yet to come,
That they may sing the praises
  of the Lord;
The strength of God, the deeds
  the Lord has done.

5 For Jacob, God established a decree,
Ordained this word be taught in Israel:
That parents tell their children
  what they heard,
6 And children yet unborn shall it retell:

7 That all may keep the precepts
  of the Lord,
That they may put their confidence
  in God;
8 And not be like their ancestors of old,
Defiant, wayward, never true to God.

9 Be not like them, be not like Ephraim,
Whose bowmen in the battle
  turned and ran.
10 They did not keep their covenant
  with God.
11 They quite forgot those mighty deeds
  and plans.

12 In Egypt they had witnessed
  how God saves:
13 The waters parted,
  they marched through the sea.
14 Throughout the day God led them
  with a cloud,
Throughout the night with fire
  so they could see.

15 In barren wilderness God split a rock,
And from the rock a stream,
  a river burst.
16 On desert land, abounding, fresh and deep,
The water flowed
  to quench the people's thirst.

17 But they went on to sin and sin again,
And in the desert God most high defied.
18 Worse, in their hearts,
  they came to testing God,
Demanding what they craved
  God must provide.

19 They grumbled, railed against the Lord,
  and said:
"Can God set us a table here to eat?"
20 Though God had brought them water,
  still they cried:
"We have no food,
  we want some bread and meat!"

21 On hearing this the Lord was filled
  with rage.
A flash of anger fell on Israel;
22 Because they had no confidence in God,
Because they did not trust the Lord
  as well.

23 But still, God told the skies to open wide
24 And manna, heaven's bread, began to fall.
25 God sent them bread,
　　　　as much as they could eat.
　　The bread of angels, now a bread for all.

26 The Lord then stirred the heavens'
　　　　winds to blow;
　　And thick as ocean's sands,
　　　　birds filled the air.
27 As in a storm the birds rained down
　　　　on them;
28 They fell around the camp,
　　　　birds everywhere.

29 The people ate their fill
　　　　of what they craved;
30 But while the food was in their mouth,
　　　　God rose,
　　To strike in wrath the strongest in the land.
31 The youth of Israel the Lord laid low.

32 In spite of all they still went on to sin;
　　In all that God had done,
　　　　would not believe.
33 And so God made their days
　　　　go by like wind.
　　Their years would end in fear,
　　　　with no reprieve.

II. READINGS & PRAYERS

WINTER

WEDNESDAY: 1ST WEEK OF THE YEAR
The Lord's concern for us:

1a. Hebrews 2:14-18.
　　He came like us to save us.

1b. I Samuel 3:1-10,19-20.
　　Speak, Lord; your servant hears.

2.　Mark 1:29-39.
　　Jesus healing and teaching.

You come to us; we come to you,
To heal our souls, our bodies, too...

SPRING

WEDNESDAY OF EASTER WEEK
The miraculous works and words go on:

1. Acts 3:1-10.
　　Peter and John heal as Jesus did.

2. Luke 24:13-35.
　　The Emmaus story.

Lord who has risen from the dead,
We meet you when we break the bread...

SUMMER

WEDNESDAY: 15TH WEEK OF THE YEAR
God wills to heal us all:

1a. Exodus 3:1-6,9-12.
　　Moses sees a burning bush.

1b. Isaiah 10:5-7,13-16.
　　God acts in the affairs of man.

2.　Matthew 11:25-27.
　　Only the Son knows the Father.

Almighty God, you see and care;
We are your children, hear our prayer...

FALL

WEDNESDAY: 28TH WEEK OF THE YEAR
The justice of God will prevail:

1a. Romans 2:1-11.
　　With God, there is no favoritism.

1b. Galatians 5:18-25.
　　Led by the spirit, not by passions.

2.　Luke 11:42-46.
　　Woe to the pharisees and lawyers.

Appearances and passions, Lord,
Are not the path to your reward...

Meditation. The Lord's Prayer. Intercessions. Personal Prayers.

EVENING PRAYER

Reflections on the Day. Thanksgiving. Reconciliation.

EVENING PSALM / PS. 13 *Let me have hope.* PAGE 6.

THE LOVE OF GOD / ROMANS 8:35-39 *Who can be against us?* PAGE 6.

Personal Prayers.

Week Seven / THURSDAY
MORNING PRAYER

I. THE PSALMS

MORNING PSALM / PS. 100
Praise God from whom all blessings flow.
PAGE 7

PSALM OF THE DAY / PS. 78:34-72
More history: II. In Egypt and the promised land.

PSALM 78:34-72 / *God merciful forgave their sin.*

34 When stricken
    they would turn to God again,
35 To seek the rock
    who had redeemed them too.
36 Yet they would lie and try to fool the Lord,
37 And to the covenant were never true.

38 But God did not give way
    to righteous wrath,
And merciful, forgave their sin again.
39 The Lord remembered all of them are flesh,
A passing breath that will not come again.

40 How often in the desert they rebelled!
And in that wasteland, how they grieved
    the Lord.
41 They tried the holy one of Israel;
42 Forgot God's might and all they owed
    the Lord.

43-4 In Egypt God turned rivers into blood,
45 And sent among them swarms of flies
    and frogs.
46 God gave their crops to locusts
    and to worms,
47 Destroyed their vines with hail,
    their trees with frost.

48 Then came the thunder,
    lightning bolts and hail;
49 The wrath of God gave way to violence.
50 On cattle, flocks, came messengers
    of death,
To visit on the land a pestilence.

51 God struck the first born child,
    the child of love,
In all of Egypt's homes
    throughout their land.

52 The Lord then brought our people out
    like sheep,
And led them like a flock
    through desert land.

53 They had no fear, for they were safe
    with God.
Their enemies behind were lost at sea.
54 God brought them to this holy
    mountain top,
The mountain God had won in victory.

55 The nations all were driven from the land,
Which then was given Israel by God.
Each tribe was given space
    to pitch its tents;
56 But even then the people tested God.

Once more the people turned against
    the Lord;
57 Dismissed divine decrees, refused to go.
And faithless like their fathers,
    turned away,
Proved treacherous, a false
    and twisted bow.

58 God saw their infidelity and cried:
    "These hillside shrines and idols
    are not mine!"
59 Enraged, the Lord rejected Israel.
60 At Shiloh God destroyed the holy shrine.

61 The fortress there surrendered to the foe.
62 The ark, their pride and joy,
    was torn from them.
63 The young men died by fire,
    the priests by swords.
64 No maiden sang,
    no widow wept for them.

65 But then the Lord awoke as from a sleep;
A soldier who had taken too much wine.
66 And struck them from behind,
put them to shame.
67 The Lord rejected them:
"They are not mine."

68 Instead, chose Judah:
"He shall be my own."
Beloved Zion was to be their home.
69 God built the temple there,
like heaven, high;
And like the earth, forever firm, on stone.

70 God's servant David, taken from his flock,
71 Would care for Jacob, Israel, God's own.
72 With faithful heart he watched his master's flock;
With skillful hands he led his people home.

II. READINGS & PRAYERS

WINTER

THURSDAY: 1ST WEEK OF THE YEAR
God wills to heal us all:

1a. Hebrews 3:7-14.
Do not grow cold in sin.

1b. I Samuel 4:1-11.
Israel is defeated in war.

2. Mark 1:40-45.
Jesus heals a leper.

A leper, outcast from his race,
The Son of man, the Lord, embraced...

SPRING

THURSDAY OF EASTER WEEK
Christ's gift to the world:

1. Acts 3:11-26.
Peter explains and exhorts the people.

2. Luke 24:35-48.
Christ appears to the disciples.

You offer us your gift of peace;
Throughout the world may it increase...

SUMMER

THURSDAY: 15TH WEEK OF THE YEAR
The compassion of God:

1a. Exodus 3:11-20.
I AM sent me to you.

1b. Isaiah 26:7-19.
Let those in dust awake and sing.

2. Matthew 11:28-30.
Come to me for rest.

We are the poor, we are oppressed;
We came to you, O Lord, for rest...

FALL

THURSDAY: 28TH WEEK OF THE YEAR
See all with the eyes of God:

1a. Romans 3:21-29.
The justice of God works through faith.

1b. Ephesians 1:3-10.
God has chosen us in Christ.

2. Luke 11:47-54.
More woes to those who kill.

The world is full of men of blood,
May we, by faith, escape the flood...

Meditation. The Lord's Prayer. Intercessions. Personal Prayers.

EVENING PRAYER

Reflections on the Day. Thanksgiving. Reconciliation.

EVENING PSALM / PS. 131 *A child in your mother's arms.* PAGE 7.

THE UNSEEN GOD / COLOSSIANS 1:15-20 *First born of all creation.* PAGE 7.

Personal Prayers.

MORNING PRAYER

I. THE PSALMS

MORNING PSALM / PS. 130
Out of the depths.
PAGE 8

PSALM OF THE DAY / PS. 74
A national lament over the destruction of Jerusalem.

PSALM 74 / *Turn back and see the ruins there.*

1 O Lord, will your rejection never end?
Will you stay angry with the flock
you tend?
2 Remember us, the tribe you made
your own.
Remember Zion where you made
your home.

3 Turn back and see the ruins
standing there.
They ravaged all within your
house of prayer.
4 The shouts of all our foes
are roaring there.
The flags of enemies are everywhere.

5 They torched the doorway,
hacked the paneling.
6 On all the carvings blows of axes ring.
7 They desecrate your house
and watch it burn;
8 And say: "Let all their progeny so burn."

9 We see no sign, we have no prophet here;
No one to say how long we have to fear.
10 How long, O Lord,
will you let foes blaspheme;
11 Restrain your hand,
and tolerate their schemes?

12 O God, our King of old,
the one who saves,
13 You smashed the heads of dragons,
ruled the waves.
14 You crushed Leviathan,
fed him to sharks,
15 Created streams,
brought land from waters dark.

16 The day is yours,
yours also is the night;
You fixed the sun and moon
to give us light.
17 On earth you set the limits for us all;
The seasons, summer, winter, spring
and fall.

18 Remember, Lord, the taunts of enemies.
Do not give up your dove
to beasts like these.
19 Barbarians revile your holy name.
Do not forget your servants in their pain.

20 Recall your covenant, the land is rent;
The city dark, the country violent.
21 Let not the poor and weak
be put to shame,
But lift their heads that they may praise
your name.

22 Arise, O mighty Lord, your cause defend
Against the jeers of fools that never end.
23 Do not forget the clamor of your foes,
The roar of enemies that ever grows.

II. READINGS & PRAYERS

WINTER

FRIDAY: FIRST WEEK OF THE YEAR
The Lord gives all we could ask:

1a. Hebrews 4:1-5, 11.
   Be eager for your final rest.

1b. I Samuel 8:4-7, 10-22.
   The people want a king.

2. Mark 2:1-12.
   Jesus now forgives sins.

Not only limbs and bodies, Lord.
But souls recover at your word...

SPRING

FRIDAY OF EASTER WEEK.
Christ feeds his disciples:

1. Acts 4:1-12.
   Peter's answer for his acts.

2. John 21:1-14.
   The appearance in Galilee.

When you appear the catch is great;
Your presence, Lord, we celebrate...

SUMMER

FRIDAY: 15TH WEEK OF THE YEAR
The Lord is in charge:

1a. Exodus 11:10-12:14.
   Instructions for the Passover.

1b. Isaiah 38:1-8.
   Sickness and recovery of Hezekiah.

2. Matthew 12:1-8.
   Jesus is Lord of the Sabbath.

We seek your word in all we do.
Because you love, we trust in you...

FALL

FRIDAY: 28TH WEEK OF THE YEAR
We can rely on God:

1a. Romans 4:1-8.
   Abraham was justified by faith.

1b. Ephesians 1:11-14.
   You received the promised Spirit.

2. Luke 12:1-7.
   The hairs on your head are numbered.

O God, your promises are true.
You know us all, we trust in you...

Meditation. The Lord's Prayer. Intercessions. Personal Prayers.

EVENING PRAYER

Reflections on the Day. Thanksgiving. Reconciliation.

EVENING PSALM / PS. 51 *David's prayer for forgiveness.* PAGE 8.

CANTICLE OF SIMEON / LUKE 2:29-32 *Lord, let me go in peace.* PAGE 8.

Personal Prayers.

Week Seven / SATURDAY
MORNING PRAYER

I. THE PSALMS

MORNING PSALM / PS. 141
Like incense let my prayer arise.
PAGE 9

PSALM OF THE DAY / PS. 73
The confession of one who almost lost hope.

PSALM 73 / *How good it is to be with you.*

1 How good is God to Israel,
  To those whose hearts are pure.
2 But me, my feet had almost strayed;
  My steps became unsure.

3 I watched the wicked, those who boast.
  I envied their success.
4 I saw their bodies sleek and sound,
  No struggle, no duress.

5 Unlike the rest of us who toil,
  They lie in indolence.
6 They wear their pride like jewelry.
  They cloak their violence.

7 Their eyes grow fat with greed for more;
  Their craving knows no bound.
8 They scoff, speak with impunity,
  And threaten all around.

9 Their mouths lash out at heaven too;
  Their tongues rail on at earth.
10 And people praise and follow them!
  Find what they say of worth!

11 They even say, "God doesn't know,
  He really doesn't know."
12 So this is it? The wicked win?
  They thrive, relax and grow?

13 Was it for this I kept my heart
  And hands in innocence?
14 Awoke each morn, endured each day
  Of more, new violence?

15 Had I continued on like this
  I would have been untrue.
16 I tried to understand, accept;
  It proved too hard to do.

17 But then I sought your holy place,
  And there began to see:
18 You set them on a slippery road
  To bring them to their knee.

19 How quickly they shall be destroyed;
  Be swept away in fear;
20 A nightmare that is gone with dawn,
  Dismissed when you appear.

21 When I was full of bitterness,
  My heart as dry as dust,
22 My mind was full of ignorance:
  A beast, devoid of trust.

23 But I was always with you, Lord;
  You took me by the hand.
24 You led me, and will bring me home
  To glory in your land.

25 I seek in heaven only you,
  Of earth I want no more.
26 My flesh will fail, but God will be
  My rock forevermore.

27 Those far from you will surely die.
  Destroyed because untrue.
28 But I am near, and Lord, how good
  It is to be with you.

You are my refuge, O my God,
And will be all my days.
And I shall tell of all your works,
Forever sing your praise.

II. READINGS & PRAYERS

WINTER

SATURDAY: 1ST WEEK OF THE YEAR
He was like us in all but sin:

1a. Hebrews 4:12-16.
We have a sympathetic priest.

1b. I Samuel 9:1-4, 17-9, 10:1.
Saul is anointed king.

2. Mark 2:13-17.
I have come to call sinners.

We are the ones you came to call;
You are our priest, Lord, save us all...

SUMMER

SATURDAY: 15TH WEEK OF THE YEAR
The wicked plot against the just:

1a. Exodus 12:37-42.
Israel departs from Egypt.

1b. Micah 2:1-5.
Woe to those who plan iniquity.

2. Matthew 12:14-21.
Jesus fulfills Isaiah's prophecy.

For you, for us, for all the just,
It is the same. In you we trust...

SPRING

SATURDAY OF EASTER WEEK
The admonition of the Risen Lord:

1. Acts 4:13-21.
We have to preach what we have seen.

2. Mark 16:9-15.
Proclaim the good news to all.

O Lord, increase our faith, and use
Our lives, our words, to spread the news...

FALL

SATURDAY: 28TH WEEK OF THE YEAR
When put on trial, worry not:

1a. Romans 4:13-18.
Hoping against hope, he believed.

1b. Ephesians 1:15-23.
Christ is the head, the church his body.

2. Luke 12:8-12.
The Spirit will teach you what to say.

We are your body, so we trust
Your Spirit, Lord, will speak in us...

Meditation. The Lord's Prayer. Intercessions. Personal Prayers.

EVENING PRAYER

Reflections on the Day. Thanksgiving. Reconciliation.

EVENING PSALM / PS. 143 *Lord, do not condemn.* PAGE 9.

SONG OF MOSES / REVELATION 15:3-4 *They all had harps and sang.* PAGE 9.

Personal Prayers.

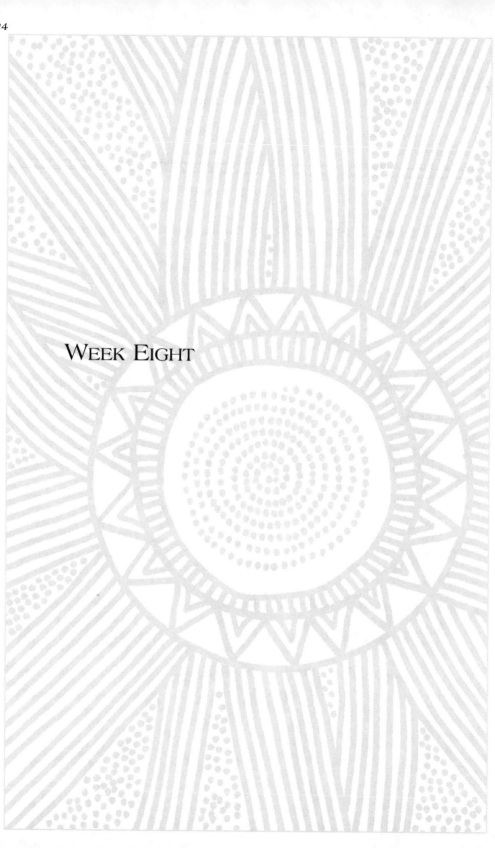

WEEK EIGHT

Week Eight / SUNDAY

MORNING PRAYER

I. THE PSALMS

MORNING PSALM / PS. 95
O my people, now listen to me.
PAGE 3

PSALMS OF THE DAY / PSS. 84 & 85
Pilgrim songs of longing.

PSALM 84 / *How lovely is your dwelling place.*

2 How lovely is your dwelling place, O God!
3 My spirit longs to see your courts, and rest.
   My being sings to you, the living God.

4 The sparrow and the swallow
       have their nests,
5 Where they may raise their young,
       O King, near you.
   Who dwell near you,
       and sing your praise, are blest.

6 Blest all who find their refuge, Lord, in you,
7 Whose minds are on their pilgrimage,
       and where,
   In valleys dry, you give them springs
       and dew.

8 They make their pilgrim way
       till they are there,
   And see the God of gods, on Zion's hill.
9 O mighty God of Jacob, hear my prayer:

10 Behold our King, our shield,
       be with him still.
11 One day outweighs a thousand
       when with you;
   A wicked house is less than heaven's sill.

12 Be sun and shade; give grace
       and glory, too,
13 Hold nothing back from those
       whose way is true.
   O Lord, how blest are all who trust in you.

PSALM 85 / *God's justice will bring peace.*

2 You once were gracious to our land,
       O Lord.
3 You took us back,
       forgave your people's sin;
4 You stayed your wrath,
       held back the angry word.

5 O saving God, restore us once again.
6 Abandon wrath; must it forever stay?
7 That we may all rejoice, give life; and then,

8 Show us once more your faithful love
       and way.
9 I long to hear God speak of peace,
       and bless
   The true of heart,
       who turn to God to stay.

10 All those who fear the Lord,
       the Lord will bless.
   Your glory then will fill our land with peace.
11 Your faithful love will meet our faithfulness.

   From that embrace
       the Lord will bring increase:
12 When faithfulness arises from the earth,
   Then justice will look down
       and bring us peace.

13 The Lord will bless our land,
       enrich the earth.
14 God's justice goes before
       and leads the way,
   And in its steps shall follow:
       peace on earth.

II. Readings & Prayers

WINTER

2ND SUNDAY OF THE YEAR
The vocation of Christ and Christians.

YEAR A

1. Isaiah 49:3-6.
   I shall make of you a light.

2. I Corinthians 1:1-3.
   Grace and peace to you from God.

3. John 1:29-34.
   This is God's chosen one.

YEAR B

1. I Samuel 3:3-10, 19.
   Speak Lord, your servant hears.

2. I Corinthians 6:13-20.
   You are members of the body of Christ.

3. John 1:35-42.
   Look: there is the lamb if God.

YEAR C

1. Isaiah 62:1-5.
   The Lord delights in you.

2. I Corinthians 12:4-11.
   Different gifts, the same Spirit.

3. John 2:1-12.
   The wedding feast at Cana.

JOHN POINTS TO YOU; YOU HEARD HIS CALL,
And Mary's call at Cana's feast.
Lord, it is good to have you here;
We, too, are called; our faith increase.

SPRING

2ND SUNDAY OF EASTER
Christ gives his Spirit to the church.

YEAR A

1. Acts 2:42-47.
   Life in the early church.

2. I Peter 1:3-9.
   A new birth of hope for salvation.

3. John 20:19-31.
   Jesus said: "Peace be with you."

YEAR B

1. Acts 4:32-35.
   Everything was held in common.

2. I John 5:1-6.
   Faith conquers the world.

3. John 20:19-31.
   Receive the Holy Spirit.

YEAR C

1. Acts 5:12-16.
   The members steadily increased.

2. Revelations 1:9-19.
   John's vision of the Lord on Patmos.

3. John 20:19-31.
   Blest are those who believe.

HOW BEAUTIFUL THAT EARLY CHURCH,
Its Spirit, peace, and faith in you;
Lord, send your Spirit once again;
May we be filled with it anew.

SUMMER
16TH SUNDAY OF THE YEAR
God's power and compassion.

Year A

1. Wisdom 12:13.16-19.
   How God uses power.

2. Romans 8:26-27.
   The Spirit helps us in our weakness.

3. Matthew 13:24-30.
   Let wheat and weeds grow side by side.

YEAR B

1. Jeremiah 23:1-6.
   Woe to wicked shepherds.

2. Ephesians 2:13-18.
   Christ's peace destroys barriers.

3. Mark 6:30-34.
   Christ's pity for the sheep.

YEAR C

1. Genesis 18:1-10.
   Hospitality earns a blessing.

2. Colossians 1:24-28.
   To suffer for you is my joy.

3. Luke 10:38-42.
   Mary chooses the better part.

ALL POWERFUL, YET PATIENT GOD:
Your heart is full of love for us.
May we be filled with love for you;
Good Shepherd, guide and care for us.

FALL
29TH SUNDAY OF THE YEAR
God's respect for those who serve.

Year A

1. Isaiah 45:1,4-6.
   Cyrus shall be my instrument.

2. Thessalonians 1:1-5.
   We thank God for your faith and hope.

3. Matthew 22:15-21.
   Give to Caesar what is Caesar's.

YEAR B

1. Isaiah 53:10-11.
   My servants shall have their reward.

2. Hebrews 4:14-16.
   Hope in Christ who understands us.

3. Mark 10:42-45.
   I came to serve, not be served.

YEAR C

1. Exodus 17:8-13.
   Moses holds his hands on high.

2. II Timothy 3:14-4:2.
   Be constant in good works.

3. Luke 18:1-18.
   The need to pray and not lose heart.

O SON OF MAN, YOU UNDERSTAND,
Respect and value those who serve.
For you yourself showed us the way;
Just Lord, give them what they deserve.

Meditation. The Lord's Prayer. Intercessions. Personal Prayers.

EVENING PRAYER

Reflections on the Day. Thanksgiving. Reconciliation.

EVENING PSALM / PS. 23 *The Lord will give me rest.* PAGE 3.

CANTICLE OF MARY / LUKE 1:46-55 *Behold the handmaid of the Lord.* PAGE 3.

Personal Prayers.

Week Eight / MONDAY
MORNING PRAYER

I. THE PSALMS

MORNING PSALM / PS. 24
Let the King of glory in.
PAGE 4

PSALM OF THE DAY / PS. 80
A lament for the nation in ruins.

PSALM 80 / *Lord, return; let your face shine on us.*

2 Hear us, Shepherd of Israel, listen to us;
You are leader of Joseph your flock.
3 From your throne on the Cherubim,
look upon Ephraim,
Manasseh and Benjamin's stock.

4 O Lord, stir up your power, and save us,
O God;
8 Lord come down;
let your face shine on us.
5 Lord, how long will your anger
continue to burn,
And our prayers bring no mercy on us?

6 You have fed us, O Lord,
with the bread of our tears;
We drink deep in full measure each day.
7 All our neighbors regard us
with loathing and scorn;
All our enemies mock us at play.

9 Lord, you brought us from Egypt,
a vine you would plant.
All the nations you drove from the land.
10 Then you cleared off the ground
for the vine of your choice;
It took root and it spread in the land.

11 Soon it covered the mountains
and cedars with shade,
With its branches as great as a tree's.
12 It extended its roots to the river to drink,
And its branches reached out to the seas.

13 So, Lord, why have you broken its walls,
torn them down,
So that all who pass by steal its fruit?
14 All the beasts of the forest are ravaging it;
All that move in the fields follow suit.

15 Mighty God, gracious Lord,
turn again to your own.
From above look below; hear our prayer.
16 Dear Lord, see what they've done to it;
look to the vine
That you planted with love and with care.

17 They have set it afire;
all its branches they cut.
Let them die by the wrath
of your glance!
18 May your hand be with him
who now stands at your side.
Let him strike with the might
you enhanced.

19 Lord, we never shall turn from you ever again.
Now we call on your name in this strife,
20 To restore us, O Lord; God of hosts, bring us back;
Let your face shine on us; give us life.

II. Readings & Prayers

WINTER
MONDAY: 2ND WEEK OF THE YEAR
The day will come when we shall fast:

1a. Hebrews 5:1-10.
   Christ, the source of salvation.

1b. I Samuel 15:16-23.
   The Lord requires obedience.

2. Mark 2:18-22.
   New wine requires new skins.

O Christ, our priest, you bring new wine,
But you remain our Lord and vine...

SPRING
MONDAY: 2ND WEEK OF EASTER
You must be born anew:

1. Acts 4:23-31.
   As they prayed, the Spirit came.

2. John 3:1-8.
   Nicodemus comes to Jesus at night.

We have been born anew, O Lord.
Send us the Spirit we adore...

SUMMER
MONDAY: 16TH WEEK OF THE YEAR
The persistence of the wicked:

1a. Exodus 14:5-18.
   Pharoah pursues the Israelites.

1b. Micah 6:1-8.
   God asks us to do right, love the good.

2. Matthew 12:38-42.
   An evil generation seeks a sign.

Destroy us all, the wicked would;
But we persist in doing good...

FALL
MONDAY: 29TH WEEK OF THE YEAR
On faith in God, not wealth:

1a. Romans 4:20-25.
   As Abraham believed, so let us.

1b. Ephesians 2:1-10.
   Salvation is yours through faith.

2. Luke 12:13-21.
   Avoid greed in all its forms.

With you, we shall possess all things;
From love of money, evil springs...

Meditation. The Lord's Prayer. Intercessions. Personal Prayers.

Evening Prayer

Reflections on the Day. Thanksgiving. Reconciliation.

EVENING PSALM / PS. 4 *I go to sleep in peace.* PAGE 4.

CANTICLE OF ZACHARY / LUKE 1:68-79 *Prepare the way of the Lord.* PAGE 4.

Personal Prayers.

Week Eight / TUESDAY
MORNING PRAYER

I. THE PSALMS

MORNING PSALM / PS. 5
At dawn I pray to you.
PAGE 5

PSALMS OF THE DAY / PSS. 79 & 99

Anguish for Jerusalem, followed by praise for God's holiness.

PSALM 79 / *Avenge your servants' blood.*

1 O Lord, they have invaded your domain.
Your holy temple pagans have defiled.
Jerusalem in ruins lies, in pain.

2 Your servants' bodies in the streets
are piled.
They have become the food of bird
and beast,
And we by all our neighbors are reviled.

3 Their blood ran out like water in the street,
4 And even for their burial no one came.
We have become the scorn
of all we meet.

5 How long, O Lord? Your anger burns
like flame.
6 Pour out your wrath on those
who know you not,
On kingdoms that do not invoke your name.

7 They eat at Jacob, desolate our lot!
8 Have mercy, Lord, for we are very low.
Our parents' sins and ours remember not.

9 O God of our salvation, help us now!
Let not the nations cry,
"Where is their God?"
To glorify your name, forgive us now.

10 So all can see, make clear to them,
O God,
That you avenge your servants' blood
who die.
11 The cries of prisoners are heard by God.

You hear the pleas of those condemned,
their sighs.
12 Return upon our neighbors seven ways
The taunts they launch at you,
O God most high.

13 Then we shall glorify you all our days;
For we are yours, your people and your flock;
In every age we shall sing out your praise!

PSALM 99 / *Holy is God*

1 The Lord, enthroned on cherubim,
is King.
Earth quakes, the people tremble
and obey.
2 In Zion you are great, the people sing;
3 They praise your name as awesome,
great, and say:
Holy is God!

4 You are a mighty King who justice loves.
On earth, Lord, you made equity
your way.
To Jacob you brought justice
from above.
5 Exalt the Lord! Bow down to God,
and say:
Holy is God!

6 First Moses, Aaron, Samuel, your priests,
  All called upon your name,
      cried out in hope.
7 You answered. They obeyed your laws,
      decrees,
  And all your words when from the cloud
      you spoke.
          Holy is God!

8 You answered them,
      were a forgiving God.
  But for their sins, O Lord,
      made all repay.
9 So on this holy mountain, bow to God;
  Exalt the Lord, give praise to God,
      and say:
          Holy is God!

II. READINGS & PRAYERS

WINTER

TUESDAY: 2ND WEEK OF THE YEAR
God looks to justice, not to law:

1a. Hebrews 6:10-20.
    God is an anchor; trust in him.

1b. I Samuel 16:1-13.
    Samuel anoints David as king.

2. Mark 2:23-28.
    The Sabbath was made for us.

Lord, we rely on you, not law,
For you are just, and know us all...

SPRING

TUESDAY: 2ND WEEK OF EASTER
Where to find unity and truth:

1. Acts 4:32-37.
    The believers had one heart, one mind.

2. John 3:7-15.
    Jesus teaches, Nicodemus questions.

Our hearts and minds, O Lord, are yours;
You have the teaching that endures...

SUMMER

TUESDAY: 16TH WEEK OF THE YEAr
How to be a child of God:

1a. Exodus 14:21-15:1.
    The Israelites march through the sea.

1b. Micah 7:14-20.
    Who is like our forgiving God?

2. Matthew 12:46-50.
    Those who do God's will are mine.

Lord Jesus, brother, we would be
Obedient to God, like thee...

FALL

TUESDAY: 29TH WEEK OF THE YEAR
Be reconciled; prepare for Christ:

1a. Romans 5:12-21.
    The just shall live by faith.

1b. Ephesians 2:12-22.
    He is our peace; he makes us one.

2. Luke 12:35-38.
    Be ready for the Lord's return.

You bring us life; you bring us peace;
Our readiness, O Lord, increase...

Meditation. The Lord's Prayer. Intercessions. Personal Prayers.

EVENING PRAYER

Reflections on the Day. Thanksgiving. Reconciliation.

EVENING PSALM / PS. 6 *My bed is wet with tears.* PAGE 5.

THE CHRIST HYMN / PHILIPPIANS 2:6-11 *The mind of Christ.* PAGE 5.

Personal Prayers.

Week Eight / WEDNESDAY
MORNING PRAYER

I. THE PSALMS

MORNING PSALM / PS. 101
A royal pledge.
PAGE 6

PSALMS OF THE DAY / PSS. 81 & 82
Two psalms that reveal the mind of God.

PSALM 81 / *I would have crushed her enemies.*

2 Sing joyfully to God our strength!
  To Jacob's God, sing out.
3 Sing lyre and harp and tambourine,
  Let trumpets blare and shout:

4 "The moon is new, the moon is full,
  It is a feast for all,
5 Decreed by God for Israel,
  Since Joseph's day, the law."

6 I heard an unfamiliar voice:
7a "I took your pain away.
8a In your distress you called on me;
7b I freed your hands that day.

8b In thunder once at Meribah,
  I put you to the test.
9 Now I admonish you again,
  O Israel, hear this:

10 You shall not serve a foreign god.
  Bow down to none but me,
11 The Lord, your God, who rescued you,
  From Egypt set you free.

My people, open up your mouths;
  I fill them; you will see.
12 But Israel would not obey,
  Instead rejected me.

13 And so I let her go her way.
14 O would it were not so!
15 I would have crushed her enemies,
  Have fought against her foe.

16 All those who hate us I would doom.
17 I would for you my flock,
  Have fed you with the finest wheat,
  With honey from the rock."

PSALM 82 / *How long will you perversely judge?*

1 God takes the throne in heaven's court,
  To render judgment on the lords:
2 "How long will you perversely judge;
  And to the wicked hand rewards?

3 Defend the orphan and the poor;
  The weak and needy: rescue them.
4 The poor and lowly vindicate;
  From wicked hands deliver them!"

5 They neither see, nor understand.
  Earth shakes, while they in darkness go.
6 I once imagined them as gods,
  The Most High's children here below,

7 But they shall fall like any prince;
  They all shall die as mortals do.
8 Arise, O God, and judge the earth!
  The nations all belong to you.

II. READINGS & PRAYERS

WINTER

WEDNESDAY: 2ND WEEK OF THE YEAR
The Son of God has power:

1a. Hebrews 7:1-3,5-17.
  The Son of God: a priest forever.

1b. I Samuel 17:32-51.
  David slays Goliath.

2. Mark 3:1-6.
  Jesus heals on the Sabbath.

O Son of God, we look to you:
A healing priest in all you do...

SPRING

WEDNESDAY: 2ND WEEK OF EASTER
God's providential care:

1. Acts 5:17-26.
  An angel releases the apostles.

2. John 3:16-21.
  God so loved the world, he sent his Son.

You care for us, you really do,
With grateful hearts we sing to you...

SUMMER

WEDNESDAY: 16TH WEEK OF THE YEAR
How shall we receive God's word?

1a. Exodus 16:1-15.
  The Israelites grumble for bread.

1b. Jeremiah 1:1-10.
  I have appointed you a prophet.

2. Matthew 13:1-9.
  The parable of the sower.

Good seed you sow in us, O Lord.
We pray it yield a rich reward...

FALL

WEDNESDAY: 29TH WEEK OF THE YEAR
Past, present, and future:

1a. Romans 6:12-18.
  Once slaves of sin, now you are free.

1b. Ephesians 3:2-12.
  The mystery of Christ is now revealed.

2. Luke 12:39-48.
  Be on guard for when he comes.

You set us free; the past is done.
The future, Lord, must still be won...

Meditation. The Lord's Prayer. Intercessions. Personal Prayers.

EVENING PRAYER

Reflections on the Day. Thanksgiving. Reconciliation.

EVENING PSALM / PS. 13 *Let me have hope.* PAGE 6.

THE LOVE OF GOD / ROMANS 8:35-39 *Who can be against us?* PAGE 6.

Personal Prayers.

Week Eight / THURSDAY
MORNING PRAYER

I. THE PSALMS

MORNING PSALM / PS. 100
Praise God from whom all blessings flow.
PAGE 7

PSALMS OF THE DAY / PSS. 83 & 87

A plea for vengeance, and a patriotic hymn.

PSALM 83 / *Lord cover them with shame.*

2 Do not be silent, God, nor still, unmoved.
3 Your enemies in rage have raised
    their head.
4 Conspiring, they lay their plans for us:
5 "Let Israel be gone, its name be dead."

6 Edom, Ishmael, Moab, Hagar too;
7 Philistia, Biblos, Amalek and all,
8 Assyria has joined with them, become
9 The arm of Lot, to make your people fall.

10 Treat them like Midian and all the rest;
11 O Lord, let them become like dung to us.
12 Like Oreb, Zeeb, Zelba, Salmana,
13 Who said, "The land of God belongs to us."

14 Make them like thistledown,
    like chaff, O God;
15 A forest fire, a mountain top ablaze.
16 Stir up a storm to drive them all away;
    Let winds of fear and terror fill their days.

17 Lord, cover them with shame, dismay, disgrace,
18 And let them die till they your name esteem.
19 And let them know your name alone is Lord
    You are most high, above the earth, supreme.

PSALM 87 / *Our roots all spring from Zion.*

1 You love the city that you built,
    Your holy mountain dwelling.
2 You love the gates of Zion more
    Than all of Jacob's dwellings.
3 O Lord, great things are said of her,
    A glory past all telling.

4 Consider Egypt, Babylon,
    They both were born of her.
Philistia and Tyre and Cush,
    They, too, were born of her.
5 Indeed it can be said of Zion:
    All were born of her.

The Lord Most High established her
    And guaranteed her care.
6 On heaven's scroll the Lord inscribes
    Beside each name: "Born there."
7 In festive dance they all will sing:
    "Our roots all spring from there."

II. READINGS & PRAYERS

WINTER

THURSDAY: 2ND WEEK OF THE YEAR
People recognize a leader:

1a. Hebrews 7:25-8:6.
   We have a new and great high priest.

1b. I Samuel 18:6-9,19:1-7.
   Saul's jealousy of David.

2. Mark 3:7-12.
   Crowds follow Jesus to be cured.

O Son of God, and David, too;
Ten thousand sing their praise of you...

SPRING

THURSDAY: 2ND WEEK OF EASTER
The testimony of God:

1. Acts 5:27-33.
   The apostles testify before the court.

2. John 3:31-36.
   The testimony of God's son.

We testify, the Spirit, too;
Let all believe, God's word is true...

SUMMER

THURSDAY: 16TH WEEK OF THE YEAR
How God communicates:

1a. Exodus 19:1-2, 9-11, 16-20.
   Israel meets God at Sinai.

1b. Jeremiah 2:1-3, 7-8, 12-13.
   My people have forsaken me.

2. Matthew 13:10-17.
   Why Jesus spoke in parables.

In smoke and fire, in parables,
We hear a world ineffable...

FALL

THURSDAY: 29TH WEEK OF THE YEAR
Choices will have to be made:

1a. Romans 6:19-23.
   The wages of sin is death.

1b. Ephesians 3:14-21.
   The riches of God's glory.

2. Luke 12:49-53.
   I came to light a fire on earth.

Not peace on earth, but peace above;
A fire on earth: such is your love...

Meditation. The Lord's Prayer. Intercessions. Personal Prayers.

EVENING PRAYER

Reflections on the Day. Thanksgiving. Reconciliation.

EVENING PSALM / PS. 131 *A child in your mother's arms.* PAGE 7.

THE UNSEEN GOD / COLOSSIANS 1:15-20 *First born of all creation.* PAGE 7.

Personal Prayers.

Week Eight / FRIDAY
MORNING PRAYER

I. THE PSALMS

MORNING PSALM / PS. 130
Out of the depths.
PAGE 8

PSALM OF THE DAY / PS. 88
The cry of one who has almost lost hope.

PSALM 88 / *I am alone, my only friend, the dark.*

2 Lord God who saves, I cry all night,
    all day;
3 Incline your ear, and hear me as I pray.
4 My soul is full of woe, is at the brink.
Before the pit I stand, about to sink.

5 I now belong with those
    consigned below.
Like them I have no strength, and so I go
6 Like those forsaken, lying in their graves,
Like those forgotten by the one
    who saves.

7 I sink in depths, in regions dark
    and deep,
8 While over me
    your waves of anger sweep.
9 You took my friends: to them I am a sin.
I am alone, without escape, shut in.

10 My eyes, O Lord,
    grow dim with sorrow too.
All day I call, I lift my hands to you.
11 Will you, O Lord, work wonders
    for the dead?
Will shadows rise
    to sing your praise instead?

12 Will those in tombs
    proclaim your faithful love?
Will faith proclaimed below
    be heard above?
13 Will miracles be seen in darkened lands?
    Or be remembered in forgotten lands?

14 O Lord, I cry to you each day at dawn.
15 Why turn away, rebuff me on and on?
16 From early on my life has been a death.
    I suffer terror, pain with every breath.

17 Your terrors have annihilated me;
18 Your wrath sweeps over me, a mighty sea.
19 Because of you my friends now all depart;
    I am alone; my only friend, the dark.

II. Readings & Prayers

WINTER
Friday: 2nd Week of the Year
Respect for those whom God has chosen:

1a. Hebrews 8:6-13.
   The mediator of a new covenant.

1b. I Samuel 24:3-21.
   David spares Saul.

2. Mark 3:13-19.
   Jesus chooses the twelve.

Lord, we respect those you anoint.
Yes, even when they disappoint...

SPRING
Friday: 2nd Week of Easter.
No obstacle impedes God's work:

1. Acts 5:34-42.
   They never stopped teaching.

2. John 6:1-15.
   Jesus feeds the multitude.

Not being whipped, not lack of food,
Will stop us, Lord, from doing good...

SUMMER
Friday: 16th Week of the Year
There is nothing that we lack:

1a. Exodus 20:1-17.
   The ten commandments.

1b. Jeremiah 3:14-17.
   I will appoint good shepherds.

2. Matthew 13:18-23.
   The sower parable explained.

Good shepherds, good commands,
      good seed,
The Lord has given all we need...

FALL
Friday: 29th Week of the Year
Have a sense of urgency:

1a. Romans 7:18-25.
   Who can free me from this death?

1b. Ephesians 4:1-6.
   One Lord, one faith, one baptism.

2. Luke 12:54-59.
   Read the signs of the times.

Awake, my soul, the hour is late;
To save yourself, your Lord await...

Meditation. The Lord's Prayer. Intercessions. Personal Prayers.

EVENING PRAYER

Reflections on the Day. Thanksgiving. Reconciliation.

Evening Psalm / Ps. 51 *David's prayer for forgiveness.* Page 8.

Canticle of Simeon / Luke 2:29-32 *Lord, let me go in peace.* Page 8.

Personal Prayers.

Week Eight / SATURDAY
MORNING PRAYER

I. THE PSALMS

MORNING PSALM / PS. 141
Like incense let my prayer arise.
PAGE 9

PSALMS OF THE DAY / PSS. 90 & 110
On the transience of life, and permanence of God's word.

PSALM 90 / *Teach us to count our days and live aright.*

1 Lord, you have been our rock
    from age to age.
Before the hills and mountains came to be,
2 Before the world was made
    and earth was born,
You are our God from all eternity.

3 O Lord, do not make us go back to dust;
Nor say to us:
    "Return, your day has passed."
4 To you a thousand years are like a day;
Or like the evening watch
    when night has passed.

5 We are like grass.
    When cut, we sleep at night,
To rise at dawn, refreshed to greet the day
6 Like grass we sprout and flourish;
    life is new.
But then by dusk we wither, fade away.

7 We are consumed by wrath,
    worn out by rage.
Our hidden sins exposed before you lie.
8 Our days are spent beneath your
    sun of wrath;
Our years come to their ending like a sigh.

9 Our span of life extends three score and ten;
Or, given strength, perhaps a decade more.
10 All spent in toil and woe,
    they quickly pass;
And then to darkness we return
    once more.

11 Who understands the fury
    of your wrath?
Let it an equal fear of you impart.
12 Teach us to count our days and live aright,
That we may grow
    in wisdom of the heart.

13 O Lord, how long? Have pity on us all.
14 Your faithful love at dawn
    will make us laugh.
15 For all the pain you gave us, give us joy;
For all the years we suffered
    from your wrath.

16 Let all your servants see your works,
    O Lord;
Your glory show the children of all lands.
17 The favor of the Lord, our God, be ours,
And bless our work,
    the service of our hands.

O bless this work, the service of our hands!

PSALM 110 / *The Lord has sworn and will not change.*

1 The Lord has spoken to the king:

"Sit here, enthroned at my right hand.
Your footstool I have made your foe."
2 Go forth from Zion, rule the land,
Armed with your mighty scepter, go!

3 Your people wait for your command.
From birth the power belongs to you.
Arrayed in splendor by God's hand,
Like dew, your youth is born anew.

4 The Lord has sworn, and will not change:

"A priest eternally are you;
 By my decree the rightful king."
5 The Lord is at your hand, with you.
 In anger God will crush the kings,

6 Will judge the nations far and wide,
 Will stack their bodies, bash their heads.
7 On heaven's throne shall you abide;
 The most high God will lift your head.

II. READINGS & PRAYERS

WINTER

SATURDAY: 2ND WEEK OF THE YEAR
On blood relationships:

1a. Hebrews 9:2-3, 11-14.
 The new covenant's blood is Christ's.

1b. II Samuel 1:1-27.
 David mourns Saul and Jonathan.

2. Mark 3:20-21.
 His family thinks Jesus mad.

Those close to us may prove untrue;
O Lord, we place our trust in you...

SPRING

SATURDAY: 2ND WEEK OF EASTER
On the providence of God:

1. Acts 6:1-7.
 The appointment of deacons.

2. John 6:16-21.
 Jesus walks on water.

You calm our fears, you calm the seas,
You care for all, you hear our pleas...

SUMMER

SATURDAY: 16TH WEEK OF THE YEAR
A patient God is also just:

1a. Exodus 24:3-8.
 The covenant, renewed with blood.

1b. Jeremiah 7:1-11.
 Has my house become a den of thieves?

2. Matthew 13:24-30.
 The parable of the wheat and weeds.

A den of thieves, a field of weeds;
A patient Lord will judge all deeds...

FALL

SATURDAY: 29TH WEEK OF THE YEAR
The Lord requires that we produce:

1a. Romans 8:1-11.
 The Spirit is our hope for life.

1b. Ephesians 4:7-16.
 We are the body of Christ.

2. Luke 13:1-9.
 Repent, bear fruit, or die.

Come dwell in us, O Spirit, come;
Enliven us that all be one...

Meditation. The Lord's Prayer. Intercessions. Personal Prayers.

EVENING PRAYER

Reflections on the Day. Thanksgiving. Reconciliation.

EVENING PSALM / PS. 143 *Lord, do not condemn.* PAGE 9.

SONG OF MOSES / REVELATION 15:2-4 *They all had harps and sang.* PAGE 9.

Personal Prayers.

WEEK NINE

MORNING PRAYER

I. THE PSALMS

MORNING PSALM / PS. 95
O my people, now listen to me.
PAGE 3

PSALMS OF THE DAY / PSS. 27 & 30
Two Davidic songs of confidence in God.

PSALM 27 / *In heaven I shall see your face.*

1 The Lord is light, my saving light;
   Whom should I fear?
The Lord is might, whom should I dread
   When God is near?

2 The wicked seek to swallow me
   For once and all.
But they themselves, my enemies,
   Will trip and fall.

3 Though armies camp before my gate,
   I still will hope.
Though they attack, make war on me,
   I still can cope.

4a A hundred times I've asked, O Lord,
   This gift I pray:
   To dwell with you, within your house,
   For all my days,

4b To gaze upon your loveliness,
   Your holy face;
   To wake each dawn, and find myself
   In sacred space.

5 I take my refuge in God's tent
   In times of woe.
The tent on high that shelters me
   From strife below.

6 And there above my enemy,
   My head I raise.
In it I offer sacrifice
   And sing God's praise.

7 Lord, hear my voice that cries aloud
   In fervent tones,
8 The voice within my heart that says:
   "Seek God alone."

9 I seek your face; turn not away
   In anger, Lord.
Do not abandon me, O God,
   My saving Lord.

10 Though father, mother turn from me,
   You, Lord, will not.
11 Show me a level path, your way;
   My foes will not.

12 Do not abandon me to them;
   They are unjust.
They testify with hate and lies;
   13 But you I trust.

In heaven I shall see your face;
   14 I wait for God.
Be strong; let courage fill your hearts;
   And wait for God.

PSALM 30 / *I praise you, Lord; you rescued me.*

2 I praise you, Lord,
   for you have rescued me.
You did not let my enemies prevail.
3 You brought me back, O Lord,
   from death, the grave.
4 I cried to you;
   you did not let me fail.

5 Your faithful sing and praise
   your holy name.
Your anger dies; your faithful love lives on.
6 When pleased, Lord, you bestow
   eternal life.
We shed our tears at night,
   but smile at dawn.

7 One time I thought:
  "I'll never be disturbed."
8 For, in your goodness,
  you had made me strong.
But then you hid, and I was terrified.
9 What good is death?
  My life, O Lord, prolong!

10 Can dust give thanks?
  Proclaim your faithfulness?
11 Have mercy on me, God;
  do not destroy!
12 O change my mourning
  into dancing, Lord.
Take off my rags, and dress me up in joy.

13 My soul shall sing forevermore your praise;
  Give thanks to you, my God, for endless days.

II. READINGS & PRAYERS

WINTER

3RD SUNDAY OF THE YEAR
Good news! Christ's work begins:

YEAR A

1. Isaiah 8:23-9:3.
   The people have seen a great light.

2. I Corinthians 1:10-13,17.
   Let there be no factions.

3. Matthew 4:12-17.
   Reform! The kingdom is at hand.

YEAR B

1. Jonah 3:1-5,10.
   Nineveh repents; God relents.

2. I Corinthians 7:29-31.
   Time is short; the world will pass away.

3. Mark 1:14-20.
   Jesus calls Peter, Andrew, James, and John.

YEAR C

1. Nehemiah 8:2-10.
   Ezra reads the law; the people weep.

2. I Corinthians 12:12-30.
   You are the body of Christ.

3. Luke 1:1-4; 4:14-21.
   The Spirit of the Lord is upon me.

LORD,
  WE HAVE HEARD YOUR WORD, YOUR CALL.
We see you start your work today.
The time is short; the harvest great;
Help us begin to work and pray.

SPRING

3RD SUNDAY OF EASTER
The risen Christ assigns our tasks:

YEAR A

1. Acts 2:22-28.
   Peter witnesses to the resurrection.

2. I Peter 1:17-21.
   We were ransomed by Christ's blood.

3. Luke 24:13-35.
   They knew him when he broke the bread.

YEAR B

1. Acts 3:13-19.
   Peter preaches reform.

2. I John 2:1-5.
   Christ is our offering for sins.

3. Luke 24:35-48.
   Penance must be preached to all.

YEAR C

1. Acts 5:27-32,40-41.
   Better to obey God than men.

2. Revelations 5:11-14.
   Glory and praise to the Lamb.

3. John 21:1-14.
   Feed my lambs; feed my sheep.

YOUR CONFIDENCE IN US IS GREAT;
See Peter now, the fearless one.
May we be faithful witnesses,
Dear Father, to your risen Son.

SUMMER	FALL
17TH SUNDAY OF THE YEAR	30TH SUNDAY OF THE YEAR
God's words and works:	*Jesus teaches and heals:*

YEAR A	YEAR A
1. I Kings 3:5-12.	1. Exodus 22:20-26.
Solomon prays for understanding.	*I hear the widows' and orphans' cries.*
2. Romans 8:28-30.	2. I Thessalonians 1:5-10.
God makes all things work together.	*You became a model for all.*
3. Matthew 13:44-46.	3. Matthew 22:34-40.
What God's kingdom is like.	*The two great commandments.*

YEAR B	YEAR B
1. II Kings 4:42-44.	1. Jeremiah 31:7-9.
Elisha feeds the people.	*I bring them back, the blind, the lame.*
2. Ephesians 4:1-6.	2. Hebrews 5:1-6.
One Lord, one faith, one Baptism.	*You are my son, a priest forever.*
3. John 6:1-15.	3. Mark 10:46-52.
Jesus feeds the people.	*Lord, I want to see.*

YEAR C	YEAR C
1. Genesis 18:20-32.	1. Sirach 35:12-18.
For ten good men I will relent.	*God hears the prayer of the poor.*
2. Colossians 2:12-14.	2. II Timothy 4:6-8,16-18.
He pardoned all our sins.	*I have fought the good fight.*
3. Luke 11:1-13.	3. Luke 18:9-14.
Christ teaches us to pray, persistently.	*Be merciful to me, a sinner.*

YOU FEED US WITH YOUR WORDS AND WORKS;	O DAVID'S SON, WE TOO WOULD SEE;
We pray for understanding too.	For we are blind and lame and poor.
Our faith increase; let us persist	And we have sinned, but still we love;
In prayer; do all we do for you.	Our faith is true, our hope is sure.

Meditation. The Lord's Prayer. Intercessions. Personal Prayers.

EVENING PRAYER

Reflections on the Day. Thanksgiving. Reconciliation.

EVENING PSALM / PS. 23 *The Lord will give me rest.* PAGE 3.

CANTICLE OF MARY / LUKE 1:46-55 *Behold the handmaid of the Lord.* PAGE 3.

Personal Prayers.

Week Nine / MONDAY
MORNING PRAYER

I. THE PSALMS

MORNING PSALM / PS. 24
Let the King of glory in.
PAGE 4

PSALMS OF THE DAY / PSS. 91 & 111

God's promises to the king and his people; their grateful praise.

PSALM 91 / *They shall drink their fill.*

1 O you who are enthroned before the Lord,
Who shelter in the shade of God most high,
2 Cry out to God: "You are my rock, my fort!
The one in whom I trust, to whom I fly."

3 The Lord alone can free you from the snare,
Protect you from a deadly pestilence.
4 The Lord will shelter you
beneath God's wings;
The Lord will be a shield for your defense.

5 You need not dread the arrows of the day;
You need not fear the terrors of the night,
6 The plague that in the darkness
stalks its prey,
The scourge that strikes at noon
in broad daylight.

7 For though upon your left a thousand fall,
And at your right
ten thousand more should die,
8 You will remain untouched,
and you will see
The wicked be repaid before your eye.

9 Because you made the Lord your rock
and fort,
10 No harm shall come to you,
no plague come near.
11 For God has given angels
this command:
To guard your every step
from every fear.

12 And they shall lift you up on angel hands.
No stone will be allowed
to graze your foot.
13 You shall not fear the lion with her cub;
The serpent you will trample underfoot.

14 "I keep them safe
because they know my name.
Because they cling to me I rescue them.
15 If they should call on me I will be there,
To save them from distress
and feast with them.

16 Their hopes for length of days I will fulfill;
Of my salvation they shall drink their fill."

PSALM 111 / *Praise is yours eternally.*

1 ALLELUIA!

With all my heart I praise you, God,
In the assembly of the just.
2 How great are all the works of God
To those who study them, and trust.

3 Your deeds are splendid, glorious.
Your goodness, Lord, will ever last.
4 Your works are known to all of us;
Your kindness and compassion vast.

5 Who fear the Lord, the Lord will feed;
For you have not forgotten us.
6 You show your might in every deed;
You gave the nations' land to us.

7 Your handiwork is true and just,
Established once, forever there.
8 Your words are worthy of our trust,
To be observed with faithful care.

9 You sent a ransom as reward;
  You set in place a covenant
  Between you and your people, Lord;
  Ordained that it be permanent.

10 Your name, O God, is holy, awesome;
  Praise is yours eternally.
  The fear of you, the root of wisdom;
  All who practice it will see.

II. Readings & Prayers

WINTER
MONDAY: 3RD WEEK OF THE YEAR
A divided kingdom cannot stand:

1. Hebrews 9:15, 24-28.
    Christ was offered up but once.

1a. II Samuel 5:1-7, 10.
    David is elected king.

1b. Mark 3:22-30.
    Satan is finished.

O Son of David, our true King,
Save us from Satan, and from sin...

SPRING
MONDAY: 3RD WEEK OF EASTER
You must be born anew:

1. Acts 6:8-15.
   Stephen before the Sanhedrin.

2. John 6:22-9.
   Seek the food that leads to life.

Give us your Spirit, Lord of Life,
To boldly answer hate and strife...

SUMMER
MONDAY: 17TH WEEK OF THE YEAR
The depths of the people's sin:

1a. Exodus 32:15-24, 30-34.
    Israel's idolatry.

1b. Jeremiah 13:1-11.
    A graphic condemnation.

2. Matthew 13:31-35.
    Images of the kingdom.

Our people's sin are rank, O Lord;
But you can save us; say the word...

FALL
MONDAY: 30TH WEEK OF THE YEAR
Jesus breaks the rules:

1a. Romans 8:12-17.
    In the Spirit we call God "Abba."

1b. Ephesians 4:32-5:8.
    Walk in love, as Christ loved us.

2. Luke 13:10-17.
    Jesus heals on the Sabbath.

O Father, Abba, throned above,
We want to love as Jesus loves...

Meditation. The Lord's Prayer. Intercessions. Personal Prayers.

EVENING PRAYER

Reflections on the Day. Thanksgiving. Reconciliation.

EVENING PSALM / PS. 4 *I go to sleep in peace.* PAGE 4.

CANTICLE OF ZACHARY / LUKE 1:68-79 *Prepare the way of the Lord.* PAGE 4.

Personal Prayers.

Week Nine / TUESDAY
MORNING PRAYER

I. THE PSALMS

MORNING PSALM / PS. 5
At dawn I pray to you.
PAGE 5

PSALMS OF THE DAY / PSS. 86 & 112
The prayer of an afflicted one, and praise for the generous.

PSALM 86 / *A proud and brutal gang is here.*

1 Lord, hear and answer;
    I am much in need.
2 Protect your servant's life; I have been true.
    I trust in you, deliver me, O God.
3 Have mercy, Lord, I cry all day to you.

4 Make glad my heart, I lift my soul to you.
5 Forgive! And give your faithful love to all.
6 Give ear! And hear my plea
    in my distress.
7 I know that you will answer when I call.

8 There is no one like you among the gods.
    Nor are the works they do,
        O Lord, the same.
9 All nations, Lord, shall glorify your name.
10 For you alone do great
    and wondrous things.

11 Teach me your way that I may walk
    in truth.
  An undivided heart implant in me.
12 With all my heart I ever praise your name.
13 Your faithful love is great; you set me free.

14 O God, a proud and brutal gang is here.
    They seek my life; they never look above
15 To you who are a kind and gracious Lord,
    One slow to anger, rich in faithful love.

16 Have pity on me;
    turn and give me strength.
  I am your servant's child, a faithful one.
17 Lord, give a sign;
    let those who hate me see
  And be ashamed;
    console your chosen one.

PSALM 112 / *The generous are not forgotten.*

1 ALLELUIA!

How blest are those who fear the Lord,
  Who find their joy in God's command.
2 Their generation will be blest;
  Their children mighty in the land.

3 Prosperity will dwell with them;
  Their generosity will last.
4 A light in darkness for the just,
  Their kindness and their mercy vast.

5 It will go well for those who lend,
  Who tend to business honestly.
6 The generous are not forgotten,
  Are not shaken easily.

7 For them bad news is not the end;
  They trust in God for every need.
8 Their hearts are firm and unafraid;
  They know their foe will not succeed.

9 They freely give; the poor they feed.
  The Lord rewards the generous.
10 The wicked see and gnash their teeth;
  For nothing comes from selfishness.

II. Readings & Prayers

WINTER

Tuesday, 3rd Week of the Year
What makes us family:

1a. Hebrews 10:1-10.
I come to do your will, O God.

1b. II Samuel 6:12-19.
David dances before the Ark.

2. Mark 3:31-35.
Who are my family?

We are your brothers, sisters, Lord,
And we shall do your will and word...

SUMMER

Tuesday, 17th Week of the Year
The leaders plead for patience:

1a. Exodus 33:7-11; 34:5-9, 28.
Moses pleads for the people.

1b. Jeremiah 14:17-22.
The prophet does the same.

2. Matthew 13:35-43.
The parable of the weeds.

You are a patient God indeed;
Till harvest, we your patience need...

SPRING

Tuesday, 3rd Week of Easter
On what meat do these Christian feed:

1. Acts 7:51-8:1.
The martyrdom of Stephen.

2. John 6:30-35.
I myself am the bread of life.

He died like you because, O Lord,
He fed on you, and your word...

FALL

Tuesday, 30th Week of the Year
What true love is like:

1a. Romans 8:18-25.
We groan, and wait, and hope for God.

1b. Ephesians 5:21-33.
Let spouses love one another.

2. Luke 13:18-21.
Kingdom images: a seed, yeast.

Enduring, hoping, trusting, pure:
So true love slowly grows, matures...

Meditation. The Lord's Prayer. Intercessions. Personal Prayers.

Evening Prayer

Reflections on the Day. Thanksgiving. Reconciliation.

Evening Psalm / Ps. 6 *My bed is wet with tears.* Page 5.

The Christ Hymn / Philippians 2:6-11 *The mind of Christ.* Page 5.

Personal Prayers.

Week Nine / WEDNESDAY
MORNING PRAYER

I. THE PSALMS

MORNING PSALM / PS. 101
A royal pledge.
PAGE 6

PSALM OF THE DAY / PS. 105:1-27
The history of Israel.. PART I. How she came to Egypt.

¹ Come praise the Lord before the nations,
  Call upon God's name.
² Sing out your thanks, your songs of praise,
  God's miracles proclaim!

³ Let all who seek the Lord rejoice;
  Exalt the name of God.
⁴ For strength return and ever seek
  The presence of your God.

⁶ Let all the seed of Abraham,
  And Jacob's children too,
⁵ Recall the miracles God wrought,
  The judgments ever true.

⁷ The Lord is God, and is our God,
  Whose judgments cover all.
⁸ A thousand generations hence,
  They will endure for all.

⁹ The covenant with Abraham,
  To Isaac sworn as well,
¹⁰ And Jacob, too, forevermore
  Is law in Israel.

¹¹ God said: "To you I give the land,
  A heritage, your own."
¹² When they were few, and strangers too,
  Were wandering alone.

¹³ From land to land, from king to king,
  ¹⁴ God sounded this alarm:
¹⁵ "Do not oppress my chosen ones,
  Nor do my prophets harm."

¹⁶ A famine sent upon their land
  Destroyed the grain God gave.
¹⁷ A man was sent ahead of them,
  Young Joseph, sold, a slave.

¹⁸ His feet in fetters, bound with chains,
  A collar round his neck,
¹⁹ The word of God was testing him,
  And kept his dreams in check.

At last the promise made came true:
  Now purged by God's decree.
²⁰ The king sent word to turn him loose,
  The ruler set him free.

²¹ He made him master of his house
  A ruler in the kingdom,
²² The one to guide the royal sons
  And teach the elders wisdom.

²³ So Israel to Egypt came,
  And there God made them grow.
²⁴ They prospered there, became a nation,
  Stronger than their foe.

²⁵ God turned the hearts of Egypt from
  The people Israel.
  And Egypt came to hate their strength.
  They cheated them as well.

²⁶ God sent a servant, Moses, who
  With Aaron at his side,
²⁷ Performed the signs and miracles
  Their foes could not abide.

II. Readings & Prayers

WINTER

Wednesday: 3rd Week of the Year
Once, for all, forever:

1a. Hebrews 10:11-18.
One sacrifice to save to the world.

1b. II Samuel 7:4-17.
Your house shall last forever.

2. Mark 4:1-20.
The sower sowed his seed.

Our seed, our word, one season lasts;
Your word, O Lord, will never pass...

SUMMER

Wednesday: 17th Week of the Year
On total dedication:

1a. Exodus 34:29-35.

The radiance of Moses's face.

1b. Jeremiah 15:10, 16-21.
God reassures the prophet.

2. Matthew 13:44-46.
Buried treasure, a perfect pearl.

Your reign indeed is worth it, Lord,
In pain, sustain us with your word...

SPRING

Wednesday: 3rd Week of Easter
What Christians must expect:

1. Acts 8:1-8.
A persecution breaks out.

2. John 6:35-40.
For life, believe in me.

We come to life through death by faith
Through trials, Lord, increase our faith...

FALL

Wednesday: 30th Week of the Year
Who will make it to the Kingdom:

1a. Romans 8:26-30.
The Spirit guides and speaks for us.

1b. Ephesians 6:1-9.
To parents, children, masters, slaves.

2. Luke 13:22-30.
The last will be first, the first, last.

The easy way, Lord, we refuse,
The narrow door, the one we choose...

Meditation. The Lord's Prayer. Intercessions. Personal Prayers.

Evening Prayer

Reflections on the Day. Thanksgiving. Reconciliation.

Evening Psalm / Ps. 13 *Let me have hope.* Page 6.

The Love of God/ Romans 8:35-39 *Who can be against us?* Page 6.

Personal Prayers.

Week Nine / THURSDAY
MORNING PRAYER

I. THE PSALMS

MORNING PSALM / PS. 100
Praise God from whom all blessings flow.
PAGE 7

PSALMS OF THE DAY / PSS. 105:28-45 & 113
The history of Israel. PART II. How they were freed, to praise the Lord.

PSALM 105:28-45 / *The plagues their foes could not abide.*

28 God hid the sun; they could not see,
But still would not comply.
29 God turned the rivers into blood
And caused the fish to die.

30 The land was overrun with frogs,
In Pharaoh's palace, too,
31 God spoke and gnats and flies appeared.
They swarmed the country through.

32 Then hail came down instead of rain,
And lightning none could flee.
33 The vines were blighted, figs destroyed,
And shattered every tree.

34 God spoke and clouds of locusts came
In numbers none could count.
35 They stripped the land of everything,
And left the barren ground.

36 Then finally from every home
God took the first born son.
The vigor of their race was taken,
None escaped, not one.

37 God led our people forth enriched;
Not one among them fell.
Their foes were glad to see them go,
For fear of Israel.

39 God spread a cloud to cover them,
And fire to light the night.
40 They asked, were given quail to eat
And bread from heaven's height.

41 God struck a rock and water flowed,
A stream in desert land!
42 So were fulfilled the promises
Once made to Abraham.

43 God led our people forth with joy
On a triumphant road.
44 The nations' lands were given them.
They reaped what others sowed.

45 There they might keep the covenant
And so win their reward,
Obedient to God's decrees.
Amen! And praise the Lord!

PSALM 113 / *Praise God who lifts the poor!*

1 ALLELUIA!

You servants of the Lord, give praise!
All praise God's holy name.
2 Forevermore, from east to west,
3 All bless the holy name.

4 Above the nations God is Lord,
Whose glory lights the sky.
5 Who else is like the Lord our God
Who is enthroned on high?

6 Who stoops to look on earth from heaven.
Sees what goes below.
7 Who feeds the hungry, lifts the poor
From rubbish heaps and woe.

8 Who places them among the great,
Among the richly blest.
9 Who makes the barren woman's house
A happy mother's nest.

II. Readings & Prayers

WINTER

THURSDAY: 3RD WEEK OF THE YEAR
The hidden shall be revealed:

1a. Hebrews 10:19-25.
  The blood of Christ gives hope.

1b. II Samuel 7:18-19, 24-29.
  David's grateful prayer.

2. Mark 4:21-25.
  A lamp is meant to shine.

We do not see our destiny;
Lord, make us what we ought to be...

SPRING

THURSDAY: 3RD WEEK OF EASTER
God's word and bread are for all.

1. Acts 8:26-40.
  Philip baptizes a convert.

2. John 6:44-51.
  My flesh for the life of the world.

Reach out to save; reach out to all;
Through us who hold you, Lord, in awe...

SUMMER

THURSDAY: 17TH WEEK OF THE YEAR
God Speaks through metaphors:

1a. Exodus 40:16-21, 34-38.
  The glory of the Lord was there.

1b. Jeremiah 18:1-6.
  You are like clay in my hand's.

2. Matthew 13:47-53.
  More images, new and old.

Clay, a dragnet brought to land.
A cloud, Lord help us understand...

FALL

THURSDAY: 30TH WEEK OF THE YEAR
What we need to win:

1a. Romans 8:31-39.
  Nothing can keep us from Christ.

1b. Ephesians 6:10-20.
  Put on the armor God.

2. Luke 13:31-35.
  I must proceed on course.

Persistence, armor, confidence,
In Christ our strength, and our defense...

Meditation. The Lord's Prayer. Intercessions. Personal Prayers.

EVENING PRAYER

Reflections on the Day. Thanksgiving. Reconciliation.

EVENING PSALM / PS. 131 *A child in your mother's arms.* PAGE 7.

THE UNSEEN GOD / COLOSSIANS 1:15-20 *First born of all creation.* PAGE 7.

Personal Prayers.

Week Nine / FRIDAY
MORNING PRAYER

I. THE PSALMS

MORNING PSALM / PS. 130
Out of the depths.
PAGE 8

PSALM OF THE DAY / PS. 102

¹ *The prayer of an afflicted one, poured out before the Lord.*

² Lord, hear my prayer, my call for help.
³ In my distress turn not away.
  Incline your ear and heed my plea,
  Come quickly, answer me today!

⁴⁻⁶My heart is withered, dry as grass,
  My days are smoke, my body burns.
  I groan aloud, am skin and bones.
  I cannot eat, my stomach churns.

⁷⁻⁸Alone atop a ruined roof,
  I sit here like a desert owl.
  I keep my watch and all day long
  My foes look up at me and scowl.

⁹ The mockers have a feast on me;
  They curse and taunt me endlessly.
¹⁰My food: the ashes of my life;
  My drink: the tears that flow from me.

¹¹You are the reason, Lord, that I,
  Once lifted up, am now downcast.
¹²Your anger, Lord, has made of me
  A fading shadow, withered grass.

¹³But you, Lord, reign eternally,
  Your throne endures from age to age.
¹⁴Arise to save your city, Lord!
  The time has come, forget your rage.

¹⁵Your servants love her very stones;
  Her dust alone moves us to tears.
¹⁶The nations will revere your name,
  Be filled with fear when you appear.

Your glory all the kings of earth.
Will see and pay the tribute due,
¹⁷When you rebuild on Zion's hill,
  When you reveal yourself anew.

¹⁸You, Lord, will hear your people's cry;
  The destitute must not despair.
¹⁹Let this be told in every age;
  The yet unborn shall praise you there.

²⁰For from the heights the Lord looked down,
  God saw the earth and heard its cry,
²¹The mournful groans of prisoners,
  The pleas of those condemned to die.

²²In Zion tell the fame of God.
  Jerusalem, sing out your praise.
²³Wherever people gather let
  Their kingdoms serve for all their days.

²⁴O Lord, you broke me in my prime,
  Cut short the time allotted me.
²⁵O God, you live eternally,
  Take not my fleeting life from me.

²⁶Long long ago you made the world;
  Your hands created heaven, too.
²⁷When they are gone, like garments worn,
  You will remain forever new.

²⁸For you, O Lord, remain the same;
  And those who serve you dwell secure.
²⁹Your years, O God, will never end;
  Your children too shall long endure.

II. READINGS & PRAYERS

WINTER

FRIDAY: 3RD WEEK OF THE YEAR
At harvest time the Lord will come.

1a. Hebrews 10:32-39.
   Do not lose confidence.

1b. II Samuel 11:1-17.
   David's sins: adultery and murder.

2. Mark 4:26-34.
   Images of the kingdom.

Whatever evil we have done,
Have hope, for God will overcome...

SPRING

FRIDAY: 3RD WEEK OF EASTER.
God picks his instruments:

1. Acts 9:1-20.
   The conversion of Saul to Paul.

2. John 6:52-59.
   Christ reaffirms: he is our food.

How hard for Paul, for us to see,
The hand of God in life for me...

SUMMER

FRIDAY: 17TH WEEK OF THE YEAR
Are we ready to listen to God?

1a. Leviticus 23:4-16, 27, 34-37.
   Instructions for the festivals.

1b. Jeremiah 26:1-9.
   Instructions for the prophet.

2. Matthew 13:54-58.
   Jesus was too much for them.

How people love to go their way!
Help us to follow what you say...

FALL

FRIDAY: 30TH WEEK OF THE YEAR
The feelings in a pastor's heart:

1a. Romans 9:1-5.
   Grief and pain are in my heart.

1b. Philippians 1:1-11.
   Joy and longing in my heart.

2. Luke 14:1-6.
   Jesus heals on the Sabbath.

You see and feel our pain, O Lord,
Speak to us, too, your healing word...

Meditation. The Lord's Prayer. Intercessions. Personal Prayers.

EVENING PRAYER

Reflections on the Day. Thanksgiving. Reconciliation.

EVENING PSALM / PS. 51 *David's prayer for forgiveness.* PAGE 8.

CANTICLE OF SIMEON / LUKE 2:29-32 *Lord, let me go in peace.* PAGE 8.

Personal Prayers.

Week Nine / SATURDAY
MORNING PRAYER

I. THE PSALMS

MORNING PSALM / PS. 141
Like incense let my prayer arise.
PAGE 9

PSALM OF THE DAY / PS. 94

A bold call for condemnation of the wicked.

PSALM 94 / *Bring justice, Lord, to judgement.*

1 You are the God of justice, Lord, appear!
2 Rise up to judge the proud
    as they deserve.
3 How long will you endure
    the wicked's jeer,
4 Their insolence, their boast:
    "We will not serve!"

5 They crush your people,
    Lord; your chosen slay.
6 They kill the widow,
    strangers, orphans, too.
7 They think, "The Lord will never see."
    They say:
    "The God of Jacob has no care for you."

8 You stupid fools, wise up.
    When will you see?
9 The one who made the ear
    must surely hear;
The one who made the eye
    must surely see.
10 God disciplines the world;
    should you not fear?

You teach the nations
    and their peoples, Lord.
11 You know the plans of men
    are empty breath.
12 How blest are those you teach
    and chasten, Lord;
13 You hear them in distress,
    snatch them from death.

The wicked? Lord,
    you dig a pit for them,
14 But you will not forsake
    your chosen one.
15 Bring justice, Lord,
    to judgment once again.
    The just will follow; justice will be done.

16 Against the wicked
    who will stand with me?
17 Alone, I would be silent in the grave.
19 But as my cares increase
    you comfort me;
18 If I should fall,
    your faithful love will save.

20 Can wicked judges, Lord,
    be your allies?
With wicked laws
    they strangle honest breath.
21 They plot to kill the just;
    they plan their lies;
And then condemn the innocent
    to death.

22 The Lord has been my refuge
    where I flee.
The Lord has been my saving rock
    throughout.
23 God will repay my foes' iniquity;
For all their sins the Lord will
    wipe them out.

II. Readings & Prayers

WINTER

SATURDAY: 3RD WEEK OF THE YEAR
Faith and Fear:

1a. Hebrews 11:1-2, 8-19.
   What faith is, and does.

1b. II Samuel 12:1-17.
   Nathan accuses, David repents.

2. Mark 4:35-41.
   The wind and seas obey him.

Storm tossed and frightened, Lord, are we;
Come once again to calm the sea...

SPRING

SATURDAY: 3RD WEEK OF EASTER
The primacy of Peter:

1. Acts 9:31-42.
   The Church grows; Peter's miracle.

2. John 6:60-69.
   You have the words of life.

Lord, Peter speaks for us and you;
We shall obey, your work shall do...

SUMMER

SATURDAY: 17TH WEEK OF THE YEAR
Do only good and trust in God:

1a. Leviticus 25:1, 8-17.
   Celebrate a year of jubilee.

1b. Jeremiah 26:11-16, 24.
   The prophet is attacked, and saved.

2. Matthew 14:1-12.
   Herod kills John the Baptist.

God's justice in the end will come
For all the good or evil done...

FALL

SATURDAY: 30TH WEEK OF THE YEAR
The humble shall be exalted:

1a. Romans 1:1-2, 11-12, 25-29.
   God's call is irrevocable.

1b. Philippians 1:18-26.
   To live is Christ, to die is gain.

2. Luke 14:1,7-11.
   Friend, come up higher.

O Lord, I seek the lowest seat,
Content to serve, be at your feet...

Meditation. The Lord's Prayer. Intercessions. Personal Prayers.

EVENING PRAYER

Reflections on the Day. Thanksgiving. Reconciliation.

EVENING PSALM / Ps. 143 *Lord, do not condemn.* PAGE 9.

SONG OF MOSES / REVELATION 15-3-4 *They all had harps and sang.* PAGE 9.

Personal Prayers.

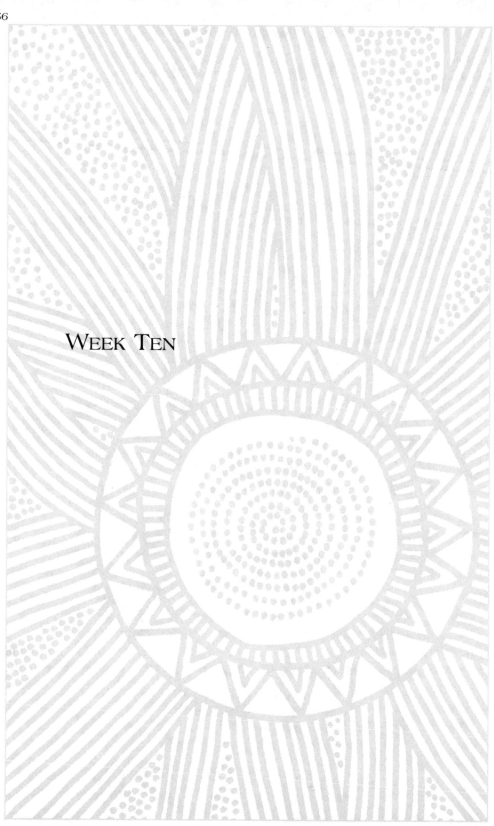

WEEK TEN

MORNING PRAYER

I. THE PSALMS

MORNING PSALM / PS. 95

O my people, now listen to me.

PAGE 3

PSALMS OF THE DAY / PSS. 28 & 92

Hymns contrasting the fate of the wicked and the just.

PSALM 28 / *O Shepherd, tend your flock.*

1 O God, my rock, I cry to you;
  Do not be deaf to me.
 I shall go down among the lost
  If you stand far from me.

2 Lord, listen to me, hear my plea
  For mercy when I cry.
 I lift my hands to you above,
  Your holy place on high.

3 Among the wicked count me not,
  Those skilled in evil arts.
 They speak of peace to all the world
  With malice in their hearts.

4 According to their wicked ways
  Repay their deeds, O Lord.
 According to their handiwork
  Give them their just reward.

5 They never think of all the good
  Your hands, O Lord, have done.
 Destroy their works, undo each one,
  To never be redone.

6 The Lord has heard my cry for help,
  How blest the Lord, and true!
7 O God, you are my strength and shield;
  My heart will trust in you.

 I am renewed, I leap for joy;
  I sing my praise to God!
8 A refuge for the chosen ones,
  Their strength will come from God.

9 O Shepherd, bless your heritage;
  Forever tend your flock.

PSALM 92 / *Your enemies will die; the righteous thrive.*

2 How good it is to praise you, Lord,
  To ever bless your name;
3 To sing your faithful love at dawn,
  At dusk to do the same,

4 With music from the lute and lyre,
  The murmur of the harp.
5 Your works, O Lord, have made me glad;
  Your joy is in my heart.

6 Magnificent your works, O Lord;
  Profound your every thought.
7 The dull will never understand;
  The fool cannot be taught.

8 The wicked sprout and grow like weeds;
  But they are doomed to die.
9 While you, O Lord, forevermore
  Shall live and reign on high.

10 Your enemies will perish, Lord;
  And scattered be their spoil.
11 But you have lifted high my head,
  Anointed me with oil.

12 My eyes have seen the ravaging
  Of all my enemies.
 My ears have heard the voice of doom
  For all who came at me.

¹³ The just will flourish like the palm,
   Like trees in Lebanon.
¹⁴ Implanted in the house of God,
   They thrive, grow on and on.

¹⁵ In age they still produce their fruit,
   Are always green and sound.
¹⁶ They show the Lord, our rock, is just;
   In God no fault is found.

II. READINGS & PRAYERS

WINTER

4TH SUNDAY OF THE YEAR
Listen humbly to God's prophets.

YEAR A

1. Zephaniah 2:3, 3:12-13.
   Seek justice; seek humility.

2. I Corinthians 1:26-31.
   God chose the weak to shame the strong.

3. Matthew 5:1-12.
   Blest are the poor and lowly.

YEAR B

1. Deuteronomy 18:15-20.
   The Lord will send a prophet.

2. I Corinthians 7:32-35.
   Be busy with the Lord's affairs.

3. Mark 1:21-28.
   Teaching with authority.

YEAR C

1. Jeremiah 1:4-5, 17-19.
   I appointed you as prophet.

2. I Corinthians 13:4-13.
   Love is patient, love is kind.

3. Luke 4:21-30.
   No prophet is received at home.

WE HONOR PROPHETS AND THEIR WORDS
That come to us from God above.
We are the weak who humbly seek
To hear your voice, your words of love.

SPRING

4TH SUNDAY OF EASTER
Good Shepherd Sunday.

YEAR A

1. Acts 2:14,36-41.
   You must reform and be baptized.

2. I Peter 2:20-25.
   Like sheep, you went astray.

3. John 10:1-10.
   Sheep follow him; they know his voice.

YEAR B

1. Acts 4:8-12.
   Salvation comes from him alone.

2. I John 3:1-2.
   We are God's children now.

3. John 10:11-18.
   I am the Good Shepherd.

YEAR C

1. Acts 13:14, 43-52.
   The preaching of Paul and Barnabas.

2. Revelations 7:9,14-17.
   The lamb will shepherd them.

3. John 10:27-30.
   They follow me; I give them life.

THE GATE, THE LAMB, GOOD SHEPHERD, LORD:
We hear your voice; we follow you.
We pray for those who shepherd us;
May they have shepherds' hearts like you.

SUMMER
18TH SUNDAY OF THE YEAR
Be hungry for the bread of life.

Year A

1. Isaiah 55:1-3.
   Come, eat and drink without cost.

2. Romans 8:35-39.
   Nothing can keep God's love from us.

3. Matthew 14:13-21.
   Jesus feeds five thousand.

Year B

1. Exodus 16:2-4,12-15.
   I will rain bread from heaven.

2. Ephesians 4:17,20-24.
   Leave the old, put on the new.

3. John 6:24-35.
   I am the bread of life.

Year C

1. Ecclesiastes 1:2, 2:21-23.
   All things are vanity.

2. Colossians 3:1-5,9-11.
   Look up to heaven, not to earth.

3. Luke 12:13-21.
   Beware of greed and wealth.

WE HUNGER FOR THE BREAD OF LIFE,
Your body, Lord, on which we feed.
All other hungers lead to death;
Save us from them, and starve our greed.

FALL
31ST SUNDAY OF THE YEAR
The love of God will never change.

Year A

1. Malachi 1:14-2:2, 8-10.
   You have not kept my ways.

2. I Thessalonians 2:7-9,13.
   We shared with you all we had.

3. Matthew 23:1-12.
   The greatest is the one who serves.

Year B

1. Deuteronomy 6:2-6.
   You shall love the Lord, your God.

2. Hebrews 7:23-28.
   Jesus' priesthood will not end.

3. Mark 12:28-34.
   You shall love the Lord, your God.

Year C

1. Wisdom 11:22-12:1.
   You, Lord, love all that is.

2. II Thessalonians 1:11-2:2.
   May God be glorified in you.

3. Luke 19:1-10.
   I came to save the lost.

YOU SEEK US OUT; YOU SAVE THE LOST.
The love of God will never change,
Nor does your law of love for us:
Our love for yours, great gift exchange.

Meditation. The Lord's Prayer. Intercessions. Personal Prayers.

EVENING PRAYER

Reflections on the Day. Thanksgiving. Reconciliation.

EVENING PSALM / PS. 23 *The Lord will give me rest.* PAGE 3.

CANTICLE OF MARY / LUKE 1:46-55 *Behold the handmaid of the Lord.* PAGE 3.

Personal Prayers.

Week Ten / MONDAY
MORNING PRAYER

I. THE PSALMS

MORNING PSALM / PS. 24

Let the King of glory in.

PAGE 4

PSALM OF THE DAY / PS. 106:1-23

Part I: Israel's liberation and abomination: "They sold their glory."

1 Give thanks, sing praise, the Lord is good;
　God's love is ever true.
2 Can any count the mighty deeds,
　Or give the praise that's due?

3 How blest are those, the truly just,
　Who always do what's right.
4 Remember as you save them, Lord,
　To keep me, too, in sight.

5 Lord, let me see prosperity
　With all your chosen ones.
　And let me feel your people's joy
　In their inheritance.

6 Lord, we have sinned like those of old,
　Done evil, gone astray.
7 From Egypt on they all forgot
　Your faithful love, your way.

　Before the Sea of Reeds they all
　8 Rebelled against you, Lord.
　Yet by your name you saved them all,
　So mighty is your word.

9 The Lord rebuked the sea. It fled.
　God led the people through.
10 Delivered them from all their foes,
　The fearful waters, too.

11 The sea returned and swamped their foe;
　Not one of them survived.
12 Then they believed God's promises,
　And praised the Lord on high.

13 But soon again, they all forgot
　God's plans for them, their need.
14 In desert lands they tested God;
　They were consumed with greed.

15 God gave them what they sought; but with
　A wasting sickness, too.
16 Then jealousy of Moses spread,
　And holy Aaron, too.

17 Earth opened, swallowed Dathan up,
　The same for Abiram.
18 God's anger blazed against them all;
　They perished in the flame.

19 They sold their glory, made a calf,
　An idol made of brass.
20 They bowed before the image of
　A bull that feeds on grass.

21 They once again forgot the God
　Who, with a mighty hand
22 Did mighty deeds to set them free,
　And turned the sea to land.

23 God would have killed them on the spot,
　But Moses intervened.
He stood between them and the Lord,
　From them, God's anger screened.

II. READINGS & PRAYERS

WINTER
MONDAY: 4TH WEEK OF THE YEAR
The power of God on our behalf:

1a. Hebrews 11:32-40.
   Through faith, they conquered all.

1b. II Samuel 15:13-14,16:5-13.
   David is betrayed and cursed.

2. Mark 5:1-20.
   Jesus casts devils into swine.

Almighty God, help me to see,
And tell how much you've done for me...

SPRING
MONDAY: 4TH WEEK OF EASTER
There shall be one flock, one shepherd:

1. Acts 11:1-18.
   Gentiles too receive the word.

2. John 10:1-10.
   For my sheep, I give my life.

Lord, no one has escaped your love,
Nor shall they ours, nor those above...

SUMMER
MONDAY: 18TH WEEK OF THE YEAR
God provides while people complain:

1a. Numbers 11:4-15.
   God sends manna; Moses complains.

1b. Jeremiah 28:1-17.
   A conflict among prophets.

2. Matthew 14:13-21.
   Jesus feeds five thousand.

For every need, the Lord provides.
In God, not self, our hope resides...

FALL
MONDAY: 31ST WEEK OF THE YEAR
The standard for our generosity:

1a. Romans 11:29-36.
   God's gifts are irrevocable.

1b. Philippians 2:1-4.
   Be unselfish; give me joy.

2. Luke 14:12-14.
   Invite the poor who can't repay.

You set the standard high, O Lord,
To give like you, for our reward...

Meditation. The Lord's Prayer. Intercessions. Personal Prayers.

EVENING PRAYER

Reflections on the Day. Thanksgiving. Reconciliation.

EVENING PSALM / PS. 4 *I go to sleep in peace.* PAGE 4.

CANTICLE OF ZACHARY / LUKE 1:68-79 *Prepare the way of the Lord.* PAGE 4.

Personal Prayers.

Week Ten / TUESDAY
MORNING PRAYER

I. THE PSALMS

MORNING PSALM / PS. 5
At dawn I pray to you.
PAGE 5

PSALM OF THE DAY / PS. 106:24-48

Part II: Israel's degradation, and God's mercy: "Lord, gather us."

24 They disbelieved God's promises,
  Despised the promised land.
25 They muttered treason in their tents,
  Refused the Lord's command.

26 Till God arose and took an oath
  To strike them then and there,
27 To scatter them
      throughout the earth,
  Disperse them everywhere.

28 They joined the pagan rites of Baal,
  Ate "banquets of the dead."
29 They further angered God and earned
  Another plague to dread.

30 Till Phinehas stood up and prayed;
  The plague came to an end.
31 All credit give this one good man
  Whose praise will never end.

32 At Meribah they angered God,
  Gave Moses troubles new.
33 Embittered, Moses spoke rash words
  That cost him dearly, too.

34 They disobeyed the Lord's command;
  They let the nations stay.
35 Instead they mingled, married them,
  And learned their pagan ways.

36 The pagan gods they came to serve
  Soon proved to be a snare.
37 They sacrificed their children to
  The demons dwelling there.

38 They shed the blood of innocents,
  Their sons' and daughters' blood.
  They sacrificed to Canaan's gods,
  Defiled the land with blood.

39 They soiled themselves
      with their own deeds,
  Became defiled by them.
40 Disgusted with the people's sins
  God's anger flared at them.

41 Once more the nations conquered them;
  Their foes ruled over them.
42 With pagan might God humbled them
  To slavery again.

43 How often he delivered them!
  But they would still rebel.
44 In their affliction God still heard
  The cry of Israel.

45 And mindful of the covenant,
  God's faithful love stayed true.
46 The Lord made sure their captors felt
  Compassion for them, too.

47 O save us, Lord, and gather us
  From pagan lands and ways,
  To celebrate your holy name,
  To glory in your praise.

48 Blest be the God of Israel,
  Who ever is our Lord.
  Let all God's people say, "Amen!"
  Sing "Alleluia, Lord!"

II. READINGS & PRAYERS

WINTER

TUESDAY: 4TH WEEK OF THE YEAR
There is nothing God cannot do:

1a. Hebrews 12:1-4.
   Keep your eyes fixed on Jesus.

1b. II Samuel 18:9-19:3.
   David mourns Absalom's death.

2. Mark 5:21-43.
   Jesus restores a girl to life.

Our eyes, O Lord, are fixed on you;
In spite of pain we look to you...

SPRING

TUESDAY: 4TH WEEK OF EASTER
No one shall snatch my sheep:

1. Acts 11:19-26.
   Greeks too become Christians.

2. John 10:22-30.
   My sheep follow me.

Your love for us is fierce, O Lord.
We trust in it, our Shepherd's word...

SUMMER

TUESDAY: 18TH WEEK OF THE YEAR
The power and fidelity of God:

1a. Numbers 12:1-13.
   God defends Moses.

1b. Jeremiah 30:1-2, 12-22.
   God chastens and forgives.

2. Matthew 14:22-36.
   Jesus walks on water.

Lord, we are weak and you are strong.
The storm is great, the night is long...

FALL

TUESDAY: 31ST WEEK OF THE YEAR
We must be so close to Christ that:

1a. Romans 12:5-16.
   We are one body in Christ.

1b. Philippians 2:5-11.
   Our mind should be the mind of Christ.

2. Luke 14:15-24.
   I want my house to be full.

Of every gift you are the font.
We want, O Lord, all that you want...

Meditation. The Lord's Prayer. Intercessions. Personal Prayers.

EVENING PRAYER

Reflections on the Day. Thanksgiving. Reconciliation.

EVENING PSALM / PS. 6 *My bed is wet with tears.* PAGE 5.

THE CHRIST HYMN / PHILIPPIANS 2:6-11 *The mind of Christ.* PAGE 5.

Personal Prayers.

Week Ten / WEDNESDAY
MORNING PRAYER

I. THE PSALMS

MORNING PSALM / PS. 101
A royal pledge.
PAGE 6

PSALM OF THE DAY / PS. 107:1-32
Four groups in different perils tell how God rescued them.

Introduction

1 The Lord is good, give thanks, praise God
    Whose mercy never ends.
2 Let those redeemed from troubles tell
    How God has rescued them.
3 God gathered them and brought them back
    From their oppressors' hand;
  From north and south, from east and west,
    From every foreign land.

I. The Wanderers

4 Some wandered in the wilderness;
    They found no welcome city.
5 Hungry, thirsty, nearing death,
    They cried to God for pity.
6 In their distress they sought the Lord
    Who saved them,
      gave them their reward.
7 God led them down an easy road;
    They found a place to dwell.
9 God satisfied their throbbing thirst,
    Their hungry mouths as well.
8 Let all give thanks to God above,
    For mighty deeds and faithful love.

II. The Imprisoned

10 Some dwelt in gloom, in prisons dark,
    In misery, in chains.
11 They had rebelled against the law;
  12 God humbled them with pain.
13 In their distress they sought the Lord
    Who saved them,
      gave them their reward.
14 But then God brought them out to light.
    Their chains were snapped in two;
16 The prison doors blown open wide,
    The iron bars cut through.
15 Let all give thanks to God above
    For mighty deeds and faithful love.

III. The Sick

17 Some lay in sickness, caused by sin,
    Afflicted for their wrong.
18 Their throats inflamed, they couldn't eat;
    Their life was almost gone.
19 In their distress they sought the Lord
    Who saved them,
      gave them their reward.
20 God gave the word, a healing word;
    It banished the disease.
22 Now they can offer gifts of thanks,
    Sing praise to God with ease.
21 Let all give thanks to God above,
    For mighty deeds and faithful love.

IV. The Storm-tossed

23 Some took to sea to see the world,
  24 The wonders of the sky.
25 A storm arose at God's command,
    With waves a mountain high
26 They climbed the crests,
      they plumbed the depths,
    Hearts fearful, faces pale.
27 Like drunken men
      they pitched and reeled,
    Their skill of no avail.
28 In their distress they sought the Lord
    Who saved them,
      gave them their reward.
29 God hushed the storm, a gentle breeze
    Blew in, the seas grew calm.
30 They all rejoiced, God brought them to
    The port for which they longed.
  The people in assembly met
  32 To hear the Lord extolled.
  The elders in their councils sat
    To hear the story told.
31 Let all give thanks to God above,
    For mighty deeds and faithful love.

II. Readings & Prayers

WINTER

Wednesday: 4th Week of the Year
Discipline, even punishment we need:

1a. Hebrews 12:4-7, 11-15.
Discipline is necessary.

1b. II Samuel 24:2, 9-17.
I sinned; punish me, not them.

2. Mark 6:1-6.
Their lack of faith distressed him.

Lord, we have sinned, we do repent,
Help us accept our punishment...

SUMMER

Wednesday: 18th Week of the Year
God's love knows no bounds:

1a. Numbers 13:25-14:1, 26-29, 34-35.
40 years in the desert.

1b. Jeremiah 31:1-7.
God's everlasting love.

2. Matthew 15:21-28.
Jesus heals a Canaanite.

Divine physician, what you do,
Looks not to race, but faith in you...

SPRING

Wednesday: 4th Week of Easter
Required of all who speak God's word:

1. Acts 12:24-13:5.
Barnabas and Paul are sent out.

2. John 12:44-50.
I speak what the Father commands.

Obedient was Christ, and Paul,
May we obey the Father's call...

FALL

Wednesday: 31th Week of the Year
On debts and possessions:

1a. Romans 13:8-10.
The only thing we owe is love.

1b. Philippians 2:12-18.
I did not run the race in vain.

2. Luke 14:25-33.
My disciples must renounce all.

O Lord, we seek your freedom, too;
Though poor in goods, yet rich in you...

Meditation. The Lord's Prayer. Intercessions. Personal Prayers.

EVENING PRAYER

Reflections on the Day. Thanksgiving. Reconciliation.

Evening Psalm / Ps. 13 *Let me have hope.* Page 6.

The Love of God / Romans 8:35-39 *Who can be against us?* Page 6.

Personal Prayers.

Week Ten / THURSDAY
MORNING PRAYER

I. THE PSALMS

MORNING PSALM / PS. 100
Praise God from whom all blessings flow.
PAGE 7

PSALMS OF THE DAY / PSS. 107:33-43 & 48

The final rescue song, and a song in praise of Zion.

PSALM 107:33-43 / *The poor were raised from misery.*

33 The Lord cut off the rivers' flow,
  And dried up every spring.
34 God turned the land to salty waste
  As penalty for sin.

35 Then, turning deserts back to pools,
  Restoring springs to earth,
36 God placed a hungry people there,
  Who gave a city birth.

37 They sowed their grain and planted vines,
  And reaped a heavy yield.
38 God blessed them and they multiplied,
  Increased their herds and fields.

39 Oppression, sorrow disappeared;
  For tyrants lost their place.
40 Despised by God,
    they were condemned
  To wander trackless waste.

41 The poor were raised from misery;
  Their families increased.
42 The just observed and they rejoiced;
  The wicked ground their teeth.

43 Let wise men think upon these things:
  The faithful love of God their King.

PSALM 48 / *The city of the king is Zion.*

2 The Lord is great, and greatly praised
 In this God's city, on this mountain.
3 Fair is she, the joy of earth,
 The city of the king is Zion.

4 The Lord is Zion's citadel;
 God proved to be her sure defense.
5 When earthly kings advanced on her,
6 They took one look and scattered hence.

 A fit of trembling came on them;
7 And, terror stricken, they grew pale,
 As with a woman caught in labor,
8 Or a ship caught in a gale.

9 In it, the city of the Lord,
  What we had heard we now have seen.
 In this the city of the Lord,
  May God preserve us safe, serene.

10 We gather in your temple, Lord
  To ponder here your faithful love.
11 O God, your name and praises reach
  The ends of earth and skies above.

12 Your hand is ever generous;
  In Zion let your praises ring.
  Because of you, your care for us,
  Let all the towns of Judah sing.

13 O look at Zion, walk around her;
14 Count her towers, ramparts, bays.
15 And tell all future generations:
  Such is God who guides our ways.

II. READINGS & PRAYERS

WINTER

THURSDAY: 4TH WEEK OF THE YEAR
We are sent to do God's work:

1a. Hebrews 12:18-24.
   Our God is accessible.

1b. I Kings 2:1-4, 10-12.
   David dies, Solomon succeeds.

2. Mark 6:7-13.
   Instructions for disciples in mission.

Lord, two be two, they showed your way;
We follow, too; you lead the way...

SPRING

THURSDAY: 4TH WEEK OF EASTER
The chain of salvation:

1. Acts 13:13-25.
   Paul gives a history lesson.

2. John 13:16-20.
   He who hears you, hears me.

We know the Father sent you, Lord;
And you send us, we speak God's word...

SUMMER

THURSDAY: 18TH WEEK OF THE YEAR
Christ gives Peter primacy:

1a. Numbers 20:1-13.
   Moses gives the people water.

1b. Jeremiah 31:31-34.
   God promises a new covenant.

2. Matthew 16:13-23.
   Upon this rock I build my church.

You built your church on rock, O Lord;
We living stones accept your Word...

FALL

THURSDAY: 31ST WEEK OF THE YEAR
Heaven's standards are different:

1a. Romans 14:7-12.
   In life and death we are the Lord's.

1b. Philippians 3:3-8.
   All is loss that is not Christ.

2. Luke 15:1-10.
   Heaven's joy when one repents.

Lord, help us view the world like you;
Where all is loss that is not you...

Meditation. The Lord's Prayer. Intercessions. Personal Prayers.

EVENING PRAYER

Reflections on the Day. Thanksgiving. Reconciliation.

EVENING PSALM / PS. 131 *A child in your mother's arms.* PAGE 7.

THE UNSEEN GOD / COLOSSIANS 1:15-20 *First born of all creation.* PAGE 7.

Personal Prayers.

MORNING PRAYER

I. THE PSALMS

MORNING PSALM / PS. 130
Out of the depths.
PAGE 8

PSALM OF THE DAY / PS. 109

Dreadful curses on the enemy: "He loved to curse, let him be cursed."

¹ God, whom I praise, stand not aloof!
² Deceitful mouths are at my back.
With lying tongues they speak of me;
³ Without a cause I am attacked.

⁴ They circle me with words of hate;
They even fault my prayer to you.
⁵ With hatred they return my love,
Do evil for the good I do.

⁶ O God, appoint a wicked man
To be his judge and stand with him.
⁷ When he is judged, pronounce him guilty;
Let his pleas be reckoned sin.

⁸ Cut short his days, and let another
Take his seat when he is dead;
⁹ His wife a widow, children orphans
¹⁰ Wandering to beg for bread.

¹¹ May creditors take all his wealth
Let strangers take what's left behind.
¹² Let no one show him pity, Lord;
And to his children none be kind.

¹³ Let his posterity be lost,
Their memory forgotten, too.
¹⁴ Do not forget his father's crimes;
His mother's sins remember, too.

¹⁵ Erase his name from earth, O Lord;
But ever keep his sins in mind.
¹⁶ He never gave a thought to you;
To others he was never kind.

The poor he hounded to their death,
The broken hearted got no rest.
¹⁷ He loved to curse; let him be cursed;
Would never bless, will not be blest.

¹⁸ Let him wear curses like a robe;
And let them lay his body waste.
¹⁹ As oil or water enters in,
Let him wear curses round his waist.

²⁰ So may the Lord repay with shame
All those who tell their lies of me.
²¹ But to your name be true, O God;
With faithful love come rescue me.

²² For I am poor and much in need;
My heart is pierced, within I sigh
²³ And fade away like evening shade.
They shake me off as locusts die.

²⁴ My knees are weak for want of food;
My body lean, my look is gaunt.
²⁵ They shake their heads; I have become
The object of their scorn and taunt.

²⁶ O Lord, my God, come rescue me,
In keeping with your faithful love.
²⁷ Let all men know it was your hand
That came and saved me from above.

²⁸ If you will bless, then let them curse.
Let me rejoice, let them be shamed.
²⁹ Let my accusers be disgraced,
Be wrapped, as with a robe, in shame.

³⁰ My mouth shall sing its praise to God
Before the elders, all of them,
³¹ Because the Lord defends the poor
From those who would the poor condemn.

II. READINGS & PRAYERS

WINTER

FRIDAY, 4TH WEEK OF THE YEAR
We have a debt to pay:

1a. Hebrews 13:1-8.
   Remember your leaders.

1b. Sirach 47:2-11.
   A hymn to honor David.

2. Mark 6:14-29.
   The beheading of John the Baptist.

They gave their lives for God, for us.
Let them be praised and thanked by us...

SPRING

FRIDAY, 4TH WEEK OF EASTER
Jesus' concluding promise:

1. Acts 13:26-33.
   Paul concludes his story.

2. John 14:1-6.
   I go to make a place for you.

Our way, our truth, our life are you.
We trust in you; we follow you...

SUMMER

FRIDAY, 18TH WEEK OF THE YEAR
Where much is given, much is asked:

1a. Deuteronomy 4:32-40.
   All this God has done for you.

1b. Nahum 2:1-3,3:1-7.
   Woe to the bloody city.

2. Matthew 16:24-28.
   Take up the cross and follow.

To win the world and lose one's soul
Is totally to miss our goal...

FALL

FRIDAY, 31TH WEEK OF THE YEAR
Who gets credit for what:

1a. Romans 15:14-21.
   What Christ has done through me.

1b. Philippians 3:17-4:1.
   You are my joy, my crown.

2. Luke 16:1-8.
   Christ gives credit for enterprise.

Lord, who did more for you than Paul?
Hear him: he says you did it all...

Meditation. The Lord's Prayer. Intercessions. Personal Prayers.

EVENING PRAYER

Reflections on the Day. Thanksgiving. Reconciliation.

EVENING PSALM / PS. 51 *David's prayer for forgiveness.* PAGE 8.

CANTICLE OF SIMEON / LUKE 2:29-32 *Lord, let me go in peace.* PAGE 8.

Personal Prayers.

Week Ten / SATURDAY

Morning Prayer

I. The Psalms

Morning Psalm / Ps. 141
Like incense let my prayer arise.
Page 9

Psalms of the Day / Pss. 114, 115, & 117
Three hymns of praise.

Psalm 114 / *O tremble, earth, before the Lord.*

1 When Israel from Egypt came,
  When Jacob left that foreign strand
2 For Judah, now God's holy place,
  And Israel, the promised land,

3 On seeing God the waters fled;
  The river Jordan backed away.
4 The mountains jumped
      and skipped like rams;
  The hills became like lambs at play.

5 What frightened you, O sea, to flee?
  Why, Jordan, did you back away?
6 What made the mountains
      skip like rams?
  You hills at play, what do you say?

7 O tremble, earth, before the Lord,
  Before the God of Jacob's flock,
8 Who turned the stones to limpid pools,
  Who brought a fountain out of rock.

Psalm 115 / *We shall shout and bless the Lord.*

1 Give not to us, Lord, not to us
  The glory due your name.
  Because your faithful love is great
  Give glory to your name!

2 Let not the nations ask "Where is
  Your god? What has he done?"
3 The Lord, our Lord, in heaven dwells;
  And what God wills is done.

4 Their gods are idols made of gold,
  By human hands as well.
5 Their ears and mouth are deaf and dumb;
  6 They cannot see or smell.

7 No hands to touch, no feet to walk,
  No sound will come from them.
8 Their makers and their worshippers,
  Will all become like them.

9 O Israel, and Aaron, too,
10 Trust God to be your shield.
11 Who fear the Lord must trust the Lord
  To be their help and shield.

12 The Lord remembers Israel,
    The house of Aaron, too.
13 And blesses those who fear the Lord,
    The small, the mighty, too.

14 May God increase both you and yours,
  15 The Lord bless all of us.
16 Earth, heaven both belong to God;
    The earth God trusts to us.

17 The dead will never praise the Lord;
    Their voice is heard no more.
18 But we shall shout and bless the Lord,
    Today and evermore.

PSALM 117 / *God's faithful love will never fail.*

1 Let all the nations praise the Lord!
Let all the peoples cry, "All hail!"
2 God's faithful love for us is strong;
God's faithfulness will never fail.
It lasts forever, praise the Lord!

II. READINGS & PRAYERS

WINTER
SATURDAY: 4TH WEEK OF THE YEAR
Shepherds with an understanding heart:

1a. Hebrews 13:15-21.
   A reminder and a blessing.

1b. I Kings 3:4-13.
   Solomon's prayer for understanding.

2. Mark 6:30-34.
   They were like sheep without a shepherd.

Like Solomon and Jesus, too,
We seek God's will in all we do...

SPRING
SATURDAY: 4TH WEEK OF EASTER
Like many, we are slow to see:

1. Acts 13:44-52.
   Paul encounters opposition.

2. John 14:7-14.
   Who sees me, sees the Father.

It isn't easy, Lord, to see.
But we believe, and trust in thee...

SUMMER
SATURDAY: 18TH WEEK OF THE YEAR
An astonishing promise:

1a. Deuteronomy 6:4-13.
   You shall love the Lord, your God.

1b. Habakkuk: 1:12-2:4.
   The just, by faith, shall live.

2. Matthew 17:14-20.
   With faith, nothing is impossible.

Increase our faith; help us believe,
That we your power may receive...

FALL
SATURDAY: 31ST WEEK OF THE YEAR
Farewells, and a caution:

1a. Romans 16:3-9,16,22-27.
   Greetings and praise.

1b. Philippians 4:10-19.
   Thanks for gifts received.

2. Luke 16:9-15.
   No man can serve two masters.

Detached from wealth like Paul, and free,
And grateful, too; so would I be...

Meditation. The Lord's Prayer. Intercessions. Personal Prayers.

EVENING PRAYER

Reflections on the Day. Thanksgiving. Reconciliation.

EVENING PSALM / PS. 143 *Lord, do not condemn.* PAGE 9.

SONG OF MOSES / REVELATION 15:3-4 *They all had harps and sang.* PAGE 9.

Personal Prayers.

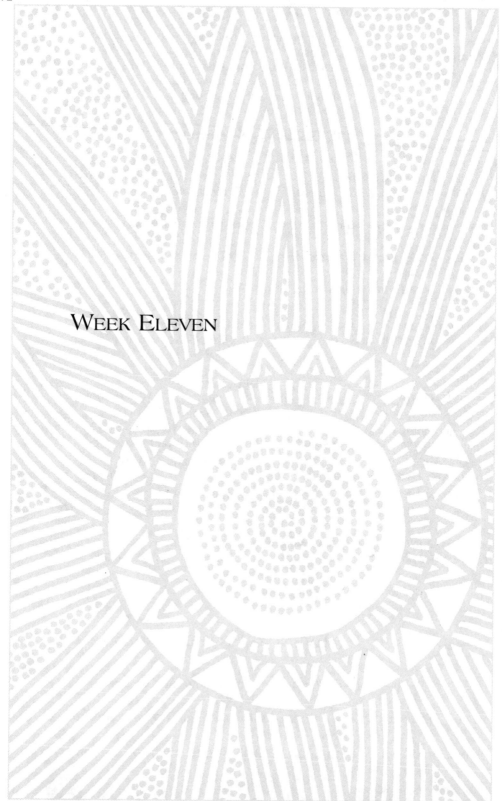

WEEK ELEVEN

MORNING PRAYER

I. THE PSALMS

MORNING PSALM / PS. 95
O my people, now listen to me.
PAGE 3

PSALM OF THE DAY / PS. 119:1-24
A week of prayer and praise of God's law.

ALEPH / *As I begin to learn.*

1 How blest are those with blameless ways,
   Who walk, O Lord, your way.
2 How blest to follow your decrees,
   With all our hearts obey.

3 They shall escape from going wrong
   Who follow in this way.
4 Your precepts have commanded us
   That we should never stray.

5 O would that I had held your law
   More firmly in my hands.
6 Then I would never have to blush
   On learning your commands.

7 I praise you with an upright heart
   As I begin to learn.
8 I will observe your statutes, Lord;
   My efforts do not spurn.

BETH / *I treasure all your promises.*

9 O God, how can the young stay pure?
   By keeping to your word.
10 With all my heart I search for you;
   Let me not stray, O Lord.

11 I treasure all your promises;
   For them I shall not sin.
12 O Lord, my God, how blest you are!
   Instill your law within.

13 I practice it; my lips rehearse
   Your rules and your commands.
14 I find my joy in your decrees,
   Like money in my hands.

15 I seek your way and study all
   The precepts I have heard.
16 I take delight in all of them,
   Do not neglect a word.

GIMEL / *I am a pilgrim on this earth.*

17 Be kind to me your servant, Lord,
   That I may live your word,
18 That I may see with open eyes
   The wonders I have heard.

19 I am a pilgrim on this earth;
   Hide not from me the way.
20 My soul cries out to know the route,
   To always see your way.

21 You curse the proud and insolent
   Who stray from your commands.
22 I keep your word, O Lord; keep me
   From taunting at their hands.

23 When rulers meet, speak ill of me,
   To you my thoughts I bend.
24 For your decrees are my delight,
   My counselor and friend.

II. READINGS & PRAYERS

WINTER

5TH SUNDAY OF THE YEAR
Our task, to bring the good news.

YEAR A

1. Isaiah 58:7-10.
   Your light will shine like dawn.

2. I Corinthians 2:1-5.
   I preached Christ crucified.

3. Matthew 5:13-16.
   You are the light of the world.

YEAR B

1. Job 7:1-7.
   Filled with sorrow, all day long.

2. I Corinthians 9:16-23.
   I am bound to preach the Gospel.

3. Mark 1:29-39.
   This is what I came to do.

YEAR C

1. Isaiah 6:1-8.
   Here I am, send me!

2. I Corinthians 15:1-11.
   This is what we preach.

3. Luke 5:1-11.
   You will be catching man.

TO SPREAD THE NEWS, YOUR GOSPEL, LORD,
To be a light, to fish for man,
What joy, responsibility!
Lord, here we are to say, "Amen!"

SPRING

5TH SUNDAY OF EASTER
Christ tells us what he is and asks.

YEAR A

1. Acts 6:1-7.
   The first deacons are chosen.

2. I Peter 2:4-9.
   You are a chosen race.

3. John 14:1-12.
   I am the way, the truth, the life.

YEAR B

1. Acts 9:26-31.
   Paul meets opposition in Jerusalem.

2. I John 3:18-24.
   Love with deeds, not talk.

3. John 15:1-8.
   I am the vine, you are the branches.

YEAR C

1. Acts 14:21-27.
   The first journey of Paul and Barnabas.

2. Revelations 21:1-5.
   I saw a new heaven, and a new earth.

3. John 13:31-35.
   A new commandment of love.

LORD, YOU HAVE CHOSEN US WITH LOVE,
And given love a meaning new.
We seek your way, embrace your truth,
Cling to the vine, for life in you.

SUMMER
19TH SUNDAY OF EASTER
Some things hard to understand.

YEAR A

1. I Kings 19:9-13.
   Elijah looks for God.

2. Romans 9:1-5.
   The pain of separation.

3. Matthew 14:22-33.
   Jesus walks on water.

YEAR B

1. I Kings 19:4-8.
   Elijah's journey to Horeb.

2. Ephesians 4:30-5:2.
   Walk in love, like Christ.

3. John 6:41-51.
   I am the living bread.

YEAR C

1. Wisdom 18:6-9.
   The people wait for God to act.

2. Hebrews 11:1-2, 8-12.
   A definition of faith.

3. Luke 12:35-40.
   Be ready when the master comes.

LORD, WE BELIEVE, THOUGH CANNOT SEE
The wondrous things you say and do.
Enough for us to walk in love,
To be prepared, and trust in you.

FALL
32ND SUNDAY OF THE YEAR
The wisdom and courage of women:

YEAR A

1. Wisdom 6:12-16.
   She comes to those who seek her.

2. I Thessalonians 4:13-14.
   Have hope for those who sleep in death.

3. Matthew 25:1-13.
   The wise and foolish bridesmaids.

YEAR B

1. I Kings 17:10-16.
   Elijah and the widow of Zarephath.

2. Hebrews 9:24-28.
   Christ died but once for sin.

3. Mark 12:41-44.
   The widow who gave all she had.

YEAR C

1. II Maccabees 7:1-14.
   The courage of the sons and mother.

2. II Thessalonians 2:16-3:5.
   May God strengthens you.

3. Luke 20:27-38.
   No marriage in the age to come.

WE PRAISE THE WISDOM, LORD, IN YOU,
And widows, bridesmaids, mothers, wives.
We thank you for a heaven, too,
Where perfect love endures. How wise.

Meditation. The Lord's Prayer. Intercessions. Personal Prayers.

EVENING PRAYER

Reflections on the Day. Thanksgiving. Reconciliation.

EVENING PSALM / PS. 23 *The Lord will give me rest.* PAGE 3.

CANTICLE OF MARY / LUKE 1:46-55 *Behold the handmaid of the Lord.* PAGE 3.

Personal Prayers.

Week Eleven / MONDAY
MORNING PRAYER

I. THE PSALMS

MORNING PSALM / PS. 24
Let the King of glory in.
PAGE 4

PSALM OF THE DAY / PS. 119:25-48
"The Psalm of the Law" continued.

DALETH / *Continue, Lord, your work in me.*

25 My body prone, I lie in dust;
Revive me with your word.
26 I spoke my piece, you answered me;
Now train me with your word.

27 Lord, help me understand your way,
That I may know your works.
28 When I am racked with grief and pain,
Sustain me with your words.

29 Remove the blinders from my eyes
And grace me with your truth.
30 I chose your way of faithfulness,
Your teaching from my youth.

31 I cling to your decrees, O Lord;
Preserve me from disgrace.
32 Enlarge my heart to know the way,
And I will run the race.

HE / *Preserve me in your ways.*

33 O teach me, Lord, your way and law.
Give me as my reward
34 The understanding to obey
Wholeheartedly, O Lord.

35 Show me the path of your commands;
For they are my concern.
36 Lord turn my heart to what you say,
And not what I can earn.

37 Avert my eyes from vanity;
Preserve me in your ways.
38 Your promise to your servant keep,
And all who give you praise.

39 Your ordinances, Lord, are good;
Remove the taunts I dread.
40 O see how much I long for you,
And give me life instead.

WAW / *My hope is in your way.*

41 Lord, touch me with your faithful love,
The love you promised us.
42 Then I can answer those who taunt
That I shall ever trust.

43 Take not your word of truth from me;
My hope is in your way.
44 Your teaching I shall always keep;
Your law I will obey.

45 Relying on your precepts, Lord,
I walk about with ease.
46 Before the kings I'm not ashamed
To speak of your decrees.

47 In your commandments I delight,
Your precepts that I love.
48 I lift my hands to your commands;
I study what I love.

II. READINGS & PRAYERS

WINTER

MONDAY: 5TH WEEK OF THE YEAR
Creation, presence, healing:

1a. Genesis 1:1-19.
   God spoke and it was done.

1b. I Kings 8:1-13.
   The dedication of the temple.

2. Mark 6:53-56.
   All who touched him got well.

Your word, your touch are marvelous,
Here in your house come dwell with us...

SPRING

MONDAY: 5TH WEEK OF EASTER
We need help:

1. Acts 14:5-18.
   The Apostles are mistaken for gods.

2. John 14:21-26.
   The Holy Spirit will instruct you.

We make mistakes, are slow to see,
Await your Spirit eagerly...

SUMMER

MONDAY: 19TH WEEK OF THE YEAR
Give everyone the honor due:

1a. Deuteronomy 10:12-22.
   Fear the Lord; follow his way.

1b. Ezekiel 1:2-5,24-28.
   A vision of God's glory.

2. Matthew 17:22-27.
   Jesus pays taxes.

Our God is glorious and true;
Let us pay God the glory due...

FALL

MONDAY: 32ND WEEK OF THE YEAR
Requirements for wisdom, office, forgiveness:

1a. Wisdom 1:1-7.
   Wisdom makes us friends of God.

1b. Titus 1:1-9.
   Qualities required for office.

2. Luke 17:1-6.
   If he repents, forgive him.

We ask your pardon, Lord; forgive.
May we repent that we may live...

Meditation. The Lord's Prayer. Intercessions. Personal Prayers.

EVENING PRAYER

Reflections on the Day. Thanksgiving. Reconciliation.

EVENING PSALM / PS. 4 *I go to sleep in peace.* PAGE 4.

CANTICLE OF ZACHARY / LUKE 1:68-79 *Prepare the way of the Lord.* PAGE 4.

Personal Prayers.

Week Eleven / TUESDAY

MORNING PRAYER

I. THE PSALMS

MORNING PSALM / PS. 5

At dawn I pray to you.

PAGE 5

PSALM OF THE DAY / PS. 119:49-72

"The Psalm of the Law" continued.

ZAIN / *All through the night I keep my*

49 Remember, Lord, your word to me,
 Your word, my hope for life.
50 My comfort in affliction, Lord;
 Your word sustains my life.

51 The arrogant deride and mock;
 From you I shall not swerve.
52 For I recall your ancient law,
 My comfort while I serve.

53 The wicked who ignore your laws
 Fill me with rage as well.
54 Your laws are songs of strength to me,
 Wherever I may dwell.

55 All through the night I keep my watch,
 Recall your law and name.
56 Because I keep your precepts, Lord,
 My lot has been this shame.

HETH / *Your words I hold in awe.*

57 I promise, Lord, to keep your word;
 My portion you shall be.
58 With all my heart I ask of you
 The mercy promised me.

59 My ways I have considered, Lord;
 To yours I have come back,
60 Without delay, indeed with haste,
 To get me back on track.

61 The wicked's snares abound, but I
 Will not forget your law.
62 I rise at night to sing your praise;
 Your words I hold in awe.

63 To those who fear you, keep your word,
 I am a friend indeed.
64 Your faithful love, Lord, fills the earth.
 Teach us the truth we need.

TETH / *Your punishment was good for me.*

65 Your servant, Lord, I have received
 The best from you, your hands.
66 Lord, teach me knowledge, wisdom, too;
 I trust in your commands.

67 Before your chastening I strayed;
 But now I keep your word.
68 For you are good, do only good;
 Teach me your laws, O Lord.

69 Though wicked men smear me with lies,
 To you I pledge my heart.
70 In you my mind finds its delight;
 Their minds are gross as lard.

71 Your punishment was good for me,
 That I might learn your law.
72 Than silver, gold, a thousand times
 More precious is your law.

II. Readings & Prayers

WINTER
TUESDAY: 5TH WEEK OF THE YEAR
Humanity, the only disappointment:

1a. Genesis 1:20-2:4.
   The creator of man and woman.

1b. I Kings 8:22-30.
   Solomon's prayer.

2. Mark 7:1-13.
   Their heart is far from me.

O God, you are enthroned above;
Below, we seek forgiving love...

SPRING
TUESDAY: 5TH WEEK OF EASTER
Paul is stoned, but carries on:

1. Acts 14:19-28.
   We must suffer many trials.

2. John 14:27-31.
   Peace is my farewell to you.

We have your peace within our hearts,
So let the persecution start...

SUMMER
TUESDAY: 19TH WEEK OF THE YEAR
Give everyone the honor due:

1a. Deuteronomy 31:1-8.
   Moses' final exhortation.

1b. Ezekiel 2:8-3:4.
   The prophet eats his words.

2. Matthew 18:1-5,10,12-14.
   Do not despise my little ones.

The very old, the very young
Have much to say to everyone...

FALL
TUESDAY: 32ND WEEK OF THE YEAR
The Lord is Lord, and will be just:

1a. Wisdom 2:23-3:9.
   The just are in the hands of God.

1b. Titus 2:1-14.
   Instructions for everybody.

2. Luke 17:7-10.
   We are only servants, doing our duty.

Your servants, in your hands, O Lord;
We pray that we be worthy, Lord...

Meditation. The Lord's Prayer. Intercessions. Personal Prayers.

EVENING PRAYER

Reflections on the Day. Thanksgiving. Reconciliation.

EVENING PSALM / PS. 6 *My bed is wet with tears.* PAGE 5.

THE CHRIST HYMN / PHILIPPIANS 2:6-11 *The mind of Christ.* PAGE 5.

Personal Prayers.

Week Eleven / WEDNESDAY
MORNING PRAYER

I. THE PSALMS

MORNING PSALM / PS. 101
A royal pledge.
PAGE 6

PSALM OF THE DAY / PS. 119:73-96
"The Psalm of the Law" continued.

YODH / *Teach me to understand.*

73 Teach me to understand your law,
    For you created me.
74 My hope, my joy is in your word;
    Let those who fear you see.

75 I know that you are fair, O Lord;
    My punishment was just.
76 Your faithful love now comforts me;
    Your promises I trust.

77 Let mercy come that I may live;
    I revel in your law.
78 Let those who slander me be shamed.
    My study is your law.

79 Let those who fear you turn to me,
    To learn of your decrees.
80 I follow them wholeheartedly,
    That shame not come on me.

KAPH / *I wait impatiently.*

81 I hope for your deliverance;
    I wait impatiently.
82 My eyes look longingly to you.
    When will you comfort me?

83 I weep like one with smoke-filled eyes,
    Yet in your law secure.
84 When will you bring my foes to task?
    How long must I endure?

85 The insolent dig pits for me
    Because they scorn your word.
86 But your commandments all are true,
    And they are liars, Lord!

87 O help me, I am almost gone;
    Though I have done your will.
88 Give faithful love that I may live
    And your decrees fulfill.

LAMEDH / *My refuge is your word.*

89 Your word is everlasting, Lord;
    It stands in heaven, too.
90 Your faithfulness more firm than earth,
    From age to age is true.

91 For all that is exists to serve,
    To carry out your word.
92 Had not your law been my delight,
    I would have perished, Lord.

93 I never will neglect your word;
    Through it you give me life.
94 Since I am yours, O save me, Lord;
    I turn to you for life.

95 The wicked seek to take my life.
    My refuge is your word.
96 I know that all is limited,
    Except, O Lord, your word.

II. READINGS & PRAYERS

WINTER

WEDNESDAY:* 5TH WEEK OF THE YEAR
It wasn't the apple that was bad:

1a. Genesis 2:5-9, 15-17.
   Eden, and God's command.

1b. I Kings 10:1-10.
   The Queen of Sheba's visit.

2. Mark 7:14-23.
   What makes a man impure.

Lord, help us watch and guard our mouth,
Not what goes in, but what comes out...

SPRING

WEDNESDAY: 5TH WEEK OF EASTER
Fruitless and fruitful relationships:

1. Acts 15:1-6.
   A dispute over circumcision starts.

2. John 15:1-8.
   The vine and the branches.

We are the branch, you are the vine;
We are the cup, you are the wine...

SUMMER

WEDNESDAY: 19TH WEEK OF THE YEAR
How many does it take?

1a. Deuteronomy 34:1-12.
   Moses dies, Joshua succeeds.

1b. Ezkiel 9:1-7, 10:18-22.
   The defiled are destroyed.

2. Matthew 18:15-20.
   The power of two or three.

A great one leaves, another comes;
But two or three in Christ are one...

FALL

WEDNESDAY: 32TH WEEK OF THE YEAR
Responsibilties of leaders and people:

1a. Wisdom 6:2-11.
   Leaders must learn wisdom.

1b. Titus 3:1-7.
   People must obey the law.

2. Luke 17:11-19.
   One came back to praise the Lord.

Good leaders, laws, give us a start;
But needed most are grateful hearts...

Meditation. The Lord's Prayer. Intercessions. Personal Prayers.

EVENING PRAYER

Reflections on the Day. Thanksgiving. Reconciliation.

EVENING PSALM / PS. 13 *Let me have hope.* PAGE 6.

THE LOVE OF GOD / ROMANS 8:35-39 *Who can be against us?* PAGE 6.

Personal Prayers.

*NOTE: If today is Ash Wednesday (see Calendar, page 234), the Readings for today and the rest of the week are on page 225.

Week Eleven / THURSDAY
MORNING PRAYER

I. THE PSALMS

MORNING PSALM / PS. 100
Praise God from whom all blessings flow.
PAGE 7

PSALM OF THE DAY / PS. 119:97-120
"The Psalm of the Law" continued.

MEM / *How sweet your word.*

97 O how I love your law's commands!
   Each day I study more.
98 They make me wiser than my foes,
   And they are mine to store.

99 I get more insight from your law
   Than from a teacher's words.
100 I gain more wisdom keeping it
   Than from my elders' words.

101 I keep my feet from evil's path
   That I may keep your word.
102 I have not swerved from your decrees,
   For you have taught me, Lord.

103 How sweet your word is in my mouth,
   Like honey on my lips.
104 Your precepts show the way to go;
   I hate the lie that trips.

NUN / *My life is in your hands.*

105 Your word is light: it shows the way,
   A lamp to guide my feet.
106 I will obey your just decrees
   That I have sworn to keep.

107 Relieve me as you promised, Lord;
   For I am deep in grief.
108 Accept my offering of praise.
   Your word be my relief

109 I ever guard your teaching, Lord;
   My life is in your hands.
110 The wicked set their traps for me.
   I stand by your commands.

111 Your law is my inheritance;
   On it my joy depends.
112 I am resolved to keep your law
   Forever, to the end.

SAMEKH / *Your word I hold in awe.*

113 How I despise hypocrisy!
   And how I love your law.
114 You are my refuge and my shield;
   I hope in you, your law.

115 You evildoers, let me be,
   That I may keep God's word.
116 O Lord, sustain my hope for life
   According to your word.

117 O save me, Lord, that I may dwell
   On your eternal word.
118 Reject the false who stray from you,
   Who do not keep your word.

119 The wicked you reject as dross.
   I rightly love your law.
120 My body shakes in fear of you;
   Your word I hold in awe.

II. READINGS & PRAYERS

WINTER

THURSDAY: 5TH WEEK OF THE YEAR
How often the favored fail:

1a. Genesis 2:18-25.
   The creation of Eve.

1b. I Kings 11:4-13.
   Solomon's sin and punishment.

2. Mark 7:24-30.
   Jesus grants a pagan's request.

A pagan trusted, won her prize;
But not the king considered wise...

SPRING

THURSDAY: 5TH WEEK OF EASTER
The way to banish strife and gloom:

1. Acts 15:17-21.
   Peter and James resolve the dispute.

2. John 15:9-11.
   Live in my love, with joy.

We thank you, Lord, for peace and joy,
The fruit of love that sins destroy...

SUMMER

THURSDAY: 19TH WEEK OF THE YEAR
How often must we forgive?

1a. Joshua 3:7-17.
   Crossing over the Jordan.

1b. Ezekiel 12:1-2.
   You live in a rebellious house.

2. Mark 18:21-19:1.
   Forgive each other from the heart.

Not seven times, not seventy;
Lord, you forgive us endlessly...

FALL

THURSDAY: 32ND WEEK OF THE YEAR
Freedom, sign of the Kingdom of God:

1a. Wisdom 7:22-8:1.
   The qualities of wisdom.

1b. Philemon 7-20.
   No more a slave, a brother now.

2. Luke 17:20-25.
   The reign of God is in your midst.

Where is it Lord? Help us to see
It everywhere that we are free...

Meditation. The Lord's Prayer. Intercessions. Personal Prayers.

EVENING PRAYER

Reflections on the Day. Thanksgiving. Reconciliation.

EVENING PSALM / PS. 131 *A child in your mother's arms.* PAGE 7.

THE UNSEEN GOD / COLOSSIANS 1:15-20 *First born of all creation.* PAGE 7.

Personal Prayers.

Week Eleven / FRIDAY
MORNING PRAYER

I. THE PSALMS

MORNING PSALM / PS. 130
Out of the depths.
PAGE 8

PSALM OF THE DAY / PS. 119:121-144
"The Psalm of the Law" continued.

AIN / *The time has come to act.*

121 Defend my rights; my cause is just;
    Do not abandon me.
122 Let not the arrogant prevail.
    I seek your guarantee.

123 I look for your deliverance,
    Your promised victory.
124 In keeping with your faithful love,
    Teach me your law; hear me.

125 I am your servant; let me see
    And understand your law.
126 O Lord, the time has come to act.
    Their sinfulness you saw.

127 I rightly cherish your commands,
    More precious far than gold.
128 I hate the false, pursue the true;
    Your precepts I will hold.

PE / *My eyes are full of tears.*

129 Lord, your decrees are wonderful;
    And rightly I obey.
130 Unfold your word that sheds your light;
    Show simple folk your way.

131 I long for your commandments, Lord.
    With open mouth I cry.
132 To those who love your name, you turn;
    I turn to you and sigh.

133 Make firm my feet; you gave your word;
    Let sin not rule my way.
134 Redeem me from oppression, Lord,
    That I may live your way.

135 Instruct your servant in your law.
    Be gracious, calm my fears.
136 Because of those who break your law
    My eyes are full of tears.

ZADE / *I am consumed with rage.*

137 How straight and true are your decrees,
    For you are just, O Lord.
138 So, too, the teaching that you give
    Is just and firm, O Lord.

139 My enemies ignore your laws;
    I am consumed with rage.
140 Your words were tested; they are pure.
    Your servant loves each page.

141 Belittled and despised by foes,
    I still will cling to you.
142 Your justice is eternal, Lord;
    Your teaching will come true.

143 Though woes and anguish come to me,
    Your laws are my delight.
144 Your just decrees will never die.
    Lord, let me live; give light.

II. Readings & Prayers

WINTER

FRIDAY: 5TH WEEK OF THE YEAR
The consequences and cure of sin:

1a. Genesis 3:1-8.
   The original sin.

1b. I Kings 11:29-32, 12:19.
   Israel rebels against David's house.

2. Mark 7:31-37.
   The deaf hear, the mute speak.

Lord, we are deaf and we are dumb
Because of sin. To save us, come...

SPRING

FRIDAY: 5TH WEEK OF EASTER.
Christ calls his servants friends:

1. Acts 15:22-31.
   The solution is relayed to all.

2. John 15:12-17.
   I call you friends, not slaves.

O Master, friend, you set us free
From law, to serve you faithfully...

SUMMER

FRIDAY: 19TH WEEK OF THE YEAR
How far we have fallen:

1a. Joshua 24:1-13.
   Joshua recites what God has done.

1b. Ezekiel 16:1-15.
   From queen to prostitute.

2. Matthew 19:3-12.
   Christ's teachings on divorce.

Our God is ever faithful, true.
Help us, O Lord, to be like you...

FALL

FRIDAY: 32ND WEEK OF THE YEAR
Some ways God comes to us:

1a. Wisdom 13:1-9.
   In the beauty of creation, see God.

1b. II John 4-9.
   Let us love one another.

2. Luke 17:26-37.
   The Son of Man will come like the flood

The Lord will come from high above
Like saving rain, for God is love...

Meditation. The Lord's Prayer. Intercessions. Personal Prayers.

Evening Prayer

Reflections on the Day. Thanksgiving. Reconciliation.

EVENING PSALM / PS. 51 *David's prayer for forgiveness.* PAGE 8.

CANTICLE OF SIMEON / LUKE 2:29-32 *Lord, let me go in peace.* PAGE 8

Personal Prayers.

Week Eleven / SATURDAY
MORNING PRAYER

I. THE PSALMS

MORNING PSALM / PS. 141
Like incense let my prayer arise.
PAGE 9

PSALM OF THE DAY / PS. 119:145-176
"The Psalm of the Law" concluded.

QOPH / *You are near me still.*

145 I cry with all my heart, O God.
    Lord, let my voice be heard.
146 I call upon you. Save me, Lord!
    That I may live your word.

147 Before the dawn I rise to pray;
    I hope to hear your word.
148 And through the night at every watch,
    Your promises are heard.

149 Your faithful love will make you hear,
    For saving is your way.
150 Those who pursue intrigue are near,
    But far from you are they.

151 Lord, all of your commands are true;
    And you are near me still.
152 I know it from your laws of old
    Which stand, and always will.

RESH / *Many are my enemies.*

153 See my affliction. Rescue me!
    Your law has ruled my life.
154 Take up my cause; redeem me, Lord.
    You promised; save my life.

155 Lord, keep the wicked far from me,
    For they ignore your law.
156 Your mercies, Lord, are very great;
    Preserve me by your law.

157 Though many are my enemies,
    I have not turned away.
158 I view the faithless with disgust;
    Their minds have gone astray.

159 See how I love your precepts, Lord?
    Your faithful love I trust.
160 The essence of your word is truth;
    Your rules are ever just.

SHIN / *You know the ways I keep.*

161 They set on me without a cause;
    My heart was full of dread.
162 Then I recalled your promises,
    Found joy in them instead.

163 I hate a lie, abhor the false.
    I love your word, your law.
164 I praise you seven times a day,
    Your justice hold in awe.

165 All those who love your law succeed.
    No stumbling blocks for them!
166 I hope for your salvation, Lord,
    To your commands attend.

167 Your precepts, teachings, I obey;
    My love for them is deep.
168 Your laws and statutes I obey;
    You know the ways I keep.

TAU / *Your law: my joy and pride.*

169 I plead for understanding, Lord,
    According to your word.
170 Let my petitions come to you;
    Your promise I have heard.

171 Since you have been my teacher, Lord,
    My lips pour forth your praise.
172 My tongue declares that you are true
    And just in all your ways.

173 I choose your way, your precepts, Lord;
   Your hand be at my side.
174 I long for your deliverance;
   Your law, my joy and pride.

175 Lord, let me live to sing your praise;
   Your law will guide my hands.
176 Pursue me, Lord, a sheep that strayed,
   But still seeks your commands.

II. READINGS & PRAYERS

WINTER
SATURDAY, 5TH WEEK OF THE YEAR
Justice comes, but mercy overcomes:

1a. Genesis 3:9-24.
   Banishment from Eden.

1b. I Kings 12:26-32, 13:33-34.
   Jeroboam's idolatry.

2. Mark 8:1-10.
   Jesus feeds four thousand.

Your banished, foolish children, Lord,
Still move your heart to pity, Lord...

SPRING
SATURDAY, 5TH WEEK OF EASTER
Christians have good ears:

1. Acts 16:1-10.
   A call for help.

2. John 15:18-21.
   They will hate and harry you.

A call for help, a cry of hate:
We hear them all; we shall not wait...

SUMMER
SATURDAY: 19TH WEEK OF THE YEAR
Decision time:

1a. Joshua 24:14-19.
   Choose today whom you will serve.

1b. Ezekiel 18:1-13, 30-32.
   The virtuous will live; sinners die.

2. Matthew 19:13-15.
   Let the children come to me.

You loved the children, pampered them.
May we become a child again...

FALL
SATURDAY: 32ND WEEK OF THE YEAR
Our hope when Christ returns:

1a. Wisdom 18:14-16, 19:6-9.
   God's word came like a warrior.

1b. III John 5-8.
   You share with them the work of truth.

2. Luke 18:1-8.
   When he returns, will he find faith?

We promise, Lord, that when you come
You will find faith, and our work done...

Meditation. The Lord's Prayer. Intercessions. Personal Prayers.

EVENING PRAYER

Reflections on the Day. Thanksgiving. Reconciliation.

EVENING PSALM / PS. 143 *Lord, do not condemn.* PAGE 9.

SONG OF MOSES / REVELATION 15:3-4 *They all had harps and sang.* PAGE 9.

Personal Prayers.

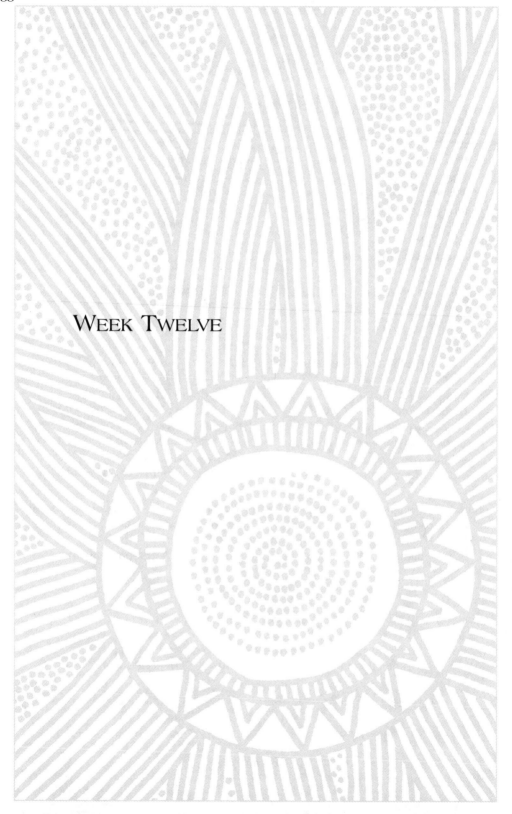

Week Twelve

Week Twelve / SUNDAY

MORNING PRAYER

I. THE PSALMS

MORNING PSALM / PS. 95

O my people, now listen to me.

PAGE 3

PSALMS OF THE DAY / PSS. 32 & 98

Songs of trust, praise, and blessing.

PSALM 32 / *Love surrounds the one who trusts in God*

.1 How blest are those
whose sins have been dismissed!
How happy those whose fault
has been released.
2 How blest are those
in whom God finds no guilt,
And those whose spirit harbors no deceit.

3 Lord, keeping silent,
save for endless groaning,
Left my body wasted, strength undone.
4 Your hand lay heavy on me night and day,
As suffocating as the summer sun.

5 Until at last I opened up my heart,
Confessed my sin, no longer hid my fall.
I said, "I will acknowledge all to God."
And so I did, and God forgave it all.

6 Let those who trust in God rely on prayer;
And mighty waters, floods will disappear.
7 Lord shelter me,
preserve me from distress;
The joyful cries of freedom let me hear.

8 My people, I will teach you,
show the way,
Will be your guide;
my eyes will be on you.
9 So listen; be not like a senseless mule
That needs a bit to make it follow you.

10 For many are the troubles of the wicked.
Love surrounds the one who trusts in God.
11 O shout for joy,
all you who trust the Lord;
Let all the just rejoice and praise our God!

PSALM 98 / *Raise a shout to the Lord, all the earth!*

1 Let us sing a new song to the Lord;
For the Lord has done marvelous things.
The right hand and the arm of the Lord
Have prevailed; see the triumph they bring.

2 God has made it quite clear to the world,
To all nations the justice of God.
3 Israel: see your Lord's faithful love;
All the earth: see the triumph of God.

4 Raise a shout to the Lord all the earth;
In a chorus of praise gladly sing.
5 With melodies sweet from the lyre,
6 With your trumpets make way for the king.

7 Let the sea and all in it resound;
Let the land and all on it rejoice.
8 Let the floods clap their hands, let the hills
Sing together in joy with one voice,

9 At the presence of God who shall come
To judge nations, with fairness for all;
Who will govern all peoples with justice,
And reign over earth, Lord of all!

II. Readings & Prayers

WINTER

6TH SUNDAY OF THE YEAR
The Lord is pushing for an answer.

YEAR A

1. Sirach 15:15-20.
   Here are life and death: choose.

2. I Corinthians 2:6-10.
   We speak God's wisdom.

3. Matthew 5:17-37.
   You have heard, but I say.

YEAR B

1. Leviticus 13:1-2, 44-46.
   The ancient treatment of lepers.

2. I Corinthians 10:31-11:1.
   Imitate me, as I do Christ.

3. Mark 1:40-45.
   Jesus cures a leper.

YEAR C

1. Jeremiah 17:5-8.
   Trust in God, not human beings.

2. I Corinthians 15:12, 16-20.
   Christ lives, or our faith is vain.

3. Luke 6:17, 20-26.
   The beatitudes and woes.

THERE IS NO DOUBT WHERE JESUS STANDS,
He reaches out his hand to us.
The Lord alone can cure our sin,
But Lord, the choice is up to us.

SPRING

6TH SUNDAY OF EASTER
Look for the Spirit, gift of God's love.

YEAR A

1. Acts 8:5-8, 14-17.
   They received the Holy Spirit.

2. I Peter 3:15-18.
   He was given life in the spirit.

3. John 14:15-21.
   The Father will send the Spirit of truth.

YEAR B

1. Acts 10:25-26, 34-35, 44-48.
   The Spirit came on all.

2. I John 4:7-10.
   God is love.

3. John 15:9-17.
   Live on in me as I live in you.

YEAR C

1. Acts 15:1-2, 22-29.
   It is the decision of the Spirit.

2. Revelations 21:10-14, 22-23.
   The new Jerusalem.

3. John 14:23-29.
   The Holy Spirit will instruct you.

O FATHER GOD, AND JESUS LORD,
Send us your Spirit from above.
Enlighten us, inflame our hearts,
Come, give yourself, the gift of love.

SUMMER

20TH SUNDAY OF THE YEAR
He came not for a few, but for all.

YEAR A

1. Isaiah 56:1,6-7.
   My house, a house of prayer for all.

2. Romans 11:13-15, 29-32.
   God's gifts are irrevocable.

3. Matthew 15:21-28.
   A pagan woman's faith is great.

YEAR B

1. Proverbs 9:1-6.
   Wisdom spreads a feast for all.

2. Ephesians 5:15-20.
   Do not act like fools.

3. John 6:51-58.
   Those who feed on me will live.

YEAR C

1. Jeremiah 38:4-10.
   The prophet is thrown into a cistern.

2. Hebrews 12:1-4.
   Let us keep our eyes fixed on Jesus.

3. Luke 12:49-53.
   I have come to light a fire.

O LORD, YOU ARE IMPATIENT WITH
Our petty mediocrity.
You seek us all, you ask for all,
You cry to all: Come feed on me!

FALL

33ND SUNDAY OF THE YEAR
The day of judgment is not far away.

YEAR A

1. Proverbs 31:10-13, 19-20, 30-31.
   The value of a worthy wife.

2. I Thessalonians 5:1-6.
   The day of the Lord is coming.

3. Matthew 25:14-30.
   A day of reckoning will come.

YEAR B

1. Daniel 12:1-3.
   At that time the wise will shine.

2. Hebrews 10:11-14, 18.
   He died but once, and now he waits.

3. Mark 13:24-32.
   Then they shall see the Son of Man.

YEAR C

1. Malachi. 3:19-20.
   The day is coming, like an oven.

2. II Thessalonians 3:7-12.
   Who would not work, should not eat.

3. Luke 21:5-19.
   There will be signs and omens.

O LORD, WE TRUST YOUR FAITHFUL LOVE
To bring us through alive.
The wise shall shine like stars above;
The patient will survive.

Meditation. The Lord's Prayer. Intercessions. Personal Prayers.

EVENING PRAYER

Reflections on the Day. Thanksgiving. Reconciliation.

EVENING PSALM / PS. 23 *The Lord will give me rest.* PAGE 3.

CANTICLE OF MARY / LUKE 1:46-55 *Behold the handmaid of the Lord.* PAGE 3.

Personal Prayers.

Week Twelve / MONDAY
MORNING PRAYER

I. THE PSALMS

MORNING PSALM / Ps. 24
Let the King of glory in.
PAGE 4

PSALMS OF THE DAY / Pss. 116 & 125
Thanksgiving for past blessings, and a prayer for more.

PSALM. 116 / *How can I repay the Lord?*

1 I love the Lord who hears my voice,
  And listens to my plea.
2 Whenever I cry out, the Lord
  Will turn and answer me.

3 The cords of death encompassed me,
  The torments of Sheol.
4 In grief and woe I cried to you:
  "O Lord, redeem my soul!"

5 The Lord is gracious, merciful;
  Our God is ever just.
6 The one who guards the innocent,
  Then raised me from the dust.

7 Return, my soul, and be at rest;
  The Lord was good to you.
8 Your eyes from tears, your feet from falls,
  From death God rescued you.

9 Now I can walk before the Lord,
  With those who live, stand tall.
10 Now I can trust, though in my pain,
  11 I called them liars all.

12 O how can I repay the Lord
  For life brought back to me?
14 I will fulfill the vows I made
  For all the world to see.

13 And I shall raise salvation's cup
  And call upon God's name.
15 To God the death of faithful ones
  Is full of costly pain.

16 O Lord, I am your servant's child;
  I am your servant too.
 The cords that bound me you have loosed.
17 I give my thanks to you.

18 I will fulfill my vows to you,
  And call upon your name.
19 Before them all, within your courts,
  Here in Jerusalem.

PSALM 125 / *O Lord, bless Israel, your people.*

1 Who trust in God stand firm as Zion,
  They shall not be moved forever.
2 As hills surround Jerusalem,
  The Lord surrounds the people ever.

3 Let not the wicked rule in lands
  That have been given to the faithful,
For fear the just will reach their hands
  To doing wrong, and prove unfaithful.

4 O Lord, do good to faithful hearts;
  But let the wicked, bent on evil,
5 Go the way of evildoers.
  Bless your Israel, your people.

II. Readings & Prayers

WINTER

Monday: 6th Week of the Year
Questions from Cain, and from Christ:

1a. Genesis 4:1-15.
   Am I my brother's keeper?

1b. James 1:1-11.
   Count it joy to be tested.

2. Mark 8:11-13.
   You seek a sign? None will be given.

God sees the heart, not just the gift;
Who comes to argue gets short shrift...

SPRING

Monday: 6th Week of Easter
Welcomed or persecuted, we rely on God:

1. Acts 16:11-15.
   A convert makes an invitation.

2. John 15:26-16:4.
   I will send the Spirit of truth.

Whatever, Lord, the future brings,
Your Spirit conquers everything...

SUMMER

Monday: 20th Week of the Year
The demands of God are great:

1a. Judges 2:11-19.
   God's anger at Israel's idolatry.

1b. Ezekiel 24:15-24.
   God takes the prophet's wife .

2. Matthew 19:16-22.
   Seek your treasure in heaven.

You ask for much, but give us more;
Increase our faith in heaven's store...

FALL

Monday: 33rd Week of the Year
End time draws near for God's people:

1a. I Maccabees 1:10-15, 41-43, 54-57, 62-63.
   Terrible affliction falls on Israel.

1b. Revelations 1:1-4, 2:1-5.
   Judgements on the churches.

2. Luke 18:35-43.
   Lord, that I may see.

O Son of David, grant that we
May see you, too, and darkness flee...

Meditation. The Lord's Prayer. Intercessions. Personal Prayers.

EVENING PRAYER

Reflections on the Day. Thanksgiving. Reconciliation.

Evening Psalm / Ps. 4 *I go to sleep in peace.* Page 4.

Canticle of Zachary / Luke 1:68-79 *Prepare the way of the Lord.* Page 4.

Personal Prayers.

Week Twelve / TUESDAY
MORNING PRAYER

I. THE PSALMS

MORNING PSALM / PS. 5
At dawn I pray to you.
PAGE 5

PSALMS OF THE DAY / PSS. 120, 121, & 122
The songs of a lover of peace.

PSALM 120 / *Among the violent, I stand for peace.*

1 In my distress I called upon the Lord:
2 "Save me from lying lips, deceitful tongues."
3 What profit can you gain deceitful ones?
4 A soldier's arrows,
    burning coals, the sword.

5 Alas, I dwell in Meshech, near Kedar,
6 Too long, too close to enemies of peace.
    Among the violent, I stand for peace.
7 But when I speak of peace,
    they rise for war.

PSALM 121 / *The Lord will guard your life.*

1 I lift my eyes to mountains high,
    Lord, where shall I find help?
2 From God, who made the earth and sky,
    The Lord will be my help.

5 The Lord, your guard, is shade and light;
    The Lord is at your hand.
6 From sun by day, and moon at night,
    The Lord will guard the land.

3 God will not let your foot give way;
    Your watchman never sleeps.
4 The guardian of Israel
    A careful watch will keep.

7 God is your shield from evil, sin,
    Will guard you, day and night,
8 Your going out, your coming in,
    Forevermore, for life.

PSALM 122 / *For the peace of Jerusalem, pray.*

1 I rejoiced when they asked me
        to come:
    "Let us go to the house of the Lord."
2 We arrived at Jerusalem's gate,
    At the City of Unity's door.

5 There the thrones of God's temple
        are found,
    Thrones of justice, of David the king.
6 For the peace of Jerusalem, pray.
    May all prosper who love her, and sing:

3 All the tribes on their pilgrimage came,
    As decreed for the tribes of the Lord;
4 The decree that enjoins Israel
    To give thanks to the name of the Lord.

7 "In your walls, in your palaces, peace."
8 For the sake of my family and friends,
9 For the sake of the house of the Lord,
    I pray, "Peace be with you!" without end.

II. Readings & Prayers

WINTER

TUESDAY: 6TH WEEK OF THE YEAR
The impatience of God:

1a. Genesis 6:5-8, 7:1-5, 10.
   God sends a flood on earth.

1b. James 1:12-18.
   God tempts no one; blesses all.

2. Mark 8:14-21.
   Do you still not understand?

That you are patient, Lord, we know;
Impatient too, for us to grow...

SPRING

TUESDAY: 6TH WEEK OF EASTER
All growth comes with pain:

1. Acts 16:22-34.
   Paul converts his jailer.

2. John 16:5-11.
   The Paraclete will explain all.

Lord, they were sad to see you go;
But, with the Spirit, soon will know...

SUMMER

TUESDAY: 20TH WEEK OF THE YEAR
God's servants overcome all odds:

1a. Judges 6:11-24.
   God sends Gideon to save Israel.

1b. Ezekiel 28:1-10.
   You are a man and not a god.

2. Matthew 19:23-30.
   We have left all to follow you.

With God all things are possible;
With God we are invincible...

FALL

TUESDAY: 33RD WEEK OF THE YEAR
God's eye goes to the heart, sees all:

1a. II Maccabees 6:18-31.
   Old age teaches all a lesson.

1b. Revelation 3:1-6, 14-22.
   Searing condemnation for the wicked.

2. Luke 19:1-10.
   Today salvation has come to this house.

Almighty and eternal Lord,
We look to you for our reward...

Meditation. The Lord's Prayer. Intercessions. Personal Prayers.

EVENING PRAYER

Reflections on the Day. Thanksgiving. Reconciliation.

EVENING PSALM / PS. 6 *My bed is wet with tears.* PAGE 5.

THE CHRIST SONG / PHILIPPIANS 2:6-11 *The mind of Christ.* PAGE 5.

Personal Prayers.

Week Twelve / WEDNESDAY

MORNING PRAYER

I. THE PSALMS

MORNING PSALM / PS. 101
A royal pledge.
PAGE 6

PSALMS OF THE DAY / PSS. 127 & 135
Two songs exalting God above all else.

PSALM 127 / *Unless the Lord shall build.*

1 Unless the Lord shall build the house,
The builders work in vain.
Unless the Lord shall guard the city,
Watchmen watch in vain.

2 To rise at dawn and toil till dusk
For bread to eat is vain.
The Lord provides for those God loves
In sleep, without the pain.

3 One's children are a heritage,
God's gifts, rewards desired.
4 Like arrows in a warrior's hand
Are sons a man has sired.

5 The man who has a quiver full
Will not be put to shame,
6 When he must meet his enemy
To carry on his name.

PSALM 135 / *The Lord is above all the gods.*
1 ALLELUIA!

Praise the name of the Lord,
    all you servants of God,
2 You who stand in the courts
    of the house of the Lord.
3 God is good; it is good
    to sing hymns to God's name.
4 God chose Jacob, made Israel God's,
    praise the Lord!

5 This I know, that the Lord is above
    all the gods;
6 That whatever God wills shall be done
    everywhere.
7 Clouds of rain from the ends of the earth,
    the Lord brings
And releases the winds
    from God's storehouse of air.

8 It was God who in Egypt destroyed
    the first born,
9 Who sent powerful signs,
    who did wonderful things
To make Pharaoh and all of his servants
    beware.
10 It was God who struck nations
    and slew many kings.

11 Sihon king of the Amorites,
    Og of Bashan,
And the whole royal family of Canaan
    as well.
12 God made all of their lands
    an inheritance gift
To our people, a heritage for Israel.

13 Lord, your name is eternal,
    will ever be known;
And through all generations
    your fame will endure.
14 You, the Lord, are our champion;
    you will avenge
And obtain what is just for your servants
    the poor.

15 But the gods of the nations are silver
    and gold;
They were made by their hands,
    and their lips cannot talk.
16 They have eyes that are blind;
    they have ears that are deaf;
17 They have mouths without breath,
    and their feet cannot walk.

18 Those who trust in such gods will become like their gods.
19 But for you, house of Israel, you praise the Lord!
20 House of Aaron, and Levi, and all who fear God,
21 Your Lord dwells in Jerusalem; praised be the Lord!

II. READINGS & PRAYERS

WINTER

WEDNESDAY:* 6TH WEEK OF THE YEAR
The Lord seeks only good for us:

1a. Genesis 8:6-13,20-22.
The flood recedes: God's promises.

1b. James 1:19-27.
Be quick to hear and slow to speak.

2. Mark 8:22-26.
Jesus gives sight to a blind man.

You make us see and calm our fear;
Speak, Lord, to us; your servants hear...

SPRING

WEDNESDAY: 6TH WEEK OF EASTER
Who shall be our guide:

1. Acts 17:15,22-18:1.
Paul addresses the intelligentsia.

2. John 16:12-15.
The Spirit will be your guide.

The world, so full of self and pride,
Will never let the Spirit guide...

SUMMER

WEDNESDAY: 20TH WEEK OF THE YEAR
Let all beware of power, greed:

1a. Judges 9:6-15.
The people of Shechem seek a king.

1b. Ezekiel 34:1-11.
God condemns wicked shepherds.

2. Matthew 20:1-16.
I will pay you whatever is fair.

Lord, may we not be envious
Because our God is generous...

FALL

WEDNESDAY: 33RD WEEK OF THE YEAR
See the reward of courage and faith:

1a. II Maccabees 7:1,20-31.
Seven brothers and their mother die.

1b. Revelation 4:1-11.
A vision of the throne of God.

2. Luke 19:11-28.
Whoever has, will be given more.

What more/ A vision of the Lord.
Our eyes shall see your glory, Lord...

Meditation. The Lord's Prayer. Intercessions. Personal Prayers.

EVENING PRAYER

Reflections on the Day. Thanksgiving. Reconciliation.

EVENING PSALM / PS. 13 *Let me have hope.* PAGE 6.

THE LOVE OF GOD / ROMANS 8:35-39 *Who can be against us?* PAGE 6.

Personal Prayers.

*NOTE: If today is Ash Wednesday (see Calendar, page 234) the Readings for today and the rest of the week are on page 225.

Week Twelve / THURSDAY
MORNING PRAYER

I. THE PSALMS

MORNING PSALM / PS. 100
Praise God from whom all blessings flow.
PAGE 7

PSALMS OF THE DAY / PSS. 108 & 132
Two calls to action in the service of the Lord.

PSALM 108 / *Awake my heart, awake the dawn.*

2 My heart is firm, O God, I sing this song.
  With all my soul, I chant this hymn to you.
3 Awake, my heart and harp,
        awake the dawn!

4 Among the people I give thanks to you.
  I sing your praise among the nations all.
5 The Lord above the sky is faithful, true.

  Your faithful love for us is heaven tall.
6 Above the heavens be exalted, Lord;
  On earth your glory reaches over all.

7 Let those you love be saved by you,
        O Lord,
  Let your right arm deliver
        those you own.
  O answer me; bring victory, O Lord.

8 The Lord has spoken
        from the holy throne:
  "I portion out the valley of Succoth.
  In triumph I take Shechem for my own.
9 Manasseh, Gilead, I take them both.
  My helmet Ephraim, Moab is my bowl.
  My scepter will be Judah, on my oath.

10 On Edom I will plant my sandal's sole;
   Philistia will see my victory.
11 Now, who will give me Edom's throne,
        my goal?"

12 Have you rejected us?
        Lord, march with me.
13 Against our foe no human help will do.
14 Lord, trample them; give us the victory.

PSALM 132 / *I will not rest until I find a place for God.*

1 Remember, Lord, the path that David trod;
2 And how he swore to Jacob's mighty God:
3 "I will not go back home,
        not leave my quest,
4 I will not close my eyes, I will not rest
5 Until I find a place to house my God,
  A fitting home for Jacob's mighty God."

6 We heard of it in Ephrathah, in Jaar,
7 To worship at his feet we traveled far.
8 "Arise, O Lord, and take your royal throne,
  Your mighty ark,
        and you have found a home.
9 Your priests are robed,
        a joyous song is sung.
10 For David's sake receive your chosen one."

11 To David God once swore, and will be true:
   "Upon your throne
        your sons will follow you.
12 And if they keep their covenant with me,
   It shall be theirs for all eternity.
13 For I, the Lord, chose Zion for my throne.
14 Here is my resting place; this is my home.

15 Her pilgrims I will bless; her poor I feed.
16 Her priests I vest;
        her faithful sing with glee.
   Here I will found a line of David's sons,
17 Will light a lamp for my anointed one.
18 His enemies I clothe in their disgrace;
   For him, his crown will shine
        upon his face."

II. Readings & Prayers

WINTER

THURSDAY: 6TH WEEK OF THE YEAR
Three to remember:

1a. Genesis 9:1-13.
The new covenant: the rainbow.

1b. James 2:1-9.
God chose the poor; show them respect.

2. Mark 8:27-33.
Peter shines; then stumbles.

Before my eyes these three endure:
The cross, the rainbow, and the poor...

SPRING

ASCENSION THURSDAY
His mission done, the Lord returns:

1. Acts 1:1-11.
He was lifted up before their eyes.

2. Ephesians 1:17-23.
He is seated at the right hand of the Father.

3. Mark 16:15-20.
He took his seat at God's right hand.

Your Spirit, Lord, for which we yearn,
Will be our parting gift from you.
You promised us you would return;
Till then we have your work to do.

SUMMER

THURSDAY: 20TH WEEK OF THE YEAR
Take care not to be foolish, rash:

1a. Judges 11:29-39.
Jephthah makes a rash vow.

1b. Ezekiel 36:23-28.
I will give you a new heart.

2. Matthew 22:1-14.
The King's wedding feast.

The invited are many; the chosen are few.
Let us go to the feast,
    but with hearts that are new...

FALL

THURSDAY: 33RD WEEK OF THE YEAR
A faithful family, a faithless city:

1a. I Maccabees 2:15-29.
Mattathias' family stays true.

1b. Revelation 5:1-10.
I saw the Lamb that had been slain.

2. Luke 19:41-44.
Jesus weeps over Jerusalem.

The Lamb is weeping for the flock;
A city razed, but for this rock...

Meditation. The Lord's Prayer. Intercessions. Personal Prayers.

EVENING PRAYER

Reflections on the Day. Thanksgiving. Reconciliation.

EVENING PSALM / PS. 131 *A child in your mother's arms.* PAGE 7.

THE UNSEEN GOD / COLOSSIANS 1:15-20 *First born of all creation.* PAGE 7.

Personal Prayers.

Week Twelve / FRIDAY

MORNING PRAYER

I. THE PSALMS

MORNING PSALM / PS. 130
Out of the depths.
PAGE 8

PSALMS OF THE DAY / PSS. 123, 129, & 137
Laments in captivity.

PSALM 123 / *Too long have we endured the insolent.*

1 To you enthroned on high I lift my eyes,
2 Like servants' eyes
    that watch their master's hand,
Like maidens' eyes
    that watch their mistress' hand,
Our eyes are on the Lord;
    at God's command.

3 Take pity on us, Lord, take pity soon.
For we have had our fill
    of their contempt.
4 Too long have sinners heaped on us
    their scorn,
Too long have we endured
    the insolent.

PSALM 129 / *Upon our backs the plowmen plowed.*

1 "They have oppressed me from my youth,"
    Let Israel declare.
2 "They have oppressed me from my youth,
    But I will not despair."

3 Upon our backs the farmers plowed
    Their furrows deep and long.
4 But God is just, will set us free
    From yokes however strong.

5 May they be scattered in disgrace
    Who hate your people, Lord.
6 Like grass that withers, dies and leaves
    The reapers no reward.

7 Let them return with empty hands,
    With no one there to say:
8 "We bless you in the name of God,
    The Lord bless you today!"

PSALM 137 / *Beside the streams of Babylon, we wept.*

1 We sat beside the streams of Babylon.
We sat and wept when Zion we recalled.
2 We hung our harps
    upon the willow trees.
"A song," our captors cried.
    We were appalled.
3 For their amusement,
    our tormentor's fun,
"A song of Zion, sing for us," they called.

4 How could we sing God's songs
    on foreign soil?
Jerusalem, if ever I forget,
5 Then let my hand be withered
    on my arm.

If I do not remember you, then let
  My tongue be stuck,
    struck dumb within my mouth.
6 No joy be mine, if ever I forget.

7 Remember Edom at Jerusalem?
  "Strip her," they cried,
    "To her foundation stone!"
8 O Babylon, destroyer, you are doomed!
Blest those who pay you back
    for what you've done;
9 Blest those who take your children
    by the neck
And smash their infant heads
    against a stone!

II. Readings & Prayers

WINTER

Friday: 6th Week of the Year
Do more than listen; follow:

1a. Genesis 11:1-9.
  Confusion at Babel.

1b. James 2:14-26.
  Faith without works is dead.

2. Mark 8:34-9:1.
  Take up the cross and follow me.

We babble on with endless talk.
Help us, dear Lord, to walk the walk...

SPRING

Friday: 6th Week of Easter.
On confidence in God:

1. Acts 18:9-18.
  Fear not, I am with you.

2. John 16:20-23.
  Your grief will be turned into joy.

Though we may weep, we shall not fear
Because we know that you are here...

SUMMER

Friday: 20th Week of the Year
Stories of great beauty and power:

1a. Ruth 1:1,3-6,14-16,22.
  Wherever you go, I will go.

1b. Ezekiel 37:1-14.
  The vision of the dry bones.

2. Matthew 22:34-40.
  On these two the whole law is based.

Dead bones that dance, the faith of Ruth:
They give us hope; they give us truth...

FALL

Friday: 33rd Week of the Year
Zeal for God's house cries out:

1a. I Maccabees 4:36-37, 52-59.
  Judas Maccabaeus rededicates the altar.

1b. Revelations 10:8-11.
  Eat the scroll, and prophesy.

2. Luke 19:45-48.
  Jesus cleanses the temple.

Your house of prayer, your temple, Lord,
And we, your church, must be restored...

Meditation. The Lord's Prayer. Intercessions. Personal Prayers.

EVENING PRAYER

Reflections on the Day. Thanksgiving. Reconciliation.

EVENING PSALM / Ps. 51 *David's prayer for forgiveness.* PAGE 8.

CANTICLE OF SIMEON / LUKE 2:29-32 *Lord, let me go in peace.* PAGE 8.

Personal Prayers.

Week Twelve / SATURDAY
MORNING PRAYER

I. THE PSALMS

MORNING PSALM / PS. 141
Like incense let my prayer arise.
PAGE 9

PSALMS OF THE DAY / PSS. 128 & 136
Songs of blessing and gratitude.

PSALM 128 / *Those who fear the Lord are blest.*

1 How blest are you who fear the Lord
  And follow in God's ways.
2 You shall enjoy the bread you eat,
  The blessing labor pays.
You will do well, find happiness,
  And prosper all your days.

3 Your wife is like a fruitful vine;
  At home you have been blest.
Your children are like olive plants;
  At table you are blest.
4 So everyone who fears the Lord
  Will be forever blest.

5 The Lord bless you from Zion's hill,
  To see and share as well
Jerusalem's prosperity,
  To spend your days in health,
6 And live to see your children's children!
  Peace on Israel!

PSALM 136 / *The "Great Hallel"*

"GOD'S FAITHFUL LOVE WILL NEVER END!"
(Repeat this refrain after every couplet.)

1 Give thanks to God, the Lord is good;
2 Give thanks to God above the gods:

3 The Lord of lords our people leads;
4 The Lord alone does wondrous deeds:

5 All wise, God made the heavens high,
6 And spread the earth beneath the sky:

7 It was the Lord who made the lights,
9 The moon and stars to rule the nights:

8 To light the day God made the sun;
10 The Lord took Egypt's first born son:

11 Led Israel from slavery;
12 With outstretched arm God split the sea:

13 With mighty hands God set them free,
14 Drowned Pharaoh's army in the sea:

15 God's people, Israel, were blessed;
16 God led them through the wilderness:

17 God conquered kingdoms
    just for them,
18 Slew many noble kings for them:

19 The king of Amorites was slain;
20 The leader of Bashan was slain:

21 Their lands were taken,
    lands God won,
22 For Israel God's chosen one:

23 God looked on our humility,
24 And saved us from our enemies:

25 God feeds us all, yes, everyone;
26 Come praise the Lord
    who heaven won:

"GOD'S FAITHFUL LOVE WILL NEVER END!"

II. READINGS & PRAYERS

WINTER
SATURDAY: 6TH WEEK OF THE YEAR
The path of faith: from cross to crown:

1a. Hebrews 11:1-7.
   A definition of faith.

1b. James 3:1-10.
   The tongue controls the body.

2. Mark 9:2-13.
   Jesus' transfiguration.

Our fathers' faith accomplished much;
To gain his crown, Christ suffered much...

SPRING
SATURDAY: 6TH WEEK OF EASTER
The word is all, the speaker least:

1. Acts 18:23-28.
   The eloquence of Apollos.

2. John 16:23-28.
   Ask and you shall receive.

O Lord, your word deserves our best;
We give it all, you do the rest...

SUMMER
SATURDAY: 20TH WEEK OF THE YEAR
Lives move us more than words:

1a. Ruth 2:1-11, 4:13-17.
   Boaz weds Ruth, a love story.

1b. Ezekiel 43:1-7.
   A vision of God's glory.

2. Matthew 23:1-12.
   Do as they say, not what they do.

Lord, what we say may well be true;
But louder speaks the work we do...

FALL
SATURDAY: 33RD WEEK OF THE YEAR
At death we think of what's to come:

1a. I Maccabees 6:1-13.
   A king's regrets before he dies..

1b. Revelation 11:4-12.
   Two prophets die and rise again..

2. Luke 20:27-40.
   Life in the age to come..

Like angels, we shall be, Christ said,
The Lord of those alive, not dead...

Meditation. The Lord's Prayer. Intercessions. Personal Prayers.

EVENING PRAYER

Reflections on the Day. Thanksgiving. Reconciliation.

EVENING PSALM / PS. 143 *Lord, do not condemn.* PAGE 9.

SONG OF MOSES / REVELATION 15:3-4 *They all had harps and sang.* PAGE 9.

Personal Prayers.

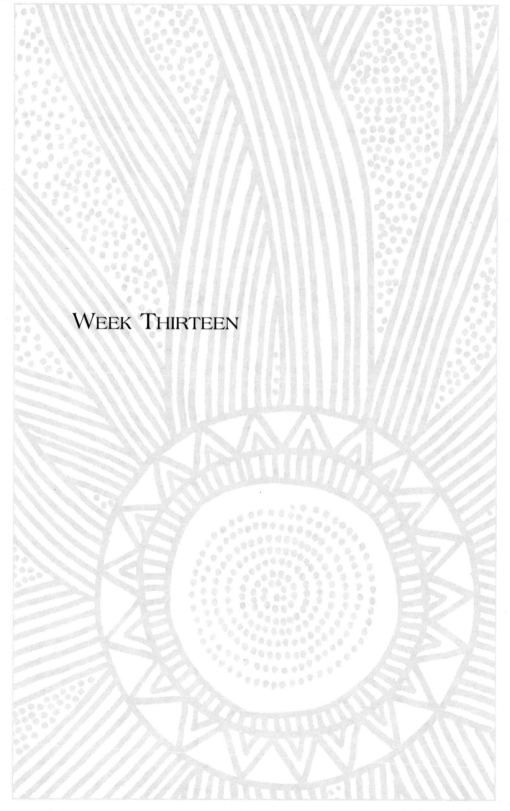

WEEK THIRTEEN

Week Thirteen / SUNDAY
Morning Prayer

I. The Psalms

Morning Psalm / Ps. 95

O my people, now listen to me.

Page 3

Psalms of the Day / Pss. 93 & 103

Psalms for the Feast of Christ the King.

Psalm 93 / *The Lord is King!*

1 The Lord is King, in glory clothed;
The Lord is robed with victory.
The earth stands firm, it shall not move.
2 Your throne as well stands firm to prove
That you are God eternally.

3 The floods have lifted up their voice,
The waves are roaring, crashing, Lord.
4 But mightier than ocean's roar,
Than pounding crashing waves, far more
Are you on high, almighty Lord!

5 Your words are firm, your house is holy,
Lord, you stand forevermore!

Psalm 103 / *Your throne is in the heavens, Lord.*

1 O bless the Lord, my soul!
O bless the Lord!

With all your being bless God's holy name.
2 Remember all the Lord has done for you,
3 God pardons all your sins
and heals your ills,
4 Redeems you from the pit with mercy true.
5 God fills your days with gifts
and faithful love,
And gives you, like an eagle, life anew.

6 The Lord is just, gives justice
to the wronged.
7 God led the way for Moses, Israel.
8 The Lord is merciful and slow to wrath,
Invites us all in faithful love to dwell.
9 The Lord does not accuse,
nor anger nurse,
10 Nor punish us for sin, nor us expel.

11 As high as heaven over earth, so high
Your faithful love for those
who fear you, Lord.
12 As far as east is from the west, so far
Our sin has been removed by you,
O Lord.
13 As parents have compassion
on their child,
So you regard all those who fear you, Lord.

14 You know how we were made,
that we are dust.
15 We are like flowers in the field,
like grass.
16 The winds blow over us
and we are gone.
17 Not so your faithful love, it will not pass.
18 For those who keep
your covenant's decrees,
Your kindness to your children ever lasts.

19 Your throne is in the heavens, Lord, on high.
You rule us all with might, we sing to you.
20 You angels, who obey the Lord's commands,
21 You armies, servants, who God's work must do,
22 All creatures of God's hands throughout the earth,
All bless the Lord! And you, my soul, bless, too.

II. Readings & Prayers

WINTER

7th Sunday of the Year
"Make our hearts like unto thine."

Year A

1. Leviticus 19:1-2,17-18.
   Love your neighbor as yourself.

2. I Corinthians 3:16-23.
   You are Christ's, and Christ is God's.

3. Matthew 5:38-48.
   Be perfect; love your enemies.

Year B

1. Isaiah 43:18-25.
   See: I am doing something new.

2. II Corinthians 1:18-22.
   God's promises come true in Christ.

3. Mark 2:1-12.
   My son, your sins are forgiven.

Year C

1. I Samuel 26:7-13, 22-23.
   David spares the life of Saul.

2. I Corinthians 15:45-49.
   Jesus is the heavenly Adam.

3. Luke 6:27-38.
   Love your enemies; be merciful.

FORGIVING GOD, FOR US TO LOVE
Like you is something new indeed.
For us to love our enemy,
The heart of Christ himself we need.

SPRING

7th Sunday of Easter
The prayer of Christ, and ours.

Year A

1. Acts 1:12-14.
   They gave themselves to constant prayer.

2. I Peter 4:13-16.
   Rejoice to share Christ's sufferings.

3. John 17:1-11.
   I pray for those you gave to me.

Year B

1. Acts 1:15-26.
   They prayed and chose Matthias.

2. I John 4:11-16.
   He who abides in love, abides in God.

3. John 17:11-19.
   May they be one as we are one.

Year C

1. Acts 7:55-60.
   As he was being stoned, he prayed.

2. Revelations 22:12-20.
   I am coming soon: Maranatha.

3. John 17:20-26.
   That all the world may believe.

O FATHER, HELP US PRAY AS JESUS PRAYED:
For all you gave to us, for unity,
Lord, may our prayer be constant, full of joy.
In life, at death, our refuge let it be.

SUMMER
21ST SUNDAY OF THE YEAR.
Of doors, and locks, and keys.

YEAR A

1. Isaiah 22:15, 19-23.
   The key of David I will give him.

2. Romans 11:33-36.
   How inscrutable God's ways!

3. Matthew 16:13-20.
   Jesus gives Peter the keys.

YEAR B

1. Joshua 24:1-2,15-18.
   We will serve the Lord, our God.

2. Ephesians 5:21-32.
   Christ loves the church with spousal love.

3. John 6:60-69.
   You have the words of eternal life.

YEAR C

1. Isaiah 66:18-21.
   I come to gather every nation.

2. Hebrews 12:5-7,11-13.
   God disciplines the beloved.

3. Luke 13:22-30.
   Come in the narrow door.

TO HEAVEN'S HOUSE, YOU ARE THE DOOR.
To Peter, Lord, you gave the key.
A man like us, who loved you much,
You trusted him, and so shall we.

FALL
THE FEAST OF CHRIST THE KING
What kind of King is Christ.

YEAR A

1. Ezekiel 34:11-12, 15-17.
   I will tend my sheep.

2. I Corinthians 15:20-28.
   Christ must reign that God be all in all.

3. Matthew 25:31-46.
   He will sit upon his royal throne.

YEAR B

1. Daniel 7:13-14.
   His kingship shall not be destroyed.

2. Revelation 1:5-8.
   Christ, the ruler of the kings of earth.

3. John 18:33-37.
   My kingdom is not here.

YEAR C

1. II Samuel 5:1-3.
   They anointed David king.

2. Colossians 1:12-20.
   The kingdom of God's Son.

3. Luke 23:35-43.
   When you enter on your reign.

LORD, ONCE YOU FLED FROM BEING KING.
But on the cross, at last we knew:
The Shepherd King had found the lost;
We are your subjects, find us too.

Meditation. The Lord's Prayer. Intercessions. Personal Prayers.

EVENING PRAYER

Reflections on the Day. Prayer for Forgiveness.

EVENING PSALM / PS. 23 *The Lord will give me rest.* PAGE 3.

CANTICLE OF MARY / LUKE 1:46-55 *Behold the handmaid of the Lord.* PAGE 3.

Personal Prayers.

Week Thirteen / MONDAY
MORNING PRAYER

I. THE PSALMS

MORNING PSALM / PS. 24
Let the King of glory in.
PAGE 4

PSALMS OF THE DAY / PSS. 124 & 144
Songs of triumph over enemies.

PSALM 124 / *Had not the Lord been on our side.*

1 Had not the Lord been on our side,
  Let Israel speak thus,
2 Had not the Lord been on our side,
  When people stormed at us,
3 They would have swallowed us alive,
  In rage engulfing us.
4 The waters would have swept aside
  And drowned the lot of us.

5 The seething waters would have swept
  The mass of us beneath.
6 But praise the Lord, who would not let
  Them tear us with their teeth.
7 We were like birds entrapped in nets;
  They broke and we are free!
8 Our hope is in the Lord who yet
  Rules earth and sky and sea.

PSALM 144 / *To God who gave victory.*

8,11 LORD, RESCUE ME FROM FOREIGNERS
WHO LIE AND SWEAR TO IT, O LORD.

1 All praise be to the Lord, my rock,
  Who trains my arms, my hands for war.
2 My fortress and my faithful one,
  My haven and my savior,
  The shield I trust, the one who makes
  The nations mine forevermore.

3 Lord what are we that you should care,
  These mortals that you think of them?
4 A puff of wind, they are no more;
  Their days pass by like shadows dim.

5 Let heaven open; Lord, come down;
  Let lightning flash from sea to sea.
6 Let mountains tremble at your touch;
  Your arrows rout my enemy.
7 Reach down your hand from heaven high,
  From raging waters rescue me.

9 A new song I shall sing to you
  Upon my harp, for you, my Lord.
10 To God who gives the victory,
  Who rescued David from the sword.

12 Our sons shall be like sturdy trees;
  Like pillars carved, our daughters stand.
13 Our storehouse full for every need,
  Our flocks in thousands fill the land.
  Our fertile fields stretch end to end;
  Our cattle fed by caring hands.

14 Let no invasion break the peace,
  No exile, outcry in the square.
15 How blest the people of the Lord;
  How blest are all within God's care.

II. Readings & Prayers

WINTER

MONDAY: 7TH WEEK OF THE YEAR
The character and power of wisdom:

1a. Sirach 1:1-10.
All wisdom comes from the Lord.

1b. James 3:13-18.
True wisdom is humble, innocent.

2. Mark 9:14-29.
Jesus exorcises an evil spirit.

May we be wise, and trust in prayer;
To conquer evil everywhere...

SPRING

MONDAY: 7TH WEEK OF EASTER
Let us pray for the Spirit to come:

1. Acts 19:1-8.
The baptism of the Holy Spirit.

2. John 16:29-33.
Be brave; I have conquered the world.

Your Spirit gives us courage, Lord.
With you, we too shall win the world...

SUMMER

MONDAY: 21ST WEEK OF THE YEAR
Praise and condemnation:

1a. I Thessalonians 1:1-5, 11-12.
Your faith in God is famous.

1b. II Thessalonians 2:1-3, 14-16.
It is for his kingdom you suffer.

2. Matthew 23:13-22.
Woe to you, blind leaders.

How welcome, praise in times adverse.
How terrible, to hear God's curse...

FALL

MONDAY: 34TH WEEK OF THE YEAR
Those who give all are worthy:

1a. Daniel 1:1-6, 8-20.
Daniel and the three young men.

1b. Revelations 14:1-5.
I saw the lamb, I heard the harps.

2. Luke 21:1-4.
The widow who gave every penny.

Lord, who is worthy of the Lamb?
These men, this widow; pray I am...

Meditation. The Lord's Prayer. Intercessions. Personal Prayers.

EVENING PRAYER

Reflections on the Day. Prayer for Forgiveness.

EVENING PSALM / PS. 4 *I go to sleep in peace.* PAGE 4.

CANTICLE OF ZACHARY / LUKE 1:68-79 *Prepare the way of the Lord.* PAGE 4.

Personal Prayers.

Week Thirteen / TUESDAY
MORNING PRAYER

I. THE PSALMS

MORNING PSALM / PS. 5
At dawn I pray to you.
PAGE 5

PSALMS OF THE DAY / PSS. 134 & 145

Blessing, Reassurance, Praise.

PSALM 134 / *A blessing from Zion.*

¹ Bless the Lord all you servants of God,
Who stand watch
in the house of the Lord.

² Lift your hands to the holy on high!
³ And may God who made heaven and earth,
Send a blessing from Zion on high.

PSALM 145 / *The Lord is near to all who call.*

¹ I will extol you, God, my King,
Forever bless your name.
² Each day I lift my arms to bless,
And ever praise your name.

³ Lord, you are great, and greatly praised,
Immeasurably great.
⁴ From age to age, all praise your works,
Your mighty deeds relate.

⁵ Your majesty and glory, Lord,
Your deeds will be my song.
⁶ O mighty King, they all shall sing,
When I your praise prolong.

⁷ Your goodness all will celebrate;
Your justice shall resound.
⁸ For you are kind, to anger slow;
Your faithful love abounds.

⁹ Your mercy is for all you made;
Lord, you are good to all.
¹⁰ Your works will ever bring you praise
From faithful servants all.

¹¹ They speak of might and majesty;
Your glory they proclaim.
¹² They show to all your mighty deeds,
The glory of your reign.

¹³ Your reign is an eternal reign;
It shall endure, O Lord.
For you are gracious in your works,
And faithful in your word.

¹⁴ The Lord supports the weak who fall;
God makes the crooked straight.
¹⁵ In hope, all eyes look to the Lord,
Whose food is never late.

¹⁶ You open wide your hands to all
To satisfy their needs.
¹⁷ Lord, you are just in all your ways,
And kind in all your deeds.

¹⁸ The Lord is near to all who call
In true sincerity.
¹⁹ God fills the hopes of all who fear;
The savior hears their plea.

²⁰ God watches over all who love;
The wicked God will shame.
²¹ My mouth will ever praise you, Lord;
All: ever bless God's name!

II. Readings & Prayers

WINTER

Tuesday: 7th Week of the Year
If we would serve the Lord:

1a. Sirach 2:1-11.
Prepare for trials.

1b. James 4:1-10.
Conflict comes from greed and pride.

2. Mark 9:30-37.
Jesus predicts his passion.

May we put greed and pride aside;
To serve the Lord, prepare to die...

SPRING

Tuesday: 7th Week of Easter
Thoughts near the end of service:

1. Acts 20:17-27.
If only I can finish my race.

2. John 17:1-11.
Christ's priestly prayer revisited.

The finish line: we're nearly there;
Like Christ, like Paul, we close with prayer...

SUMMER

Tuesday: 21st Week of the Year
More warnings, more dangers:

1a. I Thessalonians 2:1-8.
We shared with you our very lives.

1b. II Thessalonians 2:1-3, 14-16.
Let no one seduce you.

2. Matthew 23:23-26.
Woe to you, blind guides.

Beware of those who seek to scare;
Beware of frauds: seek help in prayer...

FALL

Tuesday: 34rd Week of the Year
The day of judgment is at hand:

1a. Daniel 2:31-45.
Daniel interprets the king's dream.

1b. Revelation 14:14-19.
Now is the time to reap the harvest.

2. Luke 21:5-11.
The day will come when all is gone.

The end of all earth's power is near;
The wrath of God let people fear...

Meditation. The Lord's Prayer. Intercessions. Personal Prayers.

Evening Prayer

Reflections on the Day. Prayer for Forgiveness.

Evening Psalm / Ps. 6 *My bed is wet with tears.* Page 5.

The Christ Hymn / Philippians 2:6-11 *The mind of Christ.* Page 5.

Personal Prayers.

Week Thirteen / WEDNESDAY
MORNING PRAYER

I. THE PSALMS

MORNING PSALM / PS. 101
A royal pledge.
PAGE 6

PSALM OF THE DAY / PS. 139
A prayerful meditation on the mystery of God.

PSALM 139 / *I cannot fathom it, this mystery..*

1 O Lord, you know me well;
  you tested me.
2 If I sit down, if I stand up, you see.
 You know my inmost thoughts
  from far away.
3 My comings and my goings
  you survey.
 You know my ways; you know
  my every word
4 Before it leaves my lips,
  before it's heard.
5 You are behind me and ahead of me;
 On every side I feel your hand on me.
6 It is beyond me, Lord,
  too much for me.
 I cannot fathom it, this mystery.

7 Where could I go to be away from you?
 Where could I flee
  the ever present you?
8 If I ascend to heaven you are there.
 If I descend below I find you there.
9 If I take wing and seek the farthest sea,
10 When I arrive I find you there for me,
 Your hand upholding me,
  you at my side.
11 I think: "When darkness comes,
  then I can hide."
12 But darkness is not dark for you,
  but light;
 To you the two are one,
  the day, the night.

13 You made me,
  knit me in my mother's womb.
14 How wonderful! I praise the Lord to whom
 This awesome work,
  like all your works, I owe.
15 As I was being made,
  you watched me grow.
 At night you wove the fabric of my life.
16 Your eyes beheld the stages of my life,
 Recorded in your book
  before they passed.
17 How deep is your design, O Lord,
  how vast!
18 Beyond my power to count,
  like endless sand.
 I finish, but rest ever in your hand.

19 If only you would slay my enemy!
 You murderers,
  stay far away from me!
20 They cry to you deceitfully, O Lord.
 Your enemies are false,
  their tongue a sword.
21 O Lord, you know I hate
  those who hate you.
22 Your enemies are mine;
  I hate them, too.
23 Lord, test me once again; examine me.
 And see my heart, my thoughts,
  and hear my plea:
24 Lord, let no idol hold me in its sway;
 But guide me in your everlasting way.

II. READINGS & PRAYERS

WINTER

WEDNESDAY:* 7TH WEEK OF THE YEAR
The Christian golden rule:

1a. Sirach 4:11-19.
    God loves those who love wisdom.

1b. James 4:13-17.
    To plan ahead is arrogant.

2. Mark 9:38-40.
    Anyone not against us, is with us.

Inclusive Lord, you gather all
Within your love, to hear your call...

SPRING

WEDNESDAY: 7TH WEEK OF EASTER
Final words from shepherds to shepherds:

1a. Acts 20:28-38.
    Shepherd the flock, the church of God.

2. John 17:11-19.
    I guarded them, not one was lost.

O Father, guard us to the end;
Bless every shepherd that you send...

SUMMER

WEDNESDAY: 21ST WEEK OF THE YEAR
Pet-peeves:

1a. I Thessalonians 2:9-13.
    We worked day and night for you.

1b. II Thessalonians 3:6-10, 16-18.
    Those who do not work should not eat.

2. Matthew 23:27-32.
    Woe to the hypocrites

Who angered Christ? The hypocrite.
Who got to Paul? The lazy did...

FALL

WEDNESDAY: 34TH WEEK OF THE YEAR
Visions, warnings, more suspense:

1a. Daniel 5:1-6, 13-17, 23-28.
    The hand wrote: Mene, Tekel, Peres.

1b. Revelation 15:1-4.
    The song of Moses and the Lamb.

2. Luke 21:12-19.
    By patient endurance you will survive.

The mystery grows more intense.
Lord, you will be our sole defense...

Meditation. The Lord's Prayer. Intercessions. Personal Prayers.

EVENING PRAYER

Reflections on the Day. Prayer for Forgiveness.

EVENING PSALM / PS. 13 *Let me have hope.* PAGE 6.

THE LOVE OF GOD / ROMANS 8:35-39 *Who can be against us?* PAGE 6.

Personal Prayers.

*NOTE: If today is Ash Wednesday (see Calendar, page 234) the Readings for today and the rest of the week are on page 225.

Week Thirteen / THURSDAY
MORNING PRAYER

I. THE PSALMS

MORNING PSALM / PS. 100
Praise God from whom all blessings flow.
PAGE 7

PSALMS OF THE DAY / PSS. 138 & 147
Two calls to action in the service of the Lord.

PSALM 138 / *The Lord will do all things for me.*

1 With all my heart I praise you, Lord;
  I sing before the gods above.
2 And bowing to your temple, Lord,
  I praise your name and faithful love.
  For you have lifted high, O Lord,
  Your name and promise from above.

3 When I cried out you answered, Lord;
  Your strength and courage came to me.
4 The kings of earth shall praise you, Lord;
  They heard your word, sing joyfully:
5 How great the glory of the Lord!
  How perfect God in majesty!

6 Though you are high, you look below.
  You see afar, reach out to me.
7 You save me, Lord, from every foe.
8 The Lord will do all things for me.
  Your faithful love will never go;
  Abandon not your work in me.

PSALM 147 / *How good it is to sing God's praise.*

1 SING ALLELUIA, PRAISE THE LORD!

How good it is to sing God's praise!
3 How sweet it is to chant this hymn!
  The Lord rebuilds Jerusalem,
  And gathers Israel's exiles in.

4 The one who counts and names the stars,
3 Now tends their wounds
      and mends their hearts.
5 The Lord is great, in power vast,
  In wisdom past our grasp and art.

6 The Lord lifts up, sustains the poor;
  Casts down the wicked to the ground.
7 So sing a song of thanks to God;
  And with your harps make joyful sound.

8 God covers heaven with the clouds,
  Gives rain to earth and grass to peaks.
9 The Lord gives animals their food,
  The raven's brood the food it seeks.

10 God does not prize
      the horse's strength,
  Takes no delight in runner's speed.
11 Delights in those who fear the Lord,
  Whose faithful love they seek in need.

12 O praise your Lord, Jerusalem,
13 Who made your gates a safe retreat.
  Who blest your children gathered there,
14 Who gives you peace and finest wheat.

¹⁵ The Lord sends out commands to earth;
God's words fly swiftly to their task.
¹⁶ God blankets earth with snow like wool,
And strews the earth with frost like ash.

¹⁷ God showers all with hail like crumbs;
They freeze, for who can stand the cold?
¹⁸ God speaks, the winds begin to thaw,
The waters melt. Let all behold!

¹⁹ To Jacob God proclaimed the word;
To Israel God gave the law.
²⁰ No other nation was so blest;
A law like ours they never saw.

SING ALLELUIA, PRAISE THE LORD!

II. READINGS & PRAYERS

WINTER

THURSDAY: 7TH WEEK OF THE YEAR
Procrastinators go to hell:

1a. Sirach 5:1-8.
Do not delay conversion.

1b. James 5:1-6.

A wage withheld cries out to God.

2. Mark 9:41-50.
Eradicate the source of evil.

To sacrifice an arm, an eye?
Give courage, Lord, the price is high...

SPRING

THURSDAY: 7TH WEEK OF EASTER
The universal call of Christ:

1. Acts 22:30, 23:6-11.
You must testify to me in Rome.

2. John 17:20-26.
That all may be one, as we are one.

In Rome, the center of their world:
The flag of Christ must be unfurled...

SUMMER

THURSDAY: 21TH WEEK OF THE YEAR
What we know, and what we don't:

1a. I Thessalonians 3:7-13.
Our thanks and blessings on you all.

1b. I Corinthians 1:1-9.
God will strengthen you to the end.

2. Matthew 24:42-51.
Stay awake, you do not know the day.

We know not when you, Lord, are due;
But know that we can count on you...

FALL

THURSDAY: 34RD WEEK OF THE YEAR
A faithful family, a faithless city:

1a. Daniel 6:12-28.
Daniel in the lions' den.

1b. Revelation 18:1-2, 21-23; 19:1-3, 9.
Babylon the great has fallen, Alleluia!

2. Luke 21:20-28.
Jerusalem shall fall; the end is near.

Gone Babylon, Jerusalem?
Our world, then, is soon to end...

Meditation. The Lord's Prayer. Intercessions. Personal Prayers.

EVENING PRAYER

Reflections on the Day. Prayer for Forgiveness.

EVENING PSALM / PS. 131 *A child in your mother's arms.* PAGE 7.

THE UNSEEN GOD / COLOSSIANS 1:15-20 *First born of all creation.* PAGE 7.

Personal Prayers.

Week Thirteen / FRIDAY
MORNING PRAYER

I. THE PSALMS

MORNING PSALM / PS. 130
Out of the depths.
PAGE 8

PSALMS OF THE DAY / PSS. 140 & 142
Cries for help against my enemies.

PSALM 140 / *Let coals of fire rain down on them.*

2 Lord, rescue me from evildoers
   Dealing violence.
3 Their minds are full of wicked schemes,
   Their plans for war intense.
4 Their tongues are snakes,
        their poisoned lips
   Leave us without defense.

5 Lord keep me from their wicked hands;
   From plots my life protect.
6 A hidden trap to trip my feet
   The arrogant have set.
 Beside my path they planted lures
   To catch me in their net.

7 I say to you: you are my God.
   Lord, listen to my plea.
8 In war you were
        my saving strength,
   There you protected me.
9 Let not my foes get their desire,
   Let not their plans succeed.

10 Instead, let them be covered with
   The poison of their lips.
11 Let coals of fire rain down on them;
   Let them be cast in pits,
   To never rise again; bereft,
   As slanderers befits.

12 The violent shall not escape
   The evil they pursue.
13 God's justice comes to those in need,
   I know the Lord is true.
14 The just shall praise your name, O Lord;
   The just shall dwell with you.

PSALM 142 / *Listen Lord, for I am low indeed.*
1 The prayer of David when he was in the cave.

2 I call aloud for mercy, Lord,
   Full voiced I cry, hear me.
3 My troubles are before you, Lord,
   Before you is my plea.

4 My spirit ebbs away within,
   You know my way, you see.
 Along the path I travel on
   They set a trap for me.

5 See, Lord, no one is at my side,
   No friend to stand by me.
 There is no place where I can hide,
   No one to care for me.

6 I cry to you my refuge, Lord,
   For you are all I have.
 Among the living you, O Lord,
   Alone are all I have.

7 O listen to my cry to you
   For I am low indeed.
 Save me, my enemies pursue,
   They are too strong for me.

8 That I may praise your name, O Lord
   From prison set me free.
 The just will come and see, O Lord,
   That you were good to me.

II. READINGS & PRAYERS

WINTER

FRIDAY: 7TH WEEK OF THE YEAR
Friends and spouses suffer trials:

1a. Sirach 6:5-17.
    A faithful friend is beyond price.

1b. James 5:9-12.
    As models in suffering take the prophets.

2. Mark 10:1-12.
    What God has joined let no one separate.

At home, O Lord, and in your house,
Are two dear friends: our God, our spouse...

SPRING

FRIDAY: 7TH WEEK OF EASTER.
Christ foretells Peter's life and death:

1. Acts 25:13-21.
    Roman justice serves Paul's purposes.

2. John 21:15-19.
    Jesus commissions Peter.

"Because you love me, feed my sheep;
Your life, a shepherd's, till you sleep..."

SUMMER

FRIDAY: 21ST WEEK OF THE YEAR
God's wisdom versus the world's:

1a. I Thessalonians 4:1-8.
    God calls us to holiness.

1b. I Corinthians 1:17-25.
    God's folly is better than worldly wisdom.

2. Matthew 25:1-13.
    Five were wise and five were foolish.

How tell what's wise from foolishness?
Accept God's call to holiness...

FALL

FRIDAY: 34TH WEEK OF THE YEAR
See the trees, read the signs:

1a. Daniel 7:2-14.
    First beasts, and then the Son of Man.

1b. Revelation 20:1-4, 11-21:2.
    I saw a new Jerusalem.

2. Luke 21:29-33.
    Know the reign of God is near.

Lord, ready us to see that day.
Your word will never pass away...

Meditation. The Lord's Prayer. Intercessions. Personal Prayers.

EVENING PRAYER

Reflections on the Day. Prayer for Forgiveness.

EVENING PSALM / PS. 51 *David's prayer for forgiveness.* PAGE 8.

CANTICLE OF SIMEON / LUKE 2:29-32 *Lord, let me go in peace.* PAGE 8.

Personal Prayers.

Week Thirteen / SATURDAY
MORNING PRAYER

I. THE PSALMS

MORNING PSALM / PS. 141
Like incense let my prayer arise.
PAGE 9

PSALMS OF THE DAY / PSS. 148, 149, & 150
Ending on a high note:

PSALM 148 / *Let every creature praise God's name.*

¹ SING ALLELUIA, PRAISE THE LORD!

Let all in heaven praise the Lord.
    You on the heights, you praise God, too.
² Let all the angels praise the Lord,
    Among the hosts, sing praises, too.

³ The sun and moon shall praise the Lord,
    The shining stars will praise God, too.
⁴ The clouds in heaven praise the Lord,
    The waters there sing praises, too.

⁵ Let every creature praise God's name,
    Who at God's word saw light of day,
⁶ Who stay in place forevermore;
    God's word shall never pass away.

⁷ O praise the Lord all you on earth,
    All creatures of the sea and land,
⁸ The snow and hail, the fire and smoke,
    The wind that follows God's command.

⁹ The mountains and the hills praise God,
    Trees bearing fruit, and cedars tall.
¹⁰ All beasts on earth, the tame and wild,
    Praise God all things that fly or crawl.

¹¹ All rulers, peoples of the earth,
¹² All men and women, young and old,
¹³ Let everybody praise God's name;
    That name alone must be extolled.

God's glory covers heaven, earth.
¹⁴ Our people's strength is lifted high.
You loyal servants, close to God,
O Israel, praise God on high!

SING ALLELUIA, PRAISE THE LORD!

PSALM 149 / *With timbrel, harp, and melody.*

¹ SING ALLELUIA, PRAISE THE LORD!

A song, a new one, for the Lord,
    With all the faithful gathered, sing!
² Let Israel rejoice in God,
    Let Zion's children praise their King.

³ And praise God's name with dancing, too,
    With timbrel, harp, and melody!
⁴ The Lord delights in people's joy.
    God gives the lowly victory.

⁵ So let the faithful celebrate,
    And at their feast let joy preside.
⁶ The praise of God be on their lips,
    And two edged swords be at their side.

⁷ Their task: to pay the nations back,
    To punish is their destiny.
⁸ Their kings and princes put in chains,
⁹ To carry out the Lord's decree.

It is your people's glory, Lord,

SING ALLELUIA, PRAISE THE LORD!

PSALM 150 / *Let trumpets blast, let cymbals crash!*

¹ SING ALLELUIA, PRAISE THE LORD!

Here in the temple, praise the Lord!
In heaven too, beyond the sky.
² For deeds of power praise the Lord,
For majesty that reigns on high.

³ With blasts of trumpets praise the Lord,
With harp and lyre play for God.
⁴ With timbrels, dancing, praise the Lord,
With strings and pipes give praise to God.

⁵ Let cymbals crash and ring for God!
Triumphant cymbals, praise the Lord!
Let all that breathe sing praise to God,
Sing alleluia, praise the Lord.

SING ALLELUIA, PRAISE THE LORD!

II. READINGS & PRAYERS

WINTER
SATURDAY: 7TH WEEK OF THE YEAR
We are God's children now:

1a. Sirach 17:1-15.
    The Lord made us in God's image.

1b. James 5:13-20.
    The prayer of the just is powerful.

2. Mark 10:13-16.
   Let the children come to me.

To be a child, Lord, at your knee,
No greater grace can come to me...

SPRING
SATURDAY: 7TH WEEK OF EASTER.
Two missions accomplished:

1. Acts 28:16-20, 30-31.
   Paul's life ends, preaching in Rome.

2. John 21:20-25.
   John's gospel ends; his work is done.

O Lord, now let the Spirit come
To live in us; let all be one...

SUMMER
SATURDAY: 21ST WEEK OF THE YEAR
The industrious reliable servant:

1a. I Thessalonians 4:9-12.
    God has taught you how to love.

1b. I Corinthians 1:26-31.
    Let those who boast boast of the Lord.

2. Matthew 25:14-30.
    The parable of the talents.

You gave a thousand from your store;
Let me bring you a thousand more...

FALL
SATURDAY: 34TH WEEK OF THE YEAR
Be on guard against the world's ways:

1a. Daniel 7:15-27.
    Then all shall serve the Lord.

1b. Revelation 22:1-7.
    Remember, I am coming soon.

2. Luke 21:34-36.
    The day of which I speak will come.

We pray for strength that we may stand
Before the Lord, the Son of Man...

Meditation. The Lord's Prayer. Intercessions. Personal Prayers.

EVENING PRAYER

Reflections on the Day. Prayer for Forgiveness.

EVENING PSALM / PS. 143 *Lord, do not condemn.* PAGE 9.

SONG OF MOSES / REVELATION 15:3-4 *They all had harps and sang.* PAGE 9.

Personal Prayers.

APPENDICES

Seasonal Supplements

I. Christmas Season Sundays

Sunday after Christmas (or Dec. 30):
The Feast of the Holy Family.

Psalms: Pages 80-90 (See Calendar).

Readings & Prayers:
Family values exemplified:

Years A, B, & C

1. Sirach 3:2-6,12-14.
   *The rewards of those
   who honor parents.*

2. Colossians 3:12-21.
   Bear with each other; put on love.

3. A. Matthew 2:13-15,19-23.
      The holy family flees to Egypt.

   B. Luke 2:22-40.
      They consecrate their son to God.

   C. Luke 2:41-52.
      They find Jesus in the temple.

O Lord, you chose a family
Like ours in which to grow in grace;
May families be more like yours
In every way and every place.

Sunday between January 1 & 6:
   2nd Sunday of Christmas.

Psalms: Pages 96-104 (See Calendar).

Readings & Prayers:
The ways God comes to mankind:

Years A, B, & C.

1. Sirach 24:1-4,8-12.
   Wisdom lives in God's people.

2. Ephesians 1:3-6,15-18.
   In Christ we all are blessed.

3. John 1:1-18.
   In the beginning was the Word.

You chose to dwell with us, O Lord
In wisdom, in a body, too,
And every blessing that you bring.
We give you thanks; we welcome you.

II. Christmas Season Weekdays

December 18: *(When not Sunday.)*

Psalms: Those from the day canceled out
by the 4th Sunday of Advent: Pages 64-74
(See Calendar).

Readings & Prayers:

The Prophets foretell:

1. Jeremiah 23:5-8.
   A virtuous son of David.

2. Matthew 1:18-24.
   A virgin that shall bear a child.

A virgin mother and a son:
The promises of things to come...

January 8: 2nd day after Epiphany

Psalms: Those canceled from the
3rd Week of Advent: Pages 48-56 (See
Calendar).

Readings & Prayers:
What the love of God means:

1. I John 4:7-10.
   God is love.

2. Mark 6:34-44.
   Jesus feeds five thousand.

To give us life you sent your Son;
Good Father, may your will be done...

JANUARY 9: 3RD DAY AFTER EPIPHANY

PSALMS: See January 8 or Calendar.

READINGS & PRAYERS:
He came to show the way:

1. I John 4:11-18.
   Abide in love, abide in God.

2. Mark 6:45-52.
   Jesus walks on water: Peter too.

With you, Lord Jesus, at our side,
In faith and love we shall abide...

JANUARY 10: 4TH DAY AFTER EPIPHANY

PSALMS: See January 8 or Calendar.

READINGS & PRAYERS:
Christ our brother brings good news:

1. I John 4:19-5:4.
   God's children love each other.

2. Luke 4:14-22.
   A year of favor from the Lord!

You bring good news from God above;
You fill us with your joy and love...

JANUARY 11: 5TH DAY AFTER EPIPHANY

PSALMS: See January 8 or Calendar.

READINGS & PRAYERS:
How to come to life:

1. I John 5:5-13.
   Believe that Jesus is God's son.

2. Luke 5:12-16.
   Jesus cures a leper.

The world cries out to you:
Lord Jesus, cure us, too...

JANUARY 12: 6TH DAY AFTER EPIPHANY

PSALMS: See January 8 or Calendar.

READINGS & PRAYERS:
Working together in Christ:

1. I John 5:14-21.
   God hears us whenever we ask.

2. John 3:22-30.
   Jesus begins to baptize.

You work in all: the great, the least;
You are the groom, it is your feast...

SEASONAL SUPPLEMENTS *(continued)*

III. THE 8TH WEEK OF THE YEAR

This week will occur in about a third of the years; it may fall into the Winter or Summer cycles. See the Calendar on page 234.

SUNDAY: 8TH WEEK OF THE YEAR

PSALMS: Page 173.

READINGS & PRAYERS:
On trust in God, mistrust of self:

YEAR A

1. Isaiah 49:14-15.
   I will never forget you.

2. I Corinthians 4:1-5.
   Stop passing judgment.

3. Matthew 6:24-34.
   Stop worrying.

YEAR B

1. Hosea 2:16-17, 21-22.
   I will espouse you forever.

2. II Corinthians 3:1-6.
   Our only credit comes from God.

3. Mark 2:18-22.
   Use new wineskins for new wine.

YEAR C

1. Sirach 27:4-7.

   Praise no man before he speaks.

2. I Corinthians 15:54-58.
   O death, where is your victory?

3. Luke 6:39-45.
   Each man speaks from the heart.

YOUR PEOPLE, LORD, ARE RADIANT!
We shall not worry, we shall trust.
But teach us, Lord, to mind our tongues:
To speak the truth, if speak we must.

MONDAY: 8TH WEEK OF THE YEAR

PSALMS: Page 176.

PSALMS & READINGS:
A message of hope:

1a. Sirach 17:19-27.
    Return to God who will forgive.

1b. I Peter 1:3-9.
    Rejoice in God's mercy.

2. Mark 10:17-27.
   With God all things are possible.

How hard it is, you know, O Lord;
To leave all things for your reward...

TUESDAY: 8TH WEEK OF THE YEAR

PSALMS: Page 178.

READINGS & PRAYERS:
Promises to the persecuted:

1a. Sirach 35:1-12.
    True religion is living a good life.

1b. I Peter 1:10-16.
    The prophets spoke for our sake.

2. Mark 10:28-31.
   My followers shall have eternal life.

O Lord, our confidence in you
Remains unshaken, ever true...

WEDNESDAY:* 8TH WEEK OF THE YEAR

PSALMS: Page 180.

READINGS & PRAYERS:
Jesus knew what lay ahead:

1a. Sirach 36:1, 5-6, 10-17.
    There is no god but you.

1b. I Peter 1:18-25.
    Ransomed by the blood of Christ.

2. Mark 10:32-45.
   Jesus predicts his passion.

O Lamb of God, with open eye
You went to Calvary to die...

*Note: If this is Ash Wednesday, the Readings & Prayers for today and the rest of the week are on the facing page (225).

Thursday: 8th Week of the Year

Psalms: Page 182.

Readings & Prayers:
We need to call to mind:

1a. Sirach 42:15-25.
Now will I recall God's works.

1b. I Peter 2:2-5, 9-12.
You are a chosen race.

2. Mark 10:46-52.
Jesus cures the blind.

How special you have made us, Lord!
With thanks and joy we greet your word...

Friday: 8th Week of the Year

Psalms: Page 184.

Readings & Prayers:
Some historical perspective:

1a. Sirach 44:9-13.
Remembering our ancestors.

1b. I Peter 4:7-13.
Be faithful; our end is near.

2. Mark 11:11-26.
Put your trust in God.

Midst trials we put our trust in you;
We work and pray that we be true...

Saturday: 8th Week of the Year

Psalms: Page 186.

Readings & Prayers:
Concluding admonitions:

1a. Sirach 51:12-20.
I sought wisdom; she came to me.

1b. Jude 17:20-25.
Persevere in love.

2. Mark 11:27-33.
Jesus outwits his enemies.

We do not question you, O Lord,
Your patient wisdom, our reward...

IV. The First Four Days of Lent

These days occur in the last week of the Winter Cycle, preceding the 1st Sunday of Lent. They use the Psalms of that week, whichever week it is, and the following Readings & Prayers:

Ash Wednesday
A call to fast, pray, and give alms:

1. Joel 2:12-18.
Rend your hearts, not your garments.

2. II Corinthians 5:20-6:2.
Be reconciled to God, now!

3. Matthew 6:1-6, 16-18.
Do not be like the hypocrites.

Lord, watch us; let us be on guard:
The road is long, the way is hard...

Thursday after Ash Wednesday
Decision time:

1. Deuteronomy 30:15-20.
I set before you life and death.

2. Luke 9:22-25.
Take up the cross and follow me.

Show me the way, I choose the cross;
For me, O Lord, all else is loss...

Friday after Ash Wednesday
God looks for justice and mercy:

1. Isaiah 58:1-9.
This is the fasting that I wish.

2. Matthew 9:14-15.
Why do your disciples not fast?

The time has come; the groom is gone.
Now we must fast, await the dawn...

Saturday after Ash Wednesday
Promises to the faithful:

1. Isaiah 58:9-14.
Then light shall rise for you.

2. Luke 5:27-32.
I came to serve the sick.

Salvation, health shall come from you;
We pray for strength to follow you...

Special Feasts Supplement

There are 8 feasts ("solemnities") whose special readings replace those of the day on which they fall. If they fall on a Sunday, they are transferred to the previous Saturday. The Psalms are always those of the day on which they are celebrated. The following are the Readings & Prayers:

March 19: Feast of St. Joseph,
Husband of Mary, Foster Father of Jesus.
The protector of the universal church.

1. II Samuel 7:4-5, 12-16.
   Tell David: your heir shall build my house

2. Romans 4:13-22.
   Abraham believed, so became a father

3. Matthew 1:16-24.
   Joseph did as the Lord directed.

A faithful, just, and holy man
You chose to guard your family;
His care and love be with us still
To guard the church, our family.

March 25: Annunciation of the Lord
The Incarnation of the Son of God.

1. Isaiah 7:10-14.
   The virgin shall conceive Emmanuel.

2. Hebrews 10:4-10.
   I come to do your will.

3. Luke 1:26-38.
   Let it be done to me as you say.

Hail Mary, highly favored one!
The Lord is with you, you are blest,
For at your word, the Word was fleshed,
The heavens sang, and earth was blest.

June 24: Birth of John the Baptizer
"No man born of woman is greater than John." Luke 7:24

1. Jeremiah 1:4-10.
   In the womb I knew you.

2. I Peter 1:8-12.
   They prophesied a favor meant for you.

3. Luke 1:5-17.
   Your wife will bear a son: call him John.

Lord, it was he whom you called great;
He said that he was but a voice.
"Prepare the way! Repent!" he cried.
We hear him still, and still rejoice.

June 29: Feast of Sts.. Peter & Paul
Twin pillars of the Christian church.

1. Acts 3:1-10.
   No gold have I, but what I have I give.

2. Galatians 1:11-20.
   God called me to reveal his son.

3. John 21:15-19.
   Jesus said to him: feed my sheep.

Two mighty sinners, called by you
To feed your lambs, to feed your sheep.
We owe them life; we follow them;
Lord, may our love, like theirs, be deep.

SPECIAL FEASTS SUPPLEMENT (*continued*)

AUGUST 15: THE ASSUMPTION OF MARY
The Queen is at your hand.

1. Revelations 12:1-6, 10.
   A place had been prepared for her.

2. I Corinthians 15:20-26.
   All will come to life in order.

3. Luke 1:39-56.
   My soul proclaims the greatness of the Lord

Prayer: *Salve Regina*, page 228.

NOVEMBER 1: FEAST OF ALL SAINTS
We believe in the Communion of Saints.

1. Revelations 7:2-4, 9-14.
   I saw before me a huge crowd.

2. I John 3:1-3.
   We are God's children now.

3. Matthew 5:1-12.
   Blest are they, the reign of God is theirs.

O blest communion, family divine,
We feebly struggle, you in glory shine.
Yet we are one, within the Lord's design,
Alleluia, Alleluia!

DECEMBER 8: IMMACULATE CONCEPTION
O Mary, conceived without sin.

1. Genesis 3:9-15, 20.
   I put enmity between you and the woman.

2. Ephesians 1:3-6, 11-12.
   God chose us before the world began.

3. Luke 1:26-38.
   The Lord is with you, blest are you.

Prayer: *Alma Redemptoris Mater*, page 228.

DECEMBER 12: OUR LADY OF GUADALUPE
Patroness of Christianity in the Americas.

1. Isaiah 9:2-3a, 6.
   You have brought them abundant joy.

2. Ephesians 1:3-6.
   God chose us in Christ to be holy.

3. Luke 2:41-51.
   Your father and I have searched for you.

Your mother, Lord, is searching still,
For all of us, to bring us home;
Her children ever find in her
Maternal arms their one true home.

LITURGICAL POEMS

HYMN TO THE HOLY SPIRIT

VENI SANCTE SPIRITUS
The Sequence for the Feast of Pentecost

Come, Holy Spirit, from above;
Send forth your light, your fire of love;
And kindle it within our heart.

Come good provider for the poor,
Of every gift, the Giver sure,
You are the light of every heart.

Of counselors, you are the best;
You are our soul's most welcome guest;
O sweet refreshment, with us stay.

From labor hard, you give us rest;
In summer's heat, a coolness blest;
In woe you wipe our tears away.

You are our joy, the blessed light
That banishes the dark of night
From faithful hearts, from depths within.

Without the life and strength you bring,
Lord, we cannot do anything;
We cannot even keep from sin.

All stain of sin in us erase;
The dryness in us irrigate;
And heal the wounds that bleed in us.

Lord, soften our rigidity;
Awaken our frigidity;
And straighten what is devious.

Bestow on all who trust in you,
On those who put their faith in you,
The seven gifts that come with love.

Let them have virtue's true reward;
Bestow on them salvation, Lord,
Eternal joy with you above.

THE SEASONAL MARIAN HYMNS

I. ALMA REDEMPTORIS MATER
The Advent-Christmas Antiphon

O loving Mother of the Lord,
You are the door to heaven still.
O guiding star, bring home the lost;
Arise, your people's hopes fulfill.

To all the world's astonishment
You bore the child who is your Lord.
A virgin now, a virgin then,
When Gabriel first spoke his word.

Good Mother, children cry to you.
The sinful put their hopes in you.

II. SALVE REGINA
The Antiphon Throughout the Year

Hail Queen of Mercy, Queen of Hope!
Our life, our sweetness here below.
Eve's children cry, your children cry;
With groans and tears, to you they sigh.

O turn, with a forgiving eye;
On you alone we can rely,
And when our exile here is done,
Then show us Jesus Christ, your Son.

O gentle, loving Virgin Queen,
On earth, in heaven, reign supreme.

III. REGINA COELI
The Easter Antiphon

Rejoice, O Queen above, Alleluia!
The one you bore and love, Alleluia!
Has risen from the dead, Alleluia!
Has risen as he said, Alleluia!

The Easter Proclamation

Exultet jam angelicus
In the Easter Vigil, before the Paschal Candle

Rejoice you heavens! Choirs of angels sing!
Let all creation gather round God's throne.
For Jesus Christ is risen! He is King!
Let trumpets sound; all bow to him alone.

Rejoice, O earth! The splendor of your King
Shines down on you
      as sunlight does in day.
For Christ has conquered death,
      and earth must sing.
The night is gone,
      the dawn is here to stay.

Rejoice, God's people, too, O mother church!
The Lord of Life
      to whom you prayed so long,
Has come to you; now over is your search;
Let all sing out, and hear your mighty song.

For Christ has ransomed us.
      His precious blood
Has paid for us the price of Adam's sin.
He rescued us from Egypt and the flood.
He died for us that we might live with him.

This is the night he led us through the sea,
The night when all our guilt
      was washed away.
This is the night he set his people free;
The night that has become as bright as day.

O loving Father, you who dwell above,
Your care for us will never be outdone.
How vast, how infinite your faithful love!
To ransom slaves you gave away your Son.

This candle, too, has risen from the dead.
May it dispel the darkness of our night.
When morning comes at last,
      then may it shed
On all of us the brightness of your light.

The Easter Hymn

Victimae Paschali Laudes
The Sequence for the Feast of Easter

O Christians come, your alleluias sing!
To Christ arisen, let your praises ring!

The victim lamb has saved
      the errant sheep;
The Innocent now lives, the guilty sleep.

When death fought life a duel to survive,
The Lord of life,
      once dead, came forth alive.

O Mary, tell us what you saw that morn:
The empty tomb, the burial clothes forlorn,

The angel witnesses, our hopes revived,
The glory of the Risen Lord alive.

He goes before his own to Galilee;
There we shall go, the risen Lord to see.

Triumphant King,
      who suffered in our stead,
We know that you have risen from the dead.

Amen! Alleluia!

LAUDA SION*

Sequence for the Feast of the Body of Christ.

O Zion, raise your voice and sing,
To praise your shepherd and your king
In holy hymns and sacred song.

We have not praised him near enough,
We cannot ever praise too much,
Nor ever praise the Lord too long.

Christ's body, risen from the dead,
The living and life-giving bread,
We celebrate in song today.

Remembering that sacred night,
Before the twelve would take to flight,
The gift by which the Lord would stay.

So let your praise be full and grand;
Resound with joy throughout the land;
Let happiness now fill your mind.

A solemn feast we celebrate:
The institution recreate
Of Jesus' gift to all mankind.

A banquet new, a new king too,
New laws, new customs, feasts, all new;
The old, fulfilled, now fades away.

The day must die to bring the morn;
As shadows flee, new truths are born.
The night is gone, now shines the day.

For what Christ did that sacred night,
He ordered we should do in light,
And do in memory of him.

So, following the will divine,
We consecrate the bread and wine
That liberates us all from sin.

For we believe, it is our faith,
The mystery we celebrate,
The wine is blood, the bread is flesh.

We neither see nor understand
The mystery we hold in hand,
The wine still red, the bread still fresh.

But still we know that underneath
The signs that stay, there lies beneath
The sacred, dear reality.

The flesh is food, the blood is drink;
The two are one, with Christ the link,
For he is one, who comes to me.

Consumed by me, but not destroyed;
The sacred food is now employed
To give me life: he lives in me!

Received by one, received by all,
A miracle! I stand in awe,
The Lord, our God, now dwells in me!

The just receive, the wicked too;
The difference between the two:
For one, new life; the other death.

Eternal death instead of life,
A fearful end to all this strife;
Choose life with God, and save your breath.

Fear not to break the sacrament
That feeds us all; the Lord's intent
Foresaw the need; let that suffice.

The signs divide, the body not;
They show, lest it should be forgot,
The sacramental sacrifice.

Behold the true angelic bread,
Become the food of those once dead.
Upon it once God's children fed;
Let it not be the food of beasts.

With figures God prepared this bread:
The Paschal Lamb whose blood was shed,
The manna on which Israel fed,
The offering of Salem's priest.

Good Shepherd, feed your sheep anew.
Lord Jesus, grant us mercy, too.
For living bread, we look to you,
To bring us to the feast above.

You know us all, the worst, the best;
You have the will and power to bless;
With angels, saints, your wedding guests,
Lord, share with us your faithful love.

*NOTE: A translation of the original by
Thomas Aquinas, with slight modifications.

PANGE LINGUA*

On the Good that is God

Sing, my tongue, the sacred story;
  Tell the world how God is Good.
Sing of how we share God's glory,
  How God loves, and how we should.
Sing a song of him who for me
  Died upon a cross of wood.

Slowly, slowly we are learning,
  Though the truth is far from clear.
Truth for which our hearts are yearning,
  Light we seek and darkness fear.
Visions in us churning, burning,
  Find a feeble hearing here.

Every creature, all creation,
  Is of God, a sacrament.
Each another incarnation
  Of God's Spirit, heaven sent.
Celebrate with jubilation
  World as God's embodiment.

Still, its splendor suffers doubly,
  Incomplete, and sadly rent.
Evil rules where goodness should be,
  Frustrating the Lord's intent.
We have managed badly, sadly.
  Sound the prophet's cry: repent!

Enter Jesus, sacred mystery,
  Son of man and Son of God:
Here the center of all history,
  In creation here find God,
Elsewhere, only partially;
  Here is proof that Good is God.

Christ has lead us to salvation,
  He alone, for he is God,
Goodness without reservation.
  He shall recreate this clod;
Every person, every nation's
  Feet must follow where he trod.

Jesus didn't do all for us;
  Calvary's for all to climb.
Membership in heaven's chorus
  Comes to none in space and time
Save the way of Christ, the glorious
  Paragon and paradigm.

Food is vital for a journey;
  Maps, provisions, for the just.
Let God's word and sacraments be
  Food we can rely on, must.
They are good food, God's own body,
  God's true word that we can trust.

World redeemed, our destination.
  Journey in, for our reward
Is not escape but transformation.
  We acknowledge no two lords;
One Lord, Good in all creation,
  No two cities, no two swords.

God of Christ, and God of Christians,
  Father, Mother, Son and King,
Jahweh, Spirit, Lord of nations,
  All of these, and more, we sing.
You are God of all creation,
  God the Good in everything.

*NOTE: Not a translation of the *Pange Lingua* of Aquinas, but a personal meditation of the author.

THE CHRISTIAN YEAR CALENDAR

EXPLANATORY NOTES

To accommodate the lay reader and to fit our thirteen-week seasonal cycle of Psalms, we have somewhat simplified the liturgical calendar. Still, if we want to celebrate the feasts and seasons of the year with the church, we are going to have to put up with a measure of its complexity. For those who simply want to know what week to be in and what page to be on (a good idea), we have supplied on the following pages a Calendar that does that over the next several years.

For those who want to know what choices were made in the simplification process, herewith is an explanation. As noted in the Introduction, the Year has been divided into four seasons or cycles of 13 weeks each.

The Winter or Advent-Christmas cycle begins with the first Sunday of Advent. Since Advent lasts only 3 to 4 weeks, and the Christmas season only 2 to 3 weeks, 7 "Weeks of the Year" are used to complete the normal 13 week seasonal cycle. More are needed if the start of the Spring cycle is delayed by a late Easter, or less if Easter is early.

The Spring or Lent-Easter cycle begins with the 1st Sunday of Lent and ends with the last week of Easter, which is exactly 13 weeks. It never changes.

The Summer and Fall cycles are thus normally left with 26 weeks, beginning with Pentecost Sunday and ending with the 34th week of the Year. Advent follows thereafter. Counting backwards, the Fall cycle is always 13 weeks, the 22nd through 34th weeks of the Year. The Summer cycle is left with 13 weeks too, if the Winter cycle was exactly 13 weeks, but more or less, if the Winter cycle was more or less. The difficult areas therefore are three: the Christmas

Season, the Weeks of the Year before and after the Spring cycle, and those special feasts during the year that have specific dates on the Calendar. Here is how we dealt with each.

1. *The Christmas Season.* Christmas can come on any day of the week, cutting short Advent by almost a week. The Christmas Season obviously begins on December 25, but it may end anywhere from January 7 to 13, depending on when the feast of the Baptism of Christ occurs, which begins the Weeks of the Year. We therefore made the following decisions:

a) In the Winter cycle, beginning on December 17 in Advent, we begin to follow the numbered days of the Calendar, not the days of the week. A note on page 49 and the Calendar alerts the reader when to switch. One exception: the 4th Sunday of Advent will occur between December 17 and 24, and is found on page 61-63, where one would expect December 18; when December 18 is a weekday, its readings are found on page 222; its Psalms are taken from those missed in the 3rd week of Advent. For all this period from December 17 on, use the Psalms on the facing pages, no matter what day of the week it is.

b) The Christmas Season ends the Saturday before the feast of the Baptism of Christ, which may occur any day from January 7 to 13. A set of readings for January 7 is found in the regular cycle, page 107, but the readings for January 8-12, as needed are found in the Christmas season supplements on pages 222-223. The Psalms are those missed in the 4th week of Advent.

c) Sundays in the Christmas Season may be occupied by the feasts of Christmas and Mary on December 25 and January 1, but normally they will occur on other dates. The readings for these Sundays are then found on page 222 and will replace the readings for the Calendar day on which they fall. The Psalms used are those of the day on which they fall. In all cases the Calendar will indicate the right selection for each day of the year.

2. *The weeks before and after the Spring Cycle.* The date of Easter varies widely, from March 23 to April 24, and moves the whole Spring cycle up or back with it. If Easter comes near the middle of that five week range (as, for example, April 11 in 2004), it allows for the normal 13-week Winter cycle before it, and a normal 13-week Summer cycle after it. But if Easter comes early (as on March 31 in 2002), it can cut two weeks off the Winter cycle and make the Summer cycle 15 weeks. Conversely if it comes late (as on April 23 in 2000), it can leave a two week gap between Spring and Winter, and curtail the Summer cycle.

It can become even more complex when the shorter or longer Advent and Christmas Seasons interfere, and when you figure in the extra day in the year (2 days in leap year), and when you consider that some years have 33 Weeks of the Year (2/3 of the time) and other years have 34 Weeks of the Year (1/3 of the time), requiring the dropping of one of the Sundays much of the time. A simplified layperson's prayer book cannot cope with all of this, so we made the following decisions:

a) The dropped week (which can actually be week 6, 7, 8, 9, or 10) is always number 8 for us. So we have 7 Weeks of the Year (1-7) before Lent, and 26 (9-34) after. When Week 8 is needed,

it is supplied in the Appendix on page 224. It repeats the Psalms of week 11.

b) We put Pentecost, Trinity Sunday, and Corpus Christi respectively on Sundays 9, 10, and 11 of the Year, where they always begin the Summer cycle, much like the Christian Calendar itself settled the feasts of the Baptism of Christ and Christ the King on the first and last Sundays of the Year.

c) When the Winter cycle is cut short, the omitted weeks are made up in the Summer cycle after the 11th Week of the Year. When there is a gap between Winter and Spring, it is filled with the supplemental Week 8, and if necessary the missing week(s) of the shortened Summer cycle.

d) Finally, the first 4 days of Lent, Ash Wednesday thru Saturday, will fall in whatever Week of the Year is last in the Winter cycle. The readings found on page 225 will replace the last four days of that week; but the Psalms will be the same as those in that week. Notes in the regular cycle alert the reader when they are apt to appear, and the Calendar identifies the exact date for each year.

3. *Special Feasts (with specific Calendar dates).* There are 8: St Joseph on March 19, the Annunciation on March 25, St. John the Baptist on June 24, Sts Peter and Paul on June 29, the Assumption on August 15, All Saints on November 1, Immaculate Conception on December 8 , and in America, Our Lady of Guadalupe on December 12. Readings for those 8 feasts are on pages 226 and 227. They replace the readings of the day, but use the Psalms of the day.

It works; and only occasionally are some readings not those which the church is using on that particular day.

THE CHRISTIAN CALENDAR

The capital letters, "A", "B", or "C", after the year indicate the cycle of Sunday readings used that year.

The small letters, "a" or "b", indicate which of the first weekday readings is used that year.

The *Dates* listed are for all Sundays and special *Feasts*, and for whenever the Psalms or readings for a particular day are for some reason out of sequence. The *Page* number given is for the Psalms; the readings are on the facing or following page. When two numbers, or sets of numbers, are given, the first is for Psalms, the second for readings.

1999 YEAR A,a

Date	Week Season or Feast	Page
Oct. 3	6 Fall	93
10	7	109
17	8	125
24	9	141
31	10	157
Nov. 1	All Saints	160/227
7	11	173
14	12	189
21	13	205
28	1 Winter	13
Dec. 5	2	29
8	ImmConc	36/227
12	3	45
17	3	58
18	Suplmt	56/222
19	4	61
20	4	66
25	5	77
26	Holy Fmly	80/222

2000 YEAR B,b

Date	Week Season or Feast	Page
Jan. 1		93
2	2SunXmas	96/222
8	Suplmt	64/222
9	7 Winter	109
16	8	125
23	9	141
30	10	157
Feb. 6	11	173-186
13	12	189
20	13	205
27	Suplmt Week	173/186 /22
Mar. 5	4 Summer	b 61
8-11	Ash Wed thru Sat.	68-74 /225
12	1 Spring	13
18	S. Joseph	26/226
19	2	29
25	Annunc.	42/226
26	3	45
Apr. 2	4	61
9	5	77
16	6	93
23	7	109
30	8	125
May 7	9	141
14	10	157
21	11	173
28	12	189
June 4	13	205
11	1 Summer	13
18	2	29
24	J'n B'tist	42/226
25	3	45
29	Ss.Ptr/Pl	54/226
July 2	5	77
9	6	93
16	7	109
23	8	125
30	9	141
Aug. 6	10	157
13	11	173
15	Assump'n	178/227
20	12	189
27	13	205
Sep. 3	1 Fall	13
10	2	29
17	3	45
24	4	61
Oct. 1	5	77
8	6	93
15	7	109
22	8	125
29	9	141
Nov. 1	All Saints	148/227
5	10	157
12	11	173
19	12	189
26	13	205
Dec. 3	1 Winter	13
8	ImmConc	24/227
10	2	29
12	G'dalupe	34/227
17	3	45
18	Suplmt	48/222
19	4	64
24	4	61
25	5	77
31	Holy Fmly	90/222

2001 YEAR C,a

Date	Week Season or Feast	Page
Jan. 1	6 Winter	93
7	7	109
14	8	125
21	9	141
28	10	157
Feb. 4	11	173
11	12	189
18	13	205
25	Suplmt Week	173-179 /224
28 to Mar. 3	Ash Wed. thru Sat.	180-186 /225
4	1 Spring	13
11	2	29
18	3	45
19	S. Joseph	48/226
25	4	61
Apr. 1	5	77
8	6	93
15	7	109
22	8	125
29	9	141
May 6	10	157
13	11	173
20	12	189
27	13	205
June 3	1 Summer	13
10	2	29
17	3	45
23	J'n B'tist	58/226
24	4	61
29	Ss.Ptr/Pl	70/226
July 1	5	77
8	6	93
15	7	109
22	8	125
29	9	141
Aug. 5	10	157
12	11	173
15	Assump'n	180/227
19	12	189
26	13	205
Sep. 2	1 Fall	13
9	2	29
16	3	45
23	4	61
30	5	77
Oct. 7	6	93
14	7	109
21	8	125
28	9	141
Nov.1	All Saints	150/227
4	10	157
11	11	173
18	12	189
25	13	205
Dec. 2	1 Winter	13
8	ImmConc	26/227
9	2	29
12	G'dalupe	36/227
16	3	45
17	3	58
18	Suplmt	72/222
19	4	64
23	4	61
24	4	74
25	5	77
30	Holy Fmly	88/222
31	5	90

2002 YEAR A,b

Date	Week Season or Feast	Page
Jan. 1	6 Winter	93
6	2SunXmas	104/222
7	6	106
8 to 12	Suplmt Week	48-56 /222
13	7	109
20	8	125
27	9	141
Feb. 3	10	157
10	11	173
13 to 16	Ash Wed. thru Sat.	180-186 /225
17	1 Spring	13
24	2	29
Mar. 3	3	45
10	4	61
17	5	77
19	S. Joseph	82/226
24	6	93
25	Annunc.	96/226
31	7	109
Apr. 7	8	125
14	9	141
21	10	157
28	11	173

May 5	12	189
12	13	205
19	1 Summer	13
26	2	29
June 2	3	45
9	12 Winter	189
16	13 Winter	205
23	4 Summer	61
24	J'n B'tist	64/226
29	Ss.Ptr/Pl	74/226
30	5	77
July 7	6	93
14	7	109
21	8	125
28	9	141
Aug. 4	10	157
11	11	173
15	Assump'n	182/227
18	12	189
25	13	205
Sep. 1	1 Fall	13
8	2	29
15	3	61
29	5	77
Oct. 6	6	93
13	7	109
20	8	125
27	9	141
Nov. 1	All Saints	152/227
3	10	157
10	11	173
17	12	189
24	13	205
Dec. 1	1 Winter	13
7	ImmConc	26/227
8	2	29
12	G'dalupe	38/227
15	3	45
17	3	58
18	Suplmt	70/222
19	4	64
22	4	61
25	5	77
29	Holy Fmly	86/222

2003 YEAR B,a

Date	Week Season or Feast	Page
Jan. 1	6	93
8 to 11	Suplmt	50-56 / 222
12	7	109
19	8	125
26	9	141
Feb. 2	10	157
9	11	173
16	12	189
23	13	205

Mar. 2	4 Summer	61
5 to 8	Ash Wed. thru Sat.	68-74 / 225
9	1 Spring	13
16	2	29
19	S. Joseph	36/226
23	3	45
25	Annunc.	50/226
30	4	61
Apr. 6	5	77
13	6	93
20	7	109
27	8	125
May 4	9	141
11	10	157
18	11	173
25	12	189
June 1	13	205
8	1 Summer	13
15	2	29
22	3	45
24	J'n B'tist	50/226
28	Ss.Ptr/Pl	58/226
29	5	77
July 6	6	93
13	7	109
20	8	125
27	9	141
Aug. 3	10	157
10	11	173
15	Assump'n	184/227
17	12	189
24	13	205
31	1 Fall	13
Sep. 7	2	29
14	3	45
21	4	61
28	5	77
Oct. 5	6	93
12	7	109
19	8	125
26	9	141
Nov. 1	All Saints	152/227
2	10	157
9	11	173
16	12	189
23	13	205
30	1 Winter	13
Dec. 7	2	29
8	ImmConc	32/227
12	G'dalupe	40/227
14	3	45
17	3	58
18	Suplmt	68/222
19	4	64
21	4	61
25	5	77
28	Holy Fmly	84/222

2004 YEAR C,b

Date	Week Season or Feast	Page
Jan. 1	6	93
4	2SunXmas	100/222
8 to 10	Suplmt	52-56 / 222
11	7	109
18	8	125
25	9	141
Feb. 1	10	157
8	11	173
15	12	189
22	13	205
25 to 28	Ash Wed. thru Sat.	212-218 / 225
29	1 Spring	13
Mar. 7	2	29
14	3	45
19	S. Joseph	56/226
21	4	61
25	Annunc.	70/226
28	5	77
Apr. 4	6	93
11	7	109
18	8	125
25	9	141
May 2	10	157
9	11	173
16	12	189
23	13	205
30	1 Summer	13
June 6	2	29
13	3	45
20	4	61
24	J'n B'tist	70/226
27	5	77
29	Ss.Ptr/Pl	82/226
July 4	6	93
11	7	109
18	8	125
25	9	141
Aug. 1	10	157
8	11	173
14	Assump'n	186/227
15	12	189
22	13	205
29	1 Fall	13
Sep. 5	2	29
12	3	45
19	4	61
26	5	77
Oct. 3	6	93
10	7	109
17	8	125
24	9	141
31	10	157
Nov. 1	All Saints	160/227

Nov. 7	11	173
14	12	189
21	13	205
28	1 Winter	13
Dec. 5	2	29
8	ImmConc	36/227
12	3	45
17	3	58
18	Suplmnt	64/222
19	4	61
20	4	66
5	5	77
26	Holy Fmly	80/222

2005 YEAR A,a

Date	Week Season or Feast	Page
Jan. 1	6	93
2	2SunXmas	96/222
8	Suplmnt	56/222
9	7	109
16	8	125
23	9	141
30	10	157
Feb. 6	11	173
9 to 12	Ash Wed. thru Sat.	180-186 / 225
13	1 Spring	13
20	2	29
27	3	45
Mar. 6	4	61
13	5	77
19	S. Joseph	90/226
20	6	93
27	7	109
Apr. 3	8	125
10	9	141
17	10	157
24	11	173
May 1	12	189
8	13	205
5	1 Summer	13
22	2	29
29	3	45
June 5	2 Winter	189
12	13 Winter	205
19	4 Summer	61
24	J'n B'tist	72/226
26	5	77
29	Ss.Ptr/Pl	84/226
July 3	6	93
10	7	109
17	8	125
24	9	141
31	10	157
Aug. 7	11	173
14	12	189
15	Assump'n	192/227

INDEX
OF
PSALMS